In *Mimesis and Empire* Barbara Fuchs explores the intricate dynamics of imitation and contradistinction among early modern European powers in literary and historiographical texts from sixteenth- and early seventeenth-century Spain, Italy, England, and the New World. The book considers a broad sweep of material, including European representations of New World subjects and of Islam, both portrayed as "other" in contemporary texts. It supplements the transatlantic perspective on early modern imperialism with an awareness of the situation in the Mediterranean and considers problems of reading and literary transmission; imperial ideology and colonial identities; counterfeits and forgery; and piracy.

Cambridge Studies in Renaissance Literature and Culture 40

Mimesis and Empire

Cambridge Studies in Renaissance Literature and Culture

General Editor
STEPHEN ORGEL
Jackson Eli Reynolds Professor of Humanities, Stanford University

Editorial board
Anne Barton, *University of Cambridge*
Jonathan Dollimore, *University of York*
Marjorie Garber, *Harvard University*
Jonathan Goldberg, *Johns Hopkins University*
Nancy Vickers, *Bryn Mawr College*

Since the 1970s there has been a broad and vital reinterpretation of the nature of literary texts, a move away from formalism to a sense of literature as an aspect of social, economic, political and cultural history. While the earliest New Historicist work was criticized for a narrow and anecdotal view of history, it also served as an important stimulus for post-structuralist, feminist, Marxist and psychoanalytical work, which in turn has increasingly informed and redirected it. Recent writing on the nature of representation, the historical construction of gender and of the concept of identity itself, on theatre as a political and economic phenomenon and on the ideologies of art generally, reveals the breadth of the field. Cambridge Studies in Renaissance Literature and Culture is designed to offer historically oriented studies of Renaissance literature and theatre which make use of the insights afforded by theoretical perspectives. The view of history envisioned is above all a view of our own history, a reading of the Renaissance for and from our own time.

Recent titles include

A complete list of books in the series is given at the end of the volume.

Mimesis and Empire

The New World, Islam, and European Identities

Barbara Fuchs

CAMBRIDGE
UNIVERSITY PRESS

PUBLISHED BY THE PRESS SYNDICATE OF THE UNIVERSITY OF CAMBRIDGE
The Pitt Building, Trumpington Street, Cambridge, United Kingdom

CAMBRIDGE UNIVERSITY PRESS
The Edinburgh Building, Cambridge CB2 2RU, UK
40 West 20th Street, New York NY 10011–4211, USA
477 Williamstown Road, Port Melbourne, VIC 3207, Australia
Ruiz de Alarcón 13, 28014 Madrid, Spain
Dock House, The Waterfront, Cape Town 8001, South Africa

http://www.cambridge.org

First published 2001
First paperback edition 2003

Typeface Times 10/12pt   *System* Poltype ® [VN]

A catalogue record for this book is available from the British Library

ISBN 0 521 80102 8 hardback
ISBN 0 521 54350 9 paperback

Dolus an virtus, quis in hoste requirat?
Arma dabunt ipsi.
                     – *Aeneid* II.390–1

Contents

Acknowledgments

This project owes much to the people who have fostered it through the years. Patricia Parker was throughout the most astute of readers and the kindest of mentors, and helped me see the ideological implications of rhetoric. Sepp Gumbrecht shared with me his encyclopedic knowledge of Spain and its culture. Mary Louise Pratt helped me think through the larger implications of texts, both my own and the ones I analyze. Stephen Orgel supported the project with his incisive criticism and constant enthusiasm.

The book would not have been possible without the good offices of Hippogryph, who in flights of inspiration carried the individual chapters to new and exciting places. To the members of that group, Caroline Bicks, Edmund Campos, Sujata Iyengar, Richard Menke, and Paul Saint-Amour, my deepest thanks for sustained engagement and perceptive readings. Other friends in the Bay Area provided important insights. Early on, Genevieve Bell made me see the anthropological dimension of mimesis. Tim Hampton and Albert Ascoli helped develop my readings of Tasso. Pericles Lewis, constant friend, read many versions, and infallibly provided much-needed support. Sonia Moss, of the Inter-Library Loan department at Stanford's Green Library, was consistently helpful and highly resourceful.

At the University of Washington, Marshall Brown has been my most constant and marvelously demanding reader. Srinivas Aravamudan, Jeffrey Collins, Joy Connolly, Benjamin Schmidt, Robin Stacey, and Sara van den Berg all read portions of the manuscript and provided invaluable comments. Jean Howard and Richard Helgerson generously read early chapters. To Roland Greene, Diana de Armas Wilson, and David Quint I owe special thanks, for their sustained engagement with my work.

Versions of Chapters 4 and 5 appeared in *The Journal of Spanish Cultural Studies* and *English Literary History*, respectively, and are reprinted here with permission.

This project was begun under the auspices of a Mellon Dissertation Fellowship. I am grateful also to the Stanford Humanities Center, which provided a year of stimulating exchanges as I was defining my project, and to the Simpson Center for the Humanities at the University of Washington, for the time to bring the project to completion.

My deepest thanks are due to my husband, Todd Lynch, supportive critic and editor nonpareil, and to my family, who saw me through with long-distance humor and unfailing good spirits. I dedicate this work to my families, old and new.

Note on translations

With some minor exceptions, I have cited primary texts in the original with parenthetical translations following. Translations not otherwise attributed are my own. Where I have corrected an existing translation, I have placed my emendations in brackets.

Introduction

Cuzco, Peru, 1570. As Viceroy Francisco de Toledo makes his formal entrance into the city, he is greeted with elaborate pageantry. In the main square, once site of the Inca festivals, a Moorish castle and an enchanted wood have been erected for the celebration. The mock-Moors emerge from the castle to capture young women at a fountain, only to be pursued by valiant Christian knights, who engage them in fierce mock combat. The conquistadors play "themselves." The Moors are played by the Indians.

Bristol, England, 1613. To celebrate Queen Anne's visit, the city stages a water-combat between a Christian ship and two Turkish galleys. After a lively mock battle, the "Turks" are brought as prisoners before the Queen, who laughingly observes that they are "not only like Turks by their apparell, but by their countenances."[1]

The representation of an encounter with the other is always fraught with difficulties. To mime such an encounter is also, fundamentally, to set the self adrift in a space where identity becomes nothing but props and costume. The two examples above convey some sense of the complexity of intercultural performance on early modern imperial stages. In the first, a time-honored Mediterranean script is produced in an American setting, casting the natives of the New World as the Islamic bogeymen of the Old.[2] Yet by 1570 the Indians playing Moors in Cuzco were almost certainly baptized Christians, a product of the evangelization much touted by Spaniards as their justification for the Conquista, and hardly "the infidel." The casting stretches the limits of verisimilitude, and the staging of continuity between two very different Spanish enterprises actually displays the contradictions between available story-lines and available actors. If the Indians can represent the Muslims, have the Spaniards in fact succeeded in their evangelical mission? If, on the other hand, they cannot, then at whom is the violence of Spanish conquest aimed, and why? Perhaps the "infidel" Indians are simply standing in for their unbaptized brethren, or perhaps their very participation in the Spanish performance marks the success of the Conquista. Yet the elaborate rehearsal of Old World quarrels in the

New raises important questions about the often contradictory roles that Spain plays as a colonizing power, and the identities available to its imperial others.

The second episode is even more tantalizing. Here, there is no problem with the script: a straightforward battle against a clear enemy – Islamic pirates – on a vulnerable site on the coast of England. Nor is there any difficulty in casting the right actors – or is there? The problem seems to lie in the fact that the English are only too well suited for the roles of Turks and pirates. Even when they remove their props and "apparell," they *still* look like Turks, as the Queen does not fail to point out. Are they wearing blackface, in an effort to create a racialized difference? Do they merely look uncouth, tanned by the sun and fresh from the "combat"? Or does the identification in fact go deeper? The role that sticks to these English Turks evokes the problematic afterlife of privateering in Jacobean England, where the illicit exploits of renegade corsairs threatened to collapse the distinctions between English friend and Muslim foe. Although the English had embraced state-authorized piracy as an imperial strategy during the reign of Elizabeth, James vehemently renounced such tactics. Nonetheless, English renegades continued to swell the ranks of the corsairs, crossing the geographic and religious boundary of the Mediterranean to establish their bases on the Barbary Coast. When, after the Bristol performance, James' foreign queen humorously identifies the English actors with the Turks they "merely" represent, she belies the difference between self and other that the mock-battle ostensibly stages. The imitators, Anne pointedly suggests, are too much like the imitated. Behind the humor of the moment lies a recognition of the fragility of English identity.

As the above examples suggest, scenes of elaborate cultural mimesis register the contradictions involved in translating the scripts for the emergent empires to new locales. Over the course of the sixteenth and seventeenth centuries, as Spain and England expanded into New World empires against a background of continued European struggles against Islam, the transatlantic and Mediterranean exchanges attendant upon such expansion became increasingly complex. This project proposes a critical reading of identity and difference – constantly invoked in those exchanges – as volatile and pliable relations between cultures, rather than as necessary correlatives of traits inherent within them. It exposes the intricate relations of imitation and contradistinction among the emerging European empires and would-be empires, as well as between them and their non-European others. Different national experiences – such as England's and Spain's – prove to be interconnected even as these nations pursue their own process of individuation.

The confrontation with Islam, in its many incarnations, was crucial for

Europe's cultural construction of itself as a geographic and imperial center. Spain, especially, underwent the double experience of acquiring an empire while holding Islam at bay and investing enormous energies into excising Moors and Moorish culture from the newly constituted nation. The consolidation of the state – both as unified metropole and as overseas empire – was predicated largely on the attainment of religious and ethnic homogeneity. But it was not always easy to distinguish Islamic other from Christian self, and the pertinent texts evince significant anxieties about the possibility of achieving a cohesive ethnic and religious self for the emerging nation while negotiating its expansion. Because, as the case of Spain patently shows, the dynamics of individuation and national consolidation in the Old World and in the New are so intimately connected, the study of empire in this period is best approached as an investigation of *imperium*, the Roman term that denotes a state's rule not only over colonies but also over the metropole: the "home base" and its subjects.

This book examines Europe's vision of Islam as external and internal threat in a context of nascent imperialism. It does not attempt the same for Islam's vision of Europe. Instead, it supplements the transatlantic perspective on early modern imperialism with an attention to the cultural and literary situation in the Mediterranean. The exportation of epic and romance to the Americas, the adoption of Spanish religious ideology by native American writers, and the expansion of Mediterranean piracy to the Atlantic all mark the profound interdependence of these imperial and cultural arenas. The literary problems are traditional: the status of representation in the period, the translation of established forms to new and potentially disruptive contexts. Less familiar is the overriding crux, a new conception of imitative representation. Mimesis emerges as both a powerful rhetorical weapon and a cultural – i.e. not simply literary – phenomenon.

The capacious cultural mimesis that I explore here does not, however, describe the first-order imitation among cultures which so fascinated ethnosociologists and historians of the early twentieth century.[3] Instead, it involves the deliberate representation of sameness. My reading expands mimesis from the aesthetic realm to the culture at large as it analyzes the intentionality, the power dynamics, and the political consequences of pointed imitation. The mimesis that I trace effects inclusion for marginalized subjects by challenging the construction of colonial difference, as the very distinctions on which imperial ideology depends are trumped by the production of simulacra, facsimiles, or counterfeits within the text of colonial culture. At a larger level, the deliberate imitation of both colonial and metropolitan practices and discourses threatens state legitimacy by negating its singularity. Ideology pirated or ventriloquized becomes surprisingly vulnerable – instead of reproducing it, purposeful mimesis undermines imperial claims to originary authority. Most importantly, mimetic mirrorings among emerging early modern nations challenge the process of individuation by which those nations attempt to become fully consolidated states with an exceptional claim to an imperial destiny. Imitation compromises the narratives of national distinction by emphasizing inconvenient similarities and shared heritages. In this sense, even the traditional imitation of literary precedents participates in the larger dynamics of cultural mimesis, by diluting the original force of ideology in epics that recast early modern encounters between colony and metropolis or among imperial rivals.

In our much fragmented, post-modern academy, studies of power and representation have been galvanized by careful assessments of the role of difference, both in the Saussurian–Derridian linguistic version – *différance* – and in the Lacanian/Foucauldian/post-colonial recuperations of marginalized Others. What I propose is that we consider also the political and rhetorical valence of *sameness* – identification, mimicry, reproduction. As complementary opposites, sameness and difference cannot truly be divided: the study of fidelity in representation leads necessarily to a consideration of adulteration, while accounts of imposed uniformity must generally consider the existence of subversive mimicry, the troubling same-but-different. What advantages, therefore, does the study of cultural mimesis offer? In the first place, if mimesis is defined as an act of commission, it allows for the study of the agency involved in such a gesture. How and why do individuals or states imitate? Second, and more crucially, cultural mimesis provides a bridge across that stubborn gap between the self-sufficient, institutionally reified incarnations of "literature" and "history." Both are subject to the operations of mimesis. Yet this concept is not merely another bridge for the literary to colonize the historical field: crucial to it is the redefinition of mimesis to include non-literary phenomena, designating the calculated imitation of a model, whether by subjects, polities, or texts.

The attempt to bring together literature and history as texts characterized by rhetorical figures is hardly novel – even the New Historicism must surely yield its *new* to some *newer* before long. Hayden White's revolutionary reconceptualization of history as a series of texts existing within the "Tropics of Discourse" attempted to systematize in great detail the "mode of emplotment" of historical narratives.[4] Yet his structuralist model of discourse considered mimesis inert; it was simply the "description of the 'data' found in the field of inquiry being marked out for analysis."[5] White's mimesis is inherent in the narrative of history, and devoid of agency or power. To trot out once again the most overused of the metaphors for mimesis, it is a mirror held up by no one, and before which no one in particular is preening. As such, it corresponds to the static notion of mimesis as representation of reality, richly explored in a humanistic vein in Erich Auerbach's compendious *Mimesis* (1946). What I propose instead is a concept of mimesis as the fun-house mirror, the reflection that dazzles, the impersonator, the sneaky copy, the double agent – mimesis, that is, as a deliberate performance of sameness that necessarily threatens, or at least modifies, the original.[6]

The notion of an active, aggressive imitation has been developed in very different ways by two cultural critics of an anthropological bent. Although the work of René Girard and that of Michael Taussig could not appear more dissimilar, they share a concept of mimesis as a powerful phenomenon with definite social consequences, and one which subjects harness to their particular goals. With his concept of "mimetic desire," Girard aims to remedy the exclusion of "one essential human behavior from the types subject to imitation – namely, desire and, more fundamentally still, appropriation. If one individual imitates another when the latter appropriates some object, the result cannot fail to be rivalry or conflict."[7] His analysis, although rich with insights on the workings of desire in triangulation and the tensions between models and anti-models, remains firmly focused on the individual when discussing Western texts. Although Girard addresses larger social interactions in pre-modern societies, he does not extrapolate from Western canonical texts to their political contexts.

Taussig's *Mimesis and Alterity: A Particular History of the Senses* investigates mimesis as a double phenomenon: "a copying or imitation, and a palpable, sensuous connection between the very body of the perceiver and the perceived."[8] Taussig connects the history of mimesis, and especially of nineteenth-century "mimetic machines" to the experience of European colonialism, granting mimesis a real power to undermine both hierarchies and differences:

Mastery is no longer possible. The West as mirrored in the eyes and handiwork of its Others undermines the stability which mastery needs. What remains is unsettled and unsettling interpretation in constant movement with itself – what I have elsewhere called a Nervous System – because the interpreting self is itself grafted into the object of study. The self enters into the alter against which the self is defined and sustained.[9]

As Taussig envisions it, mimesis functions as a powerful weapon for non-Western subjects, challenging both the distinctiveness and the hegemony of the West. But what of mimetic reproduction among the Western powers themselves, as they strive for imperial individuation? How can we read state-sponsored imitation, or read the state and its intentions into early modern representations?

Homi Bhabha's notion of "colonial mimicry" adroitly captures the complexity of an imitation that hovers between the colonizer and the colonized, whereby the "epic intention of the civilizing mission . . . produces a text rich in the traditions of *trompe l'oeil*, irony, mimicry and repetition."[10] Bhabha stresses the twofold power of such mimicry: "The menace of mimicry is its double vision which in disclosing the ambivalence of colonial discourse also disrupts its authority."[11] But Bhabha's account leaves little room for the agency of the colonized in producing the disruptions. How might *deliberate* imitation harness the disruptive power of colonial mimicry? As Joseph Roach has shrewdly pointed out, imitative representations are threatening in that they "raise the possibility of the replacement of the authors of the representations by those whom they imagined into existence as their definitive opposites."[12] Even more disruptively, they may suggest a substitution of the representations themselves with new imitations – *facsimiles* – that stress cultural similarity over difference.

Mimesis and Empire elaborates upon Taussig and Bhabha's key insights to study the early years of European colonialism, investigating not only the mimetic confrontations between Europe and Islam or Europe and the Americas, but also among the rival European empires, especially England and Spain. Not surprisingly, these different sets of confrontations overlap, as the Atlantic flows into the Mediterranean. Thus, for example, the English imitation of Mediterranean piracy in order to undermine the power of the Spanish empire gradually leads to increased attacks on England itself, as well as on its Atlantic colonies, by piratical subjects turned renegades. The mimetic counterfeits of pirates and renegades then complicate the attempted construction of an imperial identity based on licit transactions. As this case shows, mimesis can operate both as a weapon of the state, encouraged and promoted in the emulation of its rivals, and as a weapon against that same state, forced by imitators to relinquish its original preeminence.

Beyond the complex phenomenon of piracy, I explore the dynamics of fidelity and imitation through three principal examples of cultural mimesis in the early modern period. First, I analyze the contagion of fictionality from romance to religious texts that sorely preoccupied both moralists and writers in the Old World as well as missionaries in the New. By juxtaposing the ambivalent reception of imaginative texts in the New World to Old World literary quarrels, I suggest how the American experience altered European attitudes towards truth in literature. As Europe faced the undeniable impact of vast new territories and, increasingly, large populations of new readers, problems of authenticity and authority became ever more pressing.

Second, I explore the bitter rivalry between emerging empires, especially Spain and England, to portray themselves as the true inheritors of Rome, assuming the epic mantle of empire. The representation of *imperium* carried great weight in the late sixteenth century, at a time when England was painfully conscious of its own imperial belatedness with respect to Spain; when Philip II's Spain, though possessed of huge territories, was perennially bankrupt; and when all European empires – actual or aspiring – stood in awe of the non-European contenders, the Ottoman Turks. Whereas the European imperial rivalries have been well charted in the historical vein by Anthony Pagden, and in the literary by David Quint, I juxtapose the more self-consciously literary texts with other documents to articulate the role of Islam as a third pole in such mimetic exchanges. As the literary imitation of Roman epic intersects with the military imitation of imperial strategies on both Mediterranean and transatlantic stages, the ensuing homologies complicate European claims to national distinctiveness.

Third, I investigate the Spanish casting of the conquest of America as a reiteration of the *Reconquista* of Spanish territory from the Moors – a wishful analogy, given the unresolved conflicts between these Mediterranean antagonists in the sixteenth and early seventeenth centuries. The mimetic equation of Reconquista and Conquista is particularly vexed in its temporality. When the historian and colonial official Francisco López de Gómara writes in his early *Historia general de las Indias* that "The conquest of the Indians began after that of the Moors was completed, so that Spaniards would ever fight the infidels," he justifies the current conquest as a logical continuation of the previous one.[13] The power of the comparison thus depends on the truth of the Spanish contention that the Peninsular struggle against Islam ended with the fall of Granada in 1492. But Spain's confrontation with Islam was far from resolved in the sixteenth century; in fact, the Islamic threat seemed to be everywhere. While Spain continued to resist Ottoman encroachments on its European empire in the Eastern Mediterranean, the Peninsula itself was subject to repeated raids by Barbary corsairs. To address the relentless threat of Islam, Charles V established a series of military outposts in North Africa, which subsequently proved almost impossible for Spain to defend. Philip II's incorporation of Portugal in 1580 was a direct result of the disastrous "crusade" waged by the Portuguese in Morocco, where the young sovereign, Dom Sebastião, was killed. In Spain, the years 1568–71 saw the uprising of the Moriscos, those Moors who had remained after the fall of Granada and who were driven to revolt by the increasing pressures of cultural control. These internal others were maddeningly like, yet unlike, "true" Spaniards, an ambiguity that would not be resolved even with the final expulsion of the

Moriscos from the Peninsula in 1609. When they rebelled, Spain confronted its own invasion by the Ottoman Turks, in alliance with the Moriscos and the North African Moors, as a real and horrifying possibility.

But the problems with the Conquista/Reconquista analogy go beyond the question of temporality. There is also the contemporary obfuscation of Spanish history by critics who unquestioningly echo the sixteenth-century mimetic sleight-of-hand.[14] As María Rosa Menocal has pointed out, when researchers in our own time uncritically rehearse the supposed repetition of the Reconquista in the Conquista, and celebrate the "authentic" Spanishness of both, they participate in a construction of Spain as singlemindedly Christian, free of the Semitic "taint."[15] This negates not only the rich multicultural experience of medieval al-Andalus, which Menocal painstakingly reconstructs, but also the deliberate, calculated mimetization of one conquest into the other as a sixteenth-century strategy to encourage Spanish efforts at expansion and cultural homogenization on both the American and the Mediterranean fronts. Clearly, the version of the Reconquista on which the analogy depends is as much a fantasy as the rhetorical equation between the two phenomena. Yet while the illusory Reconquista of legend by no means corresponds to the realities of medieval Spain, the historical revival of it as a model to galvanize the Spanish not only in the New World but also in the Mediterranean is undeniable.

While the chapters that follow chart different intersections of mimesis and empire, the problems outlined above echo throughout. Chapter 1, "Truth, Fictions, and the New World," functions as a kind of preamble to discussions of the imperial rivalry between England and Spain. It analyzes Torquato Tasso's late fantasy of a Christian empire in *Gerusalemme liberata*, to suggest how the author's anxiety about the role of the marvelous in his epic can be linked to European fears about the dynamics of reading and religious truth in the New World. The Spaniards forbade imaginative literature – mainly chivalric romances – in the Americas, with statutes explaining that such fictions might confuse the natives, who were supposed to be reading biblical "truths" instead of literary lies. Yet the censorship suggests also that Spain was particularly concerned that native readers would draw their own conclusions from the tales that inspired the conquistadors. What did the Spanish fear that such readers might discover about the culture in which they were being indoctrinated? The chapter traces the metropolitan anxieties about American reading at work in Tasso's famously tortured decisions about the role of the marvelous in his Christian epic. What seems on the face of it a purely European discussion about the ideological implications of romance comes into sharper focus when juxtaposed with anxieties about the marvelous worlds that Europe was attempting to digest while Tasso wrote.

Two texts about Spain's struggle for *imperium* – Alonso de Ercilla's *La Araucana* and Ginés Pérez de Hita's *Guerras civiles de Granada* – negotiate a variety of imitative strategies in an effort to authorize their imperial narratives. Chapter 2, "Literary Loyalties, Imperial Betrayals," shows how these texts establish their own literary and historical authority by appealing, often in a contradictory fashion, to the author's witnessing, to literary models, and to the ventriloquizing of native informants. In order to narrate the Spanish campaign against the indomitable Araucanian Indians in distant Chile, Ercilla tempers the conventions of epic with ethnographic generalizations and first-hand observation. In describing the vastness of Philip's domains, on the other hand, the author ranges far afield, introducing into his narrative an account of imperial conflicts between Spain and the Turks. Amazingly, the vision of Spain's greatness elsewhere – at the battle of Lepanto, to cite one crucial example – is afforded by an Indian magician with a crystal ball. This scene of mimesis, both literary – in its allusion to the epic tradition – and ontological – in the magician's reproduction of the world, seriously undermines the account of Spanish greatness which the text ostensibly offers. As an instrument of empire, the European epic fares poorly in the New World, where it is challenged by both the irreducible difference of native customs and the insidious similarities between conquerors and conquered.

In Pérez de Hita's *Guerras civiles de Granada*, too, the lines between inside and outside Spain become ever fainter. The first part of the text – part romance, part historical novel, part ballad collection – describes wars between several factions of the Moors before their downfall in 1492. But the Moors themselves are portrayed as highly sympathetic and cultured figures, akin to Christian knights. Much like *La Araucana*, the second part of the *Guerras civiles* relates virtually contemporary events in which the author participates: in this case, the fighting in the Alpujarras, where Pérez de Hita helped quell the Morisco rebellion. Thus from one section to the next the Moors are transformed from fantastic chivalrous figures – virtual Spaniards – to actual historical enemies. Yet the sympathies of Part I continue to haunt Part II, so that the relationship between these two halves of an incongruous whole yields important insights into the role of cultural mimesis in the consolidation of Spain's internal empire.

For indigenous American authors, as for the Moriscos, imitative strategies served as a means to write themselves into Spanish debates over religion, ethnicity, and national identity. Chapter 3, "Lettered Subjects," analyzes how identity is constructed in two powerful texts that give voice to the indigenous experience before, during, and in the wake of the Conquista, in an attempt to seek redress from the Spanish Crown. In Inca Garcilaso de la Vega's *Comentarios reales de los Incas* and Felipe Guaman

Poma de Ayala's *Nueva corónica i buen gobierno*, the authors make able use of Spain's own racial and religious categories to further their own ends, inscribing themselves, chameleon-like, in Spanish mores and personas. This mimetization gets at the heart of Spanish identity, often exposing its contradictions through the very act of replicating it. Thus Inca Garcilaso constructs himself as a Spaniard based on a feudal model of individual struggle against the infidel, while resisting in general terms the Spanish identification of native Americans with Christianity's traditional Mediterranean foes. Guaman Poma, on the other hand, renames himself a nobleman and conjures the Spanish obsession with blood purity in order to condemn the increasing adulteration of Indian blood in Peru. Here, cultural mimesis, understood as the deliberate replication of Spanish ideology, provides a powerful rhetorical weapon for writers marginalized by that same ideology.

Chapter 4, "Virtual Spaniards" traces a similar mimetization within Spain itself. It analyzes both licit and illicit strategies by which the increasingly persecuted Moriscos sought inclusion within the Spanish polity. In the first case, a petition to the local authorities in Granada, the Morisco leader Francisco Núñez Muley argues for the preservation of local and regional differences – in his case, Moorish, or "Grenadine" culture – against the hegemonizing impulse of centralized authority. His argument radically dissociates nationality from ethnic or religious practices, to produce a powerful syncretic figure, the Morisco Spaniard. The second set of strategies is perhaps more complex, and suggests the Moriscos' deep and conflictive desires for inclusion in the state that ostracized them. Playing on Spain's heightened anxiety about the credibility of its Christian past, Morisco authors purveyed a series of powerful fictions to the people of Granada that attempted a synthesis of Christianity and Islam. In 1595, nineteen leaden tablets in "antiqued" Arabic and crude Latin were found in Granada, apocryphal chronicles purportedly written by Arabic disciples of St. James – patron saint of Spain in its struggle against Islam – and full of prophecies about the fate of Granada. The Moriscos' mimetic reproduction of Spanish identity thereby acquires a historico-religious pedigree: the fraudulent tablets suggest that Moriscos have always been the same as Spaniards, and that Moorish otherness in fact lies at the heart of Spain. The negotiation of identity and difference in this massive hoax – one only exposed conclusively in the late nineteenth century – suggests how cultural mimesis serves to undermine totalizing notions of national identity.

As the success of the leaden tablets suggests, what can be mimicked or imitated is oddly vulnerable to subversion. In Chapter 5, "Faithless Empires: Pirates, Renegadoes, and the English Nation," I turn to the imperial rivalry between England and Spain. Although the English proclivity for piracy was a natural continuation of the authorized privateering during the war with Spain (1587–1604), the role of pirate was hardly uncomplicated, given the tortuous maritime history of the age. Throughout the sixteenth century, Barbary corsairs carried out large-scale raids of the Mediterranean coasts, pillaging settlements and taking hundreds of captives to sell as slaves. Although these depredations were less widespread by the end of the century, the Barbary corsairs were still dangerously active. While the English had originally taken to piracy as a way to challenge the imperial might of Spain, the circulation of sensitive knowledge by English pirates who reneged quickly threatened England's own imperial aims. In the early 1600s, renegade Europeans established themselves in the Barbary States and taught the corsairs how to build and navigate ships that could sail the Atlantic. By the 1620s, the corsairs, often led by English renegades, were frequently raiding the coasts of Ireland and Newfoundland. The reflection of English piracy in this new threat to England's own empire exemplifies the unstable workings of cultural mimesis: what began as a state-sanctioned expansionist strategy eventually threatens the national borders and national identity of that very state. My argument charts the trajectory of piratical subjects' increasing independence vis-à-vis the English state – from the paradox of privateering, in which supposed private quarrels were harnessed to the service of the state, to the murky lawlessness of piracy, to, finally, the absolute break of the renegadoes. In my reading of Heywood and Rowley's *Fortune by Land and Sea*, Heywood's *The Fair Maid of the West* and Massinger's *The Renegado*, I focus on class and gender indiscretions to suggest that these plays stage the general English reluctance to abandon the aristocratic masculinity of the privateers in favor of a more fluid and performative mercantile model.

Chapter 6, "Pirating Spain," analyzes the representation of Spanish identity in literary accounts of piracy and captivity. The first part analyzes the teleological apparatus of Lope de Vega's *La Dragontea*, an epic poem on the pirate Drake. Lope's rhetorical strategy frames the English threat to Spanish possessions within the larger struggle of Catholicism against its enemies east and west, and suggests that the bedrock of Spanish identity lies precisely in the heroic endurance of their attacks. Yet while the *Dragontea*'s account of nefarious English piracy enables the discursive consolidation of a Spanish identity that is eternally committed to the Faith, other, more ambiguous narratives of piracy and captivity often challenge the integrity of that identity. By focusing on liminal characters such as renegadoes and converts to Christianity, the second part of this chapter analyzes the fragility of a Spanish identity fundamentally based on religious difference. The representation of ethnic and religious ambiguity in Cervantine narratives of piracy and kidnapping, especially, suggests that these marginal characters pose a serious threat to a Spanish identity based on an irreproducible Christianity. Cervantes' depiction of religion and nationality as flexible, performable categories suggests the porous boundaries of a "purely" Christian Spain, whose intactness is undermined by the mimetic performance of those it would exclude.

Finally, a note on the limitations of this project. It does not fully address the Islamic or Native American dimensions of the problem, but instead focuses on texts – both by Europeans and by writers who strategically claim that status – that write themselves into a European dialogue, couching their critiques in terms that make them not only readable but persuasive to European audiences.[16] I am primarily interested in how mimesis confounds the homogenizing, exclusionist goals of the state in texts that ostensibly align themselves with that state. My focus on Europe will, I hope, yield new insights about its self-construction in relation to Islam and the particular modalities of European imperialism that affected Europe's others around the globe.

1　Truth, fictions, and the New World

As the craze for romances of chivalry and other imaginative literature took hold of readers in sixteenth-century Spain, the popularity of such fictions generated a spate of moralist criticisms attacking them for their lies and impropriety. Strikingly, the first Spanish laws against imaginative literature were directed not at Peninsular readers but at those in the New World, which itself often appeared far stranger than fiction to astonished European eyes. The censorship reveals as much about European anxieties over truth and empire as about metropolitan relations to native readers. In the contact-zone, a delicate armature of romance fictions and religious truths served to assimilate the marvelous, while underwriting Spanish claims to empire. But the fragile equilibrium was disturbed by the irrepressible workings of the romance marvelous. In the Old World as in the New, the beguiling treacherousness of the *verisimilar* – the careful imitation of the true – made romance representations at one and the same time powerful displays of artistic prowess, inspiring models, and potential weapons of subversion.

In the ebullient first decades after the introduction of the printing press to Spain, the New World (especially areas of intense evangelical activity, such as New Spain) served as a testing ground for problems of reading and interpretation, even as Protestantism – by privileging direct access to texts – attacked the Roman Catholic Church's previous monopoly on truth. In the Americas, the ascription of truth to European texts had crucial religious and political implications, while the doubting of that truth could endanger the entire colonial enterprise. Yet orthodox interpretations seemed increasingly vulnerable to a contagion of fictionality, as the reproduction of the romance marvelous challenged the singular power of authorized versions.

Lying histories, sacred truths

Erasmian humanists in Spain first began to articulate a critique of chivalric romances in the 1520s and 30s, arguing that they not only provided an

13

immoral example for women and young men but lied in recounting marvelous feats that were obviously untrue.[1] Why, then, did the first legislation against imaginative literature concern not the vulnerable readers in Spain, but rather the natives of the New World? Why does the metropolitan concern so quickly find its way to a colonial stage? The Spanish monarchy's concern with the Indians' successful Christianization goes at least some way towards explaining the insistent focus on them in this body of legislation. Indian readers were under the moral tutelage of the Crown. Since Spain's claim to the New World was based largely on a pontifical grant that required the Christianization of the natives, it was vitally important to safeguard their moral welfare, even as they were infantilized or feminized by their implicit comparison to "impressionable" readers in Spain.[2]

Accounts of the censorship laws have generally ignored the intricate cultural anxieties that they express. Irving Leonard, although he stresses the emphasis on the natives' reading habits, is mainly concerned with showing that the conquistadors were quite free to read. Leonard wants to demonstrate that books were exported to the New World, in order to prove that colonial society was not the obscurantist milieu described by the Black Legend of Spain's cruel conquest, but rather a literate environment well supplied with books.[3] Thus he reads the reiteration of anti-romance laws as evidence that the ban was not obeyed, and the focus on native readers as a sign that Spaniards could read at will. Yet although Leonard convincingly establishes the presence of books in the Spanish colonies, his focus on the conquistadors as the group that managed to read around the ban precludes him from exploring what motivated the censorship in the first place.

The laws suggest certain pressing questions: what phantasmic threats to Spanish power were they intended to address? And how did the perceived threats impact Spanish policies on Indian education and evangelization, as well as attitudes towards truth in literature? Although the decrees ostensibly protect the Indians' moral welfare, they immediately establish a connection between what these subjects read and how well they can be governed. Consider this 1536 document, addressed by Empress Isabella to Antonio de Mendoza, viceroy of New Spain, for the "good government" of the province, while the Emperor was fighting the Moors in Tunis:

Algunos días ha que el Emperador y Rey mi Señor proveyó que no se llevasen a esas partes Libros de Romance de materias profanas y fábulas por que los indios que supiesen leer no se diesen a ellos dejando los libros de buena y sana doctrina, y leyéndolos no aprendiesen en ellos malas costumbres y vicios y también porque desde que supiesen que aquellos libros de historias vanas habían sido compuestos sin haber pasado así no perdiesen la autoridad y crédito de nuestra Sagrada Escritura y otros libros de doctores santos, creyendo como gente no arraigada en la fe que todos nuestros libros eran de una autoridad y manera. Y porque creemos que en la ejecución de esto no ha habido el cuidado que debría mucho os encargamos y mandamos proveáis como de aquí [en] adelante no se vendan libros algunos desta calidad ni se traigan de nuevo porque cesen estos inconvenientes, procurando que los españoles no los tengan en sus casas ni permitan que indio alguno lea en ellos. Y porque somos informados que ya comienzan a entender gramática algunos naturales de esa tierra, mandaréis a los preceptores que les enseñan que les lean siempre libros de cristiana o moral doctrina.[4]

[Some days ago the Emperor ruled that no Romance Books of profane matter and fables be sent to those lands, lest the Indians who know how to read give themselves over to them, abandoning books of good and healthy doctrine, and reading them learn bad habits and vices and also lest, once they know that those books of vain stories were composed without things really having occurred thus, they no longer place authority and credit in our Sacred Scriptures and other books by learned saints, believing, as a people not well established in the faith, that all our books are of one authority and kind. And because we fear that the proper care has not been taken in the execution of this decree we very much entreat and order you to see that from now on no books of this sort be sold or brought anew, that these unsuitable effects might cease, and to see that the Spaniards do not keep them in their houses nor permit any Indians to read them. And because we are told that some of the natives begin to understand grammar, you will order their preceptors to read them always books of Christian or moral doctrine.][5]

The problem seems to be that the Indians are not only astute readers, but dangerously formalist. Instead of merely being taken in by the "lies" of romance (as naive readers presumably would be), they extrapolate from those narrated untruths to the Bible and other sacred writings, putting the religious truths into question because they cannot – or will not – discriminate among texts according to their authority. The dangerous leveling of European cultural productions, sacred and profane, by these imagined readers, pushes the Spaniards to censorship. The motive is newly underscored in yet another, nearly identical, instance of the order, written by Prince Philip to officials in Seville, whence the dangerous books were exported, in 1543:

Sabed que de llevarse a las dichas Indias libros de romance y materias profanas y fábulas así como son libros de Amadís y otros de esta calidad de mentirosas historias se siguen muchos inconvenientes porque los indios que supieren leer dándose a ellos dejarán los libros de sana y buena doctrina y leyendo los de mentirosas historias aprenderán en ellos malas costumbres y vicios. Y además de esto, de que sepan que aquellos libros de historias vanas han sido compuestos sin haber pasado, así podría ser que perdiesen la autoridad y crédito de nuestra Sagrada Escritura y otros libros de doctores santos, creyendo como gente no arraigada en la fe que todos nuestros libros eran de una autoridad y manera.[6]

[You must know that many troubles would stem from taking romance books of profane matters and fables, such as the books of Amadís and other lying stories of this type, to the aforementioned Indies, because the Indians who know how to read, giving themselves over to these books, will abandon the books of good and healthy doctrine, and reading those books of lying histories will learn from them bad habits and vices. And moreover, once they know that these vain stories were written without having occurred, they might lose the authority and credit of our Sacred Scripture and other books by learned saints, believing, like people not well established in the faith that all our books were of the same authority and manner.]

While this decree brings up the problem of exemplarity ("they will learn from them bad habits and vices"), it quickly returns to the central source of anxiety that figured so prominently in the 1536 decree: once the Indians realize that romances lie – i.e. that they describe things that did not truly happen – they will cease to believe in the Bible. Syntax breaks down so that it becomes impossible to pinpoint agency when the Bible is discredited: the phrase "así podría ser que perdiesen la autoridad y crédito de nuestra Sagrada Escritura" collapses the text's loss of authority with the readers' loss of faith in it. The persistent problem, then, is not the generalized assumption of truth in every text, and the concomitant belief in the romance fictions (what one might term the "Don Quijote syndrome"), but rather the contagion of fictionality from imaginative to religious texts. The censorship decrees impose a kind of legislative quarantine on the romances, recent arrivals from the Old World that threaten the proper functioning of the colonies.

In challenging notions of authority and closure through their digressive structure and fantastic "lies," the romances undermine the very authority of any text, as construct.[7] If Cervantes' *Don Quijote* thematizes the problem of the naive reader, who believes that the magic world of the romances is real, then surely Ariosto's immensely popular combination of epic and chivalric romance, the *Orlando Furioso* (1516, 1532), gives the most disruptive example of the correlative problem, where fictionality contaminates all texts and all spaces.[8] Ariosto's treatment of the marvelous is more debunking than mystification, despite the fact that he exposes the mechanics of verisimilitude in the most fanciful of settings. Perhaps the most far-reaching episode in the *Furioso*, literally and figuratively, is the paladin Astolfo's famous voyage to the moon in search of Orlando's wits in Cantos 34–35. This voyage to a distant and unknown land constitutes an education in reading; Astolfo's encounter with a different new world teaches him a highly suspicious hermeneutics. The first lesson is on perspective: Astolfo expresses his surprise that the moon, which seems so small when seen from earth, should actually prove so large (34.71–72). But the more important lesson comes when St. John – the authority behind both the Gospel and the prophecies of Revelation – takes the opportunity to educate the traveling knight on the relative nature of truth. Patrons, he tells Astolfo, control the writing of history by employing poets favorable to them, and John himself is but one more such writer, with Christ as his particular patron. I quote at some length to give a sense of the passage's ironic irreverence:

> Non fu sì santo né benigno Augusto
> come la tuba di Virgilio suona.
> L'aver avuto in poesia buon gusto
> la proscrizion iniqua gli perdona.
> Nessun sapria se Neron fosse ingiusto,
> né sua fama saria forse men buona,
> avesse avuto e terra e ciel nimici,
> se gli scrittor sapea tenersi amici.
>
> Omero Agamennón vittorioso,
> e fe' i Troian parer vili et inerti;
> e che Penelopea fida al suo sposo
> dai Prochi mille oltraggi avea sofferti.
> E se tu vuoi che l'ver non ti sia ascoso,
> tutta al contrario l'istoria converti:
> che i Greci rotti, e che Troia vittrice,
> e che Penelopea fu meretrice.
>
> Da l'altra parte odi che fama lascia
> Elissa, ch'ebbe il cor tanto pudico;
> che riputata viene una bagascia,
> solo perché Maron non le fu amico.
> Non ti maravigliar ch'io n'abbia ambascia,
> e se di ciò diffusamente io dico.
> Gli scrittori amo, e fo il debito mio;
> ch'al vostro mondo fui scrittore anch'io.
>
> E sopra tutti gli altri io feci acquisto
> che non mi puó levar tempo né morte:
> e ben convenne al mio lodato Cristo
> rendermi guirardon di sì gran sorte.[9]

[Augustus was not as august and beneficent as Virgil makes him out in clarion tones – but his good taste in poetry compensates for the evil of his proscriptions. And no one would know whether Nero had been wicked – he might even, for all his enemies on earth and in heaven, have left a better name – had he known how to keep friendly with writers./ Homer made Agamemnon appear the victim and the Trojans mere poltroons; he made Penelope faithful to her husband, and victim of a thousand slights from her suitors. But if you want to know what really happened, invert the story: Greece was vanquished, Troy triumphant, and Penelope a whore./ Listen on the other hand to what reputation Dido left behind, whose heart was so chaste: she was reputed a strumpet purely because Virgil was no friend of hers.

Don't be surprised if this embitters me and if I talk about it at some length – I like writers and am doing my duty by them, for in your world I was a writer too./ And I, above all others, acquired something which neither Time nor Death can take from me: I praised Christ and merited from Him the reward of so great a good fortune.][10]

These latter-day revelations of the compromised nature of historical accounts place all writing on a continuum of fictionality, negating the truth of even divinely authorized texts.[11] As Patricia Parker has argued, St. John's admission threatens to "reduce even the Gospel to the status of a literary fiction."[12] Both historical and divine texts might seem true, the Evangelist suggests, but the authority behind them is fundamentally compromised by self-interest. Although John's own reward might be greater than all others', it is nonetheless obtained as part of a patron–writer arrangement. The Evangelist, as "imitator of Christ" (35.10), loyally reproduces his message but gives away the trick: fidelity is bought at a price.[13]

Ariosto's subversive account of two major books of the New Testament, the Gospel of John and the Book of Revelation, poses a much more direct threat to Church truth than less self-conscious romances. Yet even if the *Furioso* represents an extreme case, a similar type of danger – a less deliberate but no less dangerous leveling of the sacred and the profane – was perceived in all romances, as the decrees issued for the New World make clear. In Europe, Ariosto's poem was to become central to literary quarrels over the nature of romance that consumed critics over the course of the century. Although the quarrels often focused on the formal merits or demerits of variety and multiplicity, critics were concerned also with the ideological implications of truth and fictions – the very issue that Astolfo's voyage discovers so brazenly. On both sides of the Atlantic, then, romance itself was held under suspicion as potentially dangerous to cultural and religious truth.

Romance conquest

Before exploring precisely the ways in which readerly subversion affected Spain's interests in the New World, I will briefly describe the positive effects of chivalric romances on Spanish empire-building. A persuasive case can be made that prohibitions against imaginative literature were directed chiefly against the Indians because the Crown in fact approved of the effects it had on its main readers, the Spanish colonists. How, then, did romance further the Conquista? Viewed through the lens of chivalric romance, the conquistadors' advances in America seem the by-product of frustrated desires. Spanish expansion consists of a series of incidental conquests in a romance mode: the explorers set off for El Dorado and instead find Bolivia; they conquer Florida while seeking the Fountain of Youth.[14] The perverse refusal of the landscape to furnish the exact object of desire does not stop the expansion, but instead propels it forward. The transcendent, heroic project of imperialist expansion almost depends upon resistance from the landscape, to justify the constant advance of its own wandering desire.[15] Leonard's impression of this phenomenon is quite fanciful – he is taken with the idea of valiant conquistadors overcoming impossible odds in pursuit of impossible goals. Yet despite this idealizing tendency he provides several concrete examples of the ways in which literary constructs actively fueled a kind of mimetic discovery. Perhaps the clearest one is the powerful myth of the Amazons, newly popularized in the chivalric romance *Las sergas de Esplandián*, the first sequel to the hugely popular *Amadís de Gaula*. The Spaniards were so convinced that the warrior women would be found on the newly discovered lands that some contracts of exploration included specific instructions to search for their tribes.[16]

Clearly, quests for fictional goals within the real landscape functioned in the Crown's best interests. By imagining themselves as chivalric heroes, the Spaniards managed to digest the strangeness of their surroundings and insert themselves into a triumphalist fiction, one borne out not by attainment of ever-elusive mythical goals, but rather by the astonishing conquest and destruction wrought upon native civilizations across America. If the Christian knights of many chivalric romances – including the *Furioso* – fought Muslim enemies, in the New World version they took on the Indians. In this fashion, the romance model accommodated also the Spaniards' figuration of the Conquista as a new version of the Reconquista, the extended struggle to expel the Moors from the Peninsula: the self-designated chivalric knights saw themselves wresting territory from the infidels, as their ancestors had done in Spain.[17] Thus the romances contributed to Spain's increasing control over American territory and peoples, precisely by confusing the boundaries between truth and fiction that so exercised the metropolitan moralists. Regardless of its illusory qualities, the Don Quijote effect – albeit with a good deal less charm and humanist measure – actively benefited the imperial cause.

Why, then, legislate against the romances? Although it targeted the Indians, the ban on imports of imaginative literature would have affected both settlers and natives in America if observed. The problem is reconciling the cultural and religious conquest of the New World with its territorial conquest. The Crown contradictorily desires to achieve the successful conversion of its native subjects through careful censorship, but without dampening the expansionist imaginings of the conquistadors, fed by the same suspect fictions. Royal ambivalence about audience response is further complicated by an equal ambivalence about the texts themselves: forbidding Indians to read imaginative texts because they might confuse them with the Bible signals the Crown's recognition (almost in spite of itself) that some analogy, however slim, exists between profane and sacred narration. Prohibiting imaginative literature in order to defend biblical texts tacitly acknowledges that no text comes with a universally guaranteed, exceptional right to be considered true.

Training readers

Anxieties over the truth content of texts circulating in the New World profoundly affected Spanish policies of education and evangelization. Over the course of the sixteenth century, the Crown debated the advisability of educating the Indians. How much reading should be involved? Should they be taught in Spanish or in Latin? Could Indians be ordained? The earliest educational experiments in the Indies divided responsibilities between the Church and the *encomenderos*, Spaniards who exploited Indian labor, ostensibly in exchange for providing them with Christian instruction. The colonists were instructed to educate the "most able" among their charges.[18] Another early model established teaching by exemplarity within the native ranks: the educated Indians, sons of nobles or chiefs, were to educate the mass of the Indians in their turn.

Given these modes of education, one begins to see how the threat of unauthorized readings by the Indians coincided with that of a native hierarchy reestablishing its own values rather than transmitting those of the conquerors. The Spaniards chose to teach noble Indians in order to reinforce existing class hierarchies.[19] Yet the nobles thus taught did not learn to be willing subjects of the colonial masters, but rather their equals. Could resistant readers become resistant leaders? Without romanticizing the possibility, it is striking to note that Indians who did challenge Spanish rule in the New World invoked the ostensible equivalence of preexisting native hierarchies to those of the Spaniards as proof that the natives were capable of self-rule.[20] As the century progressed, the Spaniards became increasingly uneasy with the intellectual fluidity that the natives acquired in their studies. The Crown's determination to make full-fledged subjects of the Indians was tentative, to say the least.

Reading made the Indians disturbingly similar to their conquerors, especially when they read Latin. In New Spain, which saw perhaps the most utopian and full-fledged attempt to educate the Indians, the Franciscans conducted a large-scale effort to teach Latin, mainly at the Colegio de Santa Cruz de Tlatelolco and at the University of Mexico, founded at mid-century. There was considerable debate about whether it was prudent to Europeanize the Indians by teaching them the language of theology, and a general reluctance to give the Indians free access to texts such as the

Bible, which had confounded European intellects.[21] Direct access, it must be remembered, was one of the primary differences between the Church of Rome and the proponents of church reform, who argued for lay readership of the Bible in the vernacular. To teach the Indians to read the Scriptures in Latin was to allow them to bypass the Church hierarchy and enjoy the unmediated access to the sacred word espoused by Protestantism, albeit in the language of Rome. Again, there is the suggestion that reading – and education more generally – allowed the Indians to elude the cultural control of the very Spaniards who taught them. When the few *bachilleres* trained at Tlatelolco discussed rhetoric in Latin with the friars, they were leap-frogging over the vernacular to the classical culture that the Europeans prized so highly. At least while this utopian phase lasted, the Franciscans could imagine the transformation of the natives into their cultural peers.

Transformation through education threatened colonial hierarchies on many fronts. One magnificent example of the results of Franciscan education was Don Pablo Nazareo de Xalcotán, who wrote a series of letters in Latin to Philip II suing for the restitution of his noble privileges, including the right to bear arms and ride horses.[22] Don Pablo ably argued that he was Toltec, and not Mexica (Aztec), and had thus endured two invasions; by distancing himself from those defeated by the Spaniards, he laid claim to the same rights the Spaniards enjoyed. Don Pablo's Latin letters betray not only his careful reading of the Bible, but also a certain familiarity with Roman law and even Ovid.[23]

But whereas critics have read Don Pablo Nazareo as the "archetypal paradigm of the acculturated Indian,"[24] profoundly marked by Spanish political propaganda as well as by religious proselytism, I believe that his quest for redress may be read as a far greater challenge to Spanish authority. Don Pablo exemplifies the threats of the mimetic same-but-different: by giving him a humanist education, the Spaniards have provided the cultural materials to confute the essential difference between the conquerors and the conquered. In Michael Taussig's suggestive formulation, the copy – here the native subject himself – affects the original by taking on its properties.[25] Seen from this angle, Don Pablo's transformation is at once far more complicated and far less submissive to Spain than the notion of acculturation would suggest, for it challenges the exclusive privileges of Spanish subjects. Don Pablo's rehearsal of European culture for his own purposes ably harnesses the instability of mimesis in the colonial encounter to achieve his own ends. The Franciscans provide the knowledge, but it is the student's strategic use of what he has learned in a calculated imitation of Spanish cultural forms that reveals the true power of literacy, and especially of Latin. The self-styled noble Don Pablo treats his education in the colonists' culture as a *mode d'emploi,* which enables him to locate his own pressing local claims and demands for restitution in the interstices and fractures of their proclaimed truths. The model originally offered for the acculturation of the native becomes instead a mode of resistance, albeit of a personal and limited scope.

When Don Pablo presents himself as the equal of any native Spaniard, he proposes a formalist reading of his own merits that undermines the distinctions between colonizers and colonized. His reinterpretation of colonial hierarchies exposes the constructedness of a difference that depends on metropolitan prejudice. His suit thus suggests that only a strong hermeneutic predisposition *for* Spain can prevent contestatory readings both of and in the colonial space. The Crown's anxiety about native readers' misprision of the marvelous, with which this chapter began, betrays a grudging acknowledgment of the contingency of interpretation. As even the Crown will admit, the romance texts and sacred writings exported to the New World present similar narrated wonders; what distinguishes them is an a priori value judgment.

The threat resides in their similarity. The existence of simulacra within the larger "text" of colonial culture continuously elides the distinctions central to colonialist ideology. Romance texts for sacred ones, native subjects for colonial masters – if these are really indistinguishable, orthodox hierarchies disappear. What is more, the threat of the verisimilar recurs at the textual as at the historical level. In the textual realm, the romances of chivalry and the sacred texts share a telling symptom: the topos of treacherous duplication. While chivalric knights are lured by evil apparitions in the form of damsels in distress or wondrous palaces, religious texts warn against the beguiling artifice of that arch-fiend, Satan. In the historical realm, the problem of satanic look-alikes complicates evangelization in the New World. Even as Christianity spreads, the religious orders find it difficult to distinguish the "demonic" simulacra of self-sacrifice, pilgrimage, and purification rituals – all astutely preserved aspects of prehispanic religions – from "real" devotions.[26] When indigenous peoples profess their faith in the Christian God by performing these rites, the Spaniards cannot determine the "truth" of the performance. The dissimulation thus allows native religions, especially in more isolated areas, to survive with a minimum of syncretic adaptation.[27]

The repressive dictates of the Council of Trent (1545–63) soon cemented the New World uneasiness over educating the Indian elite. In 1563, the Council reinforced existing hierarchies by decreeing that bishops should translate the catechism and sacraments into the vernacular, so that priests could communicate them to the faithful. The immediate European rationale for such a resolution, as with so many of the Trentine decrees, was

Protestantism, which appealed to the faithful precisely because of direct access to sacred texts in the vernacular. Yet clearly the contemporary American experience of a confrontation with readers who could misinterpret sacred texts, and manipulate them for their own purposes, also made the Spaniards at home uneasy with the uncensored dissemination of religious and cultural truths.

The gradual movement to cease educating the Indians focused on problems of reading and interpretation. In New Spain, provincial religious councils convened in 1555 and 1565 decided that Indians should be excluded from the sacred orders and recommended that they be forbidden to read printed texts or manuscripts.[28] By 1580, a canon by the name of Marín urged the king to forbid the Jesuits from offering the Indians a higher education, emphasizing the dangers of heretical reading in no uncertain terms, and conjuring the specter of Lutheranism:

En la Yndia o China, que los yndios tienen colegios, y son filósophos; allí conbiene que aya otros colegios de otros mayores cathólicos, filósophos que ellos, para que confundan a sus herrores. Pero estos que están tiernos, y con esta leche de nuestra doctrina cristiana, y sus intendimientos están quietos y sosegados; no combiene meterlos en otras ciencias; no salga alguno de ellos, en el qual se rebista el demonio lo qual Dios no primita, y venga a ynbentar otras nuevas eregías, como Martín Lutero, y den otros falsos entendimientos a la letra y ciencias que deprendieron.[29]

[In India or China, where the Indians have schools, and are philosophers, there it is fit that we should have other schools, run by greater Catholics and philosophers to confound their errors. But these, who are tender with the milk of Christian doctrine, and whose intellects are quiet and calm, should not be led to other sciences, lest the devil disguise himself as one of them, God forbid, and invent new heresies, like Martin Luther, and lest they give other false meanings to the letters and sciences they have learned.]

The canon imagines an agonistic model in which Christianity fights it out with other cultures where their existence is granted, as in the ancient and highly admired cultures of the Far East or in India, but argues that the putative cultural vacuum of the American natives leaves them prey to the devil's tricks once educated. Like Martin Luther, they might come up with new, and illicit, interpretations. In fact, as the example of Don Pablo Nazareo de Xalcotán shows, the Indians were only too willing to use their learning to attempt to counteract the ravages of the Conquista. That, of course, was why their misreadings required urgent attention.

Metropolitan heroics

In the troubled climate of the Counter-Reformation, all fictions became newly suspect, and reading itself seemed fraught with dangers. The

European literary quarrels of the mid- to late-sixteenth century took place in an increasingly repressive ideological context. The new, often obsessive focus on the restrictions and specifications of Aristotle's *Poetics* went hand in hand with the Tridentine Church's deepening suspicion of the connections between humanism and Protestantism.[30] The poet whose writings conflate the two sets of constraints – classical and contemporary – in the most interesting fashion is Torquato Tasso. In an Italy that was largely a colony of Spain, Tasso continuously reworked an epic fantasy of expanding Christian empire in order to expurgate both religious and literary heterodoxy.

Although conventionally read as two distinct works, *Gerusalemme liberata* (1581) and *Gerusalemme conquistata* (1593), Tasso's poem in fact existed in a number of intermediate guises. He seemed reluctant to fix his text in any one version that could be attacked on aesthetic, religious, or political grounds; only through constant revision could he achieve the kind of "floating" text that would be infinitely responsive to criticism. Tasso's repeated defenses of his own writing exhibit a sustained anxiety about the possible effects of reading on authority that goes beyond Aristotelian aesthetic considerations. His concerns echo those of the Spanish censors, or the ambivalent teachers of New Spain, as he struggles to situate his poetry against those pernicious bestsellers that so troubled the Spanish Crown: *Orlando Furioso*, and his own father's rambling romance, *Amadigi*, a poetic version of *Amadís de Gaula*.[31] Most interesting, perhaps, is Tasso's lifelong attempt to reconcile the great literary appeal of the romance marvelous – as exemplified by Ariosto's immensely popular *Furioso* – with the historical verisimilitude and seriousness he sought for his own works. Tasso attempts to correct Ariosto's subversion of Christian truth, but finds it impossible to forgo romance, regardless of its perils. His theoretical writings document his constant efforts to attract readers by incorporating romance marvels into his epic poetry, without transgressing against the "real" Christian God.

Tasso's anxieties over truth versus romance have traditionally been read as a purely literary, purely European phenomenon. I will argue here that they project the American experience of reading, with its vagaries of authorized and unauthorized textual interpretation, onto the European literary landscape. The parameters of counter-colonial influence remain to be determined; it may be that Tasso's is a unique – though surely significant – case. The effects of New World reading may well be different for other quarrels, or other genres. Nonetheless, by analyzing the evanescent trace of the New World in Tasso's theoretical and literary production, I will suggest some ways in which to recover those effects. In recent years, critics have fruitfully explored Tasso's varying accounts of the New World;

this chapter locates those representations within the larger context of mimesis and empire, introducing a consideration of New World reading into Old World literary debates.[32]

Tasso portrays in his poem that ideal of militant Christianity from which all chivalric romances were a sad falling away: the First Crusade, under Godfrey of Bulloigne. His choice of subject matter is telling precisely for what it does *not* address: in the century of great discoveries both in the East and West Indies, and of the massive Christianization of the American natives, Tasso imagines a European empire firmly focused on the Near East. The crusade is portrayed as a return to "liberate Christ's great sepulcher" – that is, to recover what belongs by rights to a militant, expansionist Christianity. Christian warriors from all over Europe join the crusade, in a historical fantasy that permits Tasso to gloss over the contemporary rifts which so bitterly divided the Christian Church. Moreover, recent victories against the Turks, such as the battle of Lepanto, which had reinforced Spanish authority over large parts of Italy, are passed over in favor of a distant historical episode.[33] Tasso's anachronistic imagining of a unified Christian empire thus minimizes the many divisions, political and religious, of sixteenth-century Europe, as well as the contemporary confrontations between Christianity and its others. His imaginary Europe – unproblematically and univocally identified with Christendom – dissimulates the bitter imperial and religious rivalries that marked the poet's era.

This is not to say that Tasso's poem unequivocally conveys European unity and Christian superiority. The Christian leader notably lacks charisma, while the besieged city of Jerusalem and its inhabitants are sympathetically portrayed. Yet these ideological fissures are conspicuously sealed: as David Quint has shown, the poem occasionally introduces rebellious characters who might challenge religious orthodoxy, such as the mutinous knight Argillano and the Ethiopian warrior-woman Clorinda, only to contain them.[34] Moreover, the poet himself attempts to exonerate his poem through his critical writings, going to great lengths to fix the meaning of his imagery, as in the "Allegory of the Poem" that he added to *Gerusalemme liberata* after its publication. These efforts are no doubt in response to the repressive context in which the poem existed, and will not serve to settle the question of Tasso's orthodoxy.

The singularity of Tasso's project failed to please all readers. Attacks on the *Liberata* compared it unfavorably with the brilliant romance digressions of *Orlando Furioso*, and Tasso defended his poem by casting its problems in a religious and political light: Romance Multiplicity, he suggests, equals paganism and political instability, while Epic Singularity equals Christian absolutism.[35] Yet Tasso strove also to address the opposite criticism, that his poem included too many romance elements for a

Christian epic.[36] Although he criticized the *Furioso* as an "animale d'incerta natura,"[37] – a mongrel or even monstrous animal, incongruously composed of epic and romance – his own poem merits a similar description. In the "Allegory" Tasso published to accompany the *Liberata*, he states: "Heroic poetry, like a living creature in which two natures are combined, is compounded of Imitation and Allegory."[38] It is not clear that the moralizing nature of what Tasso calls "allegory" saves the poem from the same monstrosity of which he accused the *Furioso*.

In virtually all his theoretical writings on poetry – the early *Discorsi dell' Arte Poetica* (written ca. 1567), later expanded into the 1594 *Discorsi del Poema Eroico*, as well as in the *Apologia in difesa della "Gerusalemme liberata"* (1585) – Tasso wrestles with the seductive power of the romance marvelous. Already in the first *Discourses*, the poet recognizes the need of fictions to counter fictions. Although he argues that above all poetry must be verisimilar, he imagines a possible conjunction of verisimilitude and wonder:

Some works that greatly exceed the power of men the poet attributes to God, to His angels, to demons, or to those granted such power by God or by demons, like saints and wizards and fairies. If considered by themselves, these works seem wondrous; in fact, common usage calls them miracles. These same works, if attention is given to the virtue and the power that have wrought them, are deemed verisimilar. Since our people have imbibed this opinion in the cradle, along with their milk, and since it was confirmed in them by the masters of our blessed Faith (that is, that God and his ministers and demons and magicians, with his permission, can do things wondrous beyond the forces of nature) and, finally, since every day they read and hear new examples related, therefore it does not appear to them beyond verisimilitude . . . Likewise, to the ancients, who lived in the errors of their vain religion, those miracles must not have seemed impossible which not only their poets but sometimes the historians relate about their gods – for even if learned men deem them impossible (as they were), the opinion of the multitude suffices the poet in this, as in many other things; and many times, abandoning the exact truth of things, he is accustomed to, and should, hold closely to his opinion.[39]

This Tasso is more than pragmatic – he is virtually a relativist. To reproduce the immense romance appeal of the *Furioso* in a Christian context, Tasso proposes harnessing the marvelous to a Christian rationale. Hence, in his own poem, the descent of the archangel Michael in Canto 9 replaces the classical motif of the messenger-god's descent from heaven and establishes the divine purpose of what will occur on the battlefield.[40] Yet this kind of miracle-making, and especially the rationale Tasso provides, places the poet in the rather tricky theological position of mimicking God's truth, even as he opportunistically squeezes his fiction into that slim space between the truth of the Faith and readers' belief in it. In this formulation, it seems impossible for poetry to harness religious truth without relativizing it as *verisimilar*. The attempt to neutralize the marvelous by placing it in a proper theological context only mires the poet in greater controversy.

Tasso elaborates further on the problem of religious truth by suggesting that a poet should find his epic theme in "chronicles of true religion but not of such great authority as to be unalterable."[41] The proper theme for an epic poem on a religious topic seems to be something like the "not-so-true." Yet if religious truth can shade into fiction in this way, perhaps there is no essential difference between the two. It appears we have come full circle, so that Tasso's prescription for the verisimilar perversely justifies the Spanish Crown's rationale for quarantining the Indians from imaginative literature. Significantly, whereas Tasso preserves the discussion of Christian miracles in the expanded *Discourses*, he disguises the explicit recommendation to choose a semi-authoritative religious topic, dissimulating it within a forest of scholastic distinctions:

> Ecclesiastical and spiritual writings command greater authority, if one may put it so, since, as St. Thomas held, all spiritual things are sacred, although not all sacred things are spiritual. The others doubtless have less authority. The poet had better not touch histories of the first type; they may be left in their pure and simple truth, since with them discovery takes no effort and invention seems hardly permitted. And whoever does not invent or imitate, but restricts himself to the very details given, would be no poet but rather a historian.[42]

Explaining miracles as the work of God in order to preserve romance might occasionally prove a solution for the hamstrung poet, but building poetry upon religious near-truths seems a much trickier endeavor. Tasso's cagey formulation in the later *Discourses* shows full well the pitfalls of writing a Christian epic. The writer of such a text is constrained on all sides: if the epic were "invented," – i.e. merely verisimilar – it would challenge the truth of the religion upon which it was based. If, on the other hand, it replicated the "truth," it would both detract from that truth's singularity, and, moreover, lack the poetic hallmark of invention.

Even as Tasso refined his poetic theory, the propriety of the *Liberata* continued to trouble him. He defended it in his theoretical and critical writings and labored at the revised version that was to become *Gerusalemme conquistata*. Whatever liberatory energies lay in the *Liberata* were presumably laid to rest in the conquered poem, which – perhaps due to its relentless orthodoxy – has never attained the canonical status of its predecessor. If the *Liberata*'s singularity was intended to improve upon Ariostan romance, then the *Conquistata* takes Tasso's ideological single-mindedness even further: the revised poem aggressively suppresses the wandering sensuous energies of the earlier version by focusing more narrowly on the spiritual. This narrowed scope and resistance to wandering are reflected in the poem's geography, which becomes similarly restrictive.

The ideological adventurousness of Tasso's poem may be mapped by scrutinizing the poem's geography for the landmarks of a poetic praxis. What accounts for the gradual disappearance of Western exploration from the poem? To what extent does Tasso's turn to a biblical landscape resolve the problems of truth and representation that dog his poetic project? Tasso's critical writings support a symptomatic reading: in his later *Discourses*, the matter of America appears as a balm for the Christian poet's plagued creativity, by providing "recently discovered" material that is both new, and, because unknown, easily credible.[43] Yet the poetic remedy also represents the intellectual adventurousness of going beyond the Pillars of Hercules, which Tasso cannot justify:

Many people think, my illustrious lord, that the same thing has happened with the noblest arts and sciences as with peoples, provinces, lands, and oceans, a number of which were not well known to the ancients, but have recently been discovered beyond the Pillars of Hercules to the west, or indeed beyond the altars Alexander set up in the east. They compare the achievements of the poetic and rhetorical arts to the goals and other marks placed as boundaries to timid navigators. But just as I do not blame a daring that is guided by reason, so I do not praise a boldness without reflection, for I think it an insanity that anyone should wish to create an art from chance, virtue from vice, and prudence from temerity.[44]

As Sergio Zatti has observed, Tasso here uses the imagery of discovery to ponder the situation of a modern poet vis-à-vis ancient rules for poetry.[45] Yet the New World serves also as a metaphor for the poet's temerity in going beyond the ideological, as well as the formal, limitations of his project. If sailing beyond the Pillars of Hercules exposes one to the inconstancy of the changing stars, it also underscores the difficulty of navigating between truth and verisimilitude.

Tasso's ambivalence about the intellectual hubris represented by the new discoveries is reflected in the gradual disappearance of the New World from his poem. Yet there remain faint traces of the European westward impulse in the safely biblical world of the *Liberata*. The most famous are Fortuna's vatic stanzas in praise of Columbus – a prophecy announcing the dissemination of the "faith of Peter" beyond the Pillars of Hercules:

> Un uom de la Liguria avrà ardimento
> a l'incognito corso esporsi in prima;
> né 'l minaccievol fremito del vento,
> né l'inospito mar, né 'l dubbio clima,
> né s'altro di periglio o di spavento
> più grave e formidabile or si stima,

faran che 'l generoso entro a i divieti
d'Abila angusti l'alta mente accheti.

Tu spiegherai, Colombo, a un novo polo
lontane sì le fortunate antenne,
ch'a pena seguirà con gli occhi il volo
la fama c'ha mille occhi e mille penne.
Canti ella Alcide e Bacco, e di te solo
basti a i posteri tuoi ch'alquanto accenne,
ché quel poco darà lunga memoria
di poema dignissima e d'istoria.[46]

[A man of Liguria will have the daring first to set himself on the unknown course:
and not the menacing howling of the wind, nor inhospitable seas, nor doubtful
clime, nor anything else that now may be esteemed more formidable and filled with
fear or danger will make the proud spirit content his lofty mind within the narrow
proscriptions of Abyla.

You, Columbus, will spread your fortunate sails so far toward an unknown pole
that Fame [that has a thousand eyes and a thousand wings] will scarcely follow
with her eyes your flight. Let her sing of Alcides and Bacchus, and of you let it be
enough that she only give some hint for your posterity: for that little will give you a
lasting memorial most worthy of Poetry and History.]

The limited "hint for posterity" has been quite effective; readers never fail
to notice the intriguing suggestion of things to come in this passage.[47] Yet,
paradoxically, the hint actually looks back, abbreviating a discarded episode: an earlier version of the *Liberata* included a far more extensive
journey West, modeled on Pigafetta's account of Magellan's voyage
around the world.[48] Tasso's careful reworking of his sources suggests that
he was well versed in New World lore; the narrative, included as an
appendix in some modern editions,[49] combines the historical specificity of
the discoveries – the giant Patagonians, the riches of Peru – with the
romance conventions of far-flung voyages.[50]

But the geography of the standard *Liberata* does not extend to the
Americas; instead, it stops at the Fortunate Isles – i.e. the Canaries – the
location of the enchantress Armida's deceptive paradise.[51] The rescue of
the wayward crusader, Rinaldo, from Armida's spell provides the occasion
for a westward voyage, as the knights Carlo and Ubaldo set out to find him
under the firm guidance of Fortuna, here transformed into an allegory of
Christian teleology (15.6). Fortuna predicts Columbus' great adventure as
part of God's design, but the crusading knights themselves go no further
than the Canaries, and are specifically forbidden to explore or experience
the new lands before God's appointed time (15.38–39).[52] Whether coded
positively or negatively, the discoveries are tightly harnessed to a religious
framework.[53]

The limited excursion beyond the Pillars of Hercules to the Fortunate Isles – the perfect locus for personified Fortuna – betrays its own ideological status through its heavy symbolism. Tasso's earlier, specific description of America gives way to the highly allegorical landscape of Armida's island, replete with dangerous snakes and lions, rugged snowy wastes below temperate plateaus, gardens in which art improves upon nature, and fleshy temptations. What lies just beyond Europe is equivocal and dangerous; who knows what might lie further? In Zatti's terms, America remains only as metonymy, with the Fortunate Isles as the "Atlantic residue of a greater project gradually sacrificed to the changing goals of Tasso's poetics."[54] As the poet increasingly restricts the wandering energies of his text, the new worlds to the West disappear entirely: the *Conquistata* sets Armida's lair in Lebanon, well within the known world and barely outside the main scene of battle.

Within the *Liberata*, all evidence of Armida's realm disappears after Rinaldo has been rescued. Once the hero has forsaken her, the sorceress conjures "three hundred deities from Avernus" to destroy her creation, and by the time day breaks there is nothing left of her fantastic palace:

> Come imagin talor d'immensa mole
> forman nubi ne l'aria e poco dura,
> ché'l vento la disperde o solve il sole,
> come sogno se'n va ch'egro figura,
> così sparver gli alberghi, e restàr sole
> l'alpe e l'orror che fece ivi natura.

(16.70, 1–6)

[As sometimes the clouds in middle air form images of a mighty mass, and last but little time, for the wind disperses them or sun dissolves; as a dream that an invalid fashions goes away; so disappeared the buildings and only remained the mountains and [the horror] that nature had created there.]

The palace is a dangerous simulacrum – its insubstantiality alerts one not only to the possible treacherousness of the marvelous but also to the moral hazards of the verisimilitude the poet attempts. Armida's imitation-Paradise links her to that other master artificer, the poet himself, and her deceit casts a shadow over Tasso's goal of a verisimilitude that imitates Christian truth.

As I have suggested earlier, the treacherous mimicry of the New World involves not only its deceptively paradisiacal landscapes but, more crucially, its inhabitants' capacity to imitate Europeanness or Christianity.[55] Such New World mimicry also plays a central role in the *Liberata*. The satisfying moral resolution of the poem depends not only on the anticipated (and historical) defeat of the infidel, but also on the conversion of a pagan, somewhat unceremoniously yanked into the fold at the point where ideological truth takes precedence over verisimilitude. Rinaldo's attempted conversion of the enchantress Armida as she attempts to take her own life – a few stanzas before the end of the poem in Canto 20 – neutralizes the last pagan champion:[56]

> – Mira ne gli occhi miei, s'al dir non vuoi
> fede prestar, de la mia fede il zelo.
> Nel soglio, ove regnàr gli avoli tuoi,
> riporti giuro; ed oh piacesse al Cielo
> ch'a la tua mente alcun de raggi suoi
> del paganesmo dissolvesse il velo,
> com'io farei che'n Oriente alcuna
> non t'agguagliasse di regal fortuna. –
>
> Sì parla e prega, e i preghi bagna e scalda
> or di lagrime rare, or di sospiri;
> onde sì como suol nevosa falda
> dov'arda il sole o tepid'aura spiri,
> così l'ira che 'n lei parea sì salda
> solvesi e restan sol gli altri desiri.
> – Ecco l'ancilla tua; d'essa a tuo senno
> dispon, – gli disse – e le fia legge il cenno. –

(20.135–36)

["Behold in my eyes the sincerity of my faith, if you do not wish to [lend faith to] my words. I swear to restore you to the royal throne where your forefathers reigned: and oh if it should please Heaven that some of its rays should dissolve the evil of paganism from your mind, how would I see to it that nobody in the Orient should equal you for royal fortune!"

So he speaks, and prays, and bathes and warms his prayers now with his scanty tears, now with his sighs; so that, even as the flakes of snow are wont, where the sun gives heat or the warming breeze is breathing, so is dissolved the wrath that seemed in her so firm, and only her other passions are left behind. "Behold your handmaid; dispose of her at your discretion (she said), and your command shall be her law."]

Armida's short lines, with their echo of the Virgin Mary's response to Gabriel and of Clorinda's conversion in Canto 12, suggest her acceptance of Rinaldo's plea.[57] Critics have consistently been troubled by the enchantress' sudden tractability so late in the poem; Giamatti makes the strongest claim for the episode's failure to convince, calling it "too forced" and "desperate."[58]

Although powerful, Giamatti's reading does not go far enough in examining the ideological implications of the episode. By charting its rhetorical thematization of doubt and unknowability, I would like to suggest how the unconvincing conversion marks a larger faultline in Tasso's poetics. The episode not only challenges belief but marks a fissure in the poem's careful armature of "truth": the scene observes

Christian truth but *not* verisimilitude. Here we have the dark double of Tasso's Christianly explained marvels – Christian ideology that fails to convince.

Although Tasso presents Armida's passion for Rinaldo as one possible motivation for her transformation, the passage abounds with suggestions of her continuing duplicity and its powerful effects. In its figurative language, Rinaldo's plea unwittingly presents Armida with the option of "*lending* faith" rather than irrevocably *pledging* it. Moreover, when he vows to restore her to the throne of her ancestors, he refers back to the complicated story concocted by Armida in Canto 4 to woo the Christian warriors away from the battlefield. Despite all that has happened between them, his vows to her rely on her earlier fabrication rather than on an authentic bond. Still seduced by her fictions, Rinaldo imagines a time beyond the scope of the poem when he might fittingly take on Armida's entirely fraudulent cause.

There are signs, too, that Armida's powers are undiminished. In stanza 136, Armida's wrath dissipates "even as the flakes of snow are wont [to], where the sun gives heat." But the sun shines earlier in the poem, as well, without melting away all the layers of deception. In 4.84, as Armida spins her web for the knights, she merely pretends to find solace in the prospect of their help: "Serenò allora i nubilosi rai Armida,/ e sì ridente apparve fuore/ ch'innamorò di sue bellezze il cielo" [Armida then cleared her cloudy rays and shone forth so smilingly that she enamored heaven of her beauties]. Here the image expressly marks her devious agency. She herself is a sun whose brilliance blinds men to the truth. The image recurs yet again when Armida destroys her palace (16.70), leaving nothing but an empty landscape. If the fading of her palace suggests that deception vanishes with the coming of the sun – so that the image would lead one to trust the reformed Armida – the earlier instance in Canto 4 suggests that there are many layers to the fog that obscures her intentions. Lest the reader forget, Tasso reminds us elsewhere in Canto 20, when Armida, in a silent monologue, wonders whether she has exhausted her arsenal against Rinaldo: "Or qual arte novella e qual m'avanza nova forma in cui possa anco mutarmi?" (20.67) [Now what new art is left for me, or what new shape to which I might yet transform myself?]. Even as she despairs, her rhetorical questions recall her magical arts and powerful dissimulation. They anticipate the undecidability of the "conversion" scene, and suggest just how difficult it is to reconcile romance heterodoxy with the verisimilar representation of Christian orthodoxy.

If an orthodox ending requires a chastened Armida, convincingly brought to Christianity by love and cured of her duplicitous ways, what the episode in fact presents is a fragile tissue of dissimulation and confusion. Jane Tylus suggests that Armida's own talents for recreating truth complicate her late "conversion":

Does she, the consummate sorceress whose legacy includes Circe, Medea, and Ariosto's Alcina, parody the act of conversion, miming and thereby appropriating Christianity through her pagan craft? . . . Her ability, in fact, to mime so well the culture of her Western "superiors" is precisely what throws into question the status of her final appearance in the text.[59]

The undecidability of the sorceress' conversion troubles the orthodox verities of the text. The episode stages the epistemological dilemma of ascertaining when a turn to Christianity is true and when it is pro forma.[60] In the wake of the New World experience, the authenticity of Armida's conversion cannot be trusted. The episode undermines Tasso's project both ideologically and formally, with the two levels entangled in contradiction and undecidability. If Tasso cannot convince at this key moment, if the pagan cannot be successfully brought into the fold, the unassimilable other, with her endless repertory of imitations and mimicry, appears to have disarmed Christian epic.

This seems to be Tasso's own conclusion as he strives for that elusive mirage, the perfectly orthodox text, for not only does America disappear from the *Conquistata*, no trace remains of Armida's conversion. They vanish as completely, and as tellingly, as the enchantress' palace in *Gerusalemme liberata* (16). Quint perceptively relates the disappearance of conversion – as an "interpretive middle ground where the evident misdirection of paganism can be read in terms of its eventual reconciliation with Christianity" – to the increasingly polarized spiritual certainties of the *Conquistata*.[61] But declaring the pagan unredeemable is not simply the mark of renewed orthodoxy – it is Tasso's reaction to the narrative and epistemological treachery of conversion as a phenomenon that dangerously conflates truth and verisimilitude.

Conversion in Christian epic is ultimately no more reliable than the "real" conversions and readings that trouble Christianity in the New World. With the voyage to the Fortunate Isles, Tasso makes the case that Christian Fortune will tame the great American unknown through its prophetic power. Yet in that same West lies the deceptive paradise of Armida. The explanatory force of Christianity is not enough, for the possibility of satanic doubles always remains.

Can the poet ultimately recuperate romance, that most insidious of fictions, to invent a marvelous that enshrines the True? As the end of the *Liberata* suggests, even verisimilar replication of the marvels of the faith catches the poet in a trap of representation. Tasso's attempt to conserve romance by subordinating it to a Christian framework leads him only to the aporia of an unknowable pagan. The attraction of romance is undeniable – it seduces readers in the Old World as in the New, where lowly conquistadors cast themselves as chivalric knights. Yet the possibility of romance contamination, which mixes heterodoxy with orthodox truth, plagues the purveyors of texts on both sides of the Atlantic. Tasso's unconvincing recuperation of Armida eerily echoes the actual difficulties of Spanish clerics as they attempted to convert the Indians through a judicious dosage of the Christian marvelous. Both cases demonstrate the futility of legislative or literary efforts to suppress romance so that it would not lead readers – or writers themselves – astray.

I turn now to two texts on the expansion and consolidation of Spain's empire, whose allegiances to literary precursors compromise their imperial loyalties. Riven by American and European struggles, Alonso de Ercilla's *La Araucana* (1569–1597) and Ginés Pérez de Hita's *Guerras civiles de Granada* (1595, 1604) evince the difficulty of finding a rhetorical position from which to narrate empire. In their effort to both accommodate and challenge Spanish expansionism, these literary mongrels constantly combine and reshape generic parameters. Their formal legerdemain offers new insights into the ideological stakes of imitation. Do the vexed instances of ventriloquism, quotation, and allusion – i.e. of literary mimesis – in these texts accrete into a poetics of protest? Do these gestures actively dissimulate ideological questionings within the texts, or do they merely signal their deep ambivalence?

Although *La Araucana* and Part I of the *Guerras civiles de Granada* were historical contemporaries as bestsellers in the 1590s, even traveling together to the Americas,[1] they have not been examined side by side. Pairing them underscores the global character of Spanish empire in the sixteenth century and its large and uneven reach both within and without the Iberian Peninsula. It also exposes the metropole's own sense of vulnerability to the depredations of the Ottoman empire – especially during the second "guerras civiles" that Pérez de Hita chronicles – a vulnerability that contrasts sharply with our own modern sense of Spain's monolithic conquering power. By considering both the New World and Spain itself as contested sites, the comparison evinces telling similarities between the rhetorical operations of empire in the New World and in the imperfectly achieved metropole.

In very different ways, *La Araucana* and the *Guerras civiles de Granada* struggle with the difficulties of an authorial voice sympathetic to the other camp – a problem that has fruitfully vexed epic writing since its very beginnings. Yet, although both present marked characteristics of the genre, neither text is fully epic. They participate instead in a series of alternate generic conventions that make it difficult to ascribe to them the forceful imperial ideology often identified in earlier epics, such as Virgil's *Aeneid*.[2] As romance, ethnography, or ballad collection, these texts strain at the limits of genre in an effort to accommodate their unorthodox sympathies. Their generic permutations pose an intriguing set of questions: what literary resources does a sixteenth-century Spaniard actually have for presenting a sympathetic vision of Spain's others, or for occupying their subject position? More importantly, do the rhetorical maneuvers of these texts cohere into a strategy of cultural mimesis, collapsing the difference between self and other?

Faced with the need to justify their suspicious sympathies, both Ercilla and Pérez de Hita constantly thematize the search for authority in their texts. I will explore this search on three different levels: first, how do these accounts of imperial campaigns establish authority for the text itself? Second, given their fragmentation and complicated publication history, how do the texts reaffirm that authority vis-à-vis their own multiple sections, and how do they negotiate the ensuing contradictions? Third, how do they validate their own authority with respect to literary traditions? Far from remaining largely formal concerns, the shapes and literary filiations of these early modern texts expose their complicated negotiation of mimesis and imperialism.

Epic in America

As Spain's control of the New World spread ever further over the course of the sixteenth century, the monarchy faced both rebellious colonists and enduring native resistance. The conquistadors' insubordination resulted largely from long-term juridical and theological conflicts within Spain over the legitimacy of the conquest, the terms of Spain's rule, and the proper relationship of settlers to native inhabitants.[3] In the 1540s and 50s, Charles V proved especially responsive to the *indigenistas* – clerical advocates for the Indians – who recommended limiting the excessive powers of the conquistadors in order to protect the natives. The Crown had political as well as ethical motivations for reform: in order to preserve its own power, it needed to curtail attempts by early settlers to transform themselves into feudal lords in the New World.[4] Influenced by the tireless advocate Bartolomé de Las Casas, Charles passed laws both to defend the natives and to rein in the colonists in those areas where Spanish power was more established. Needless to say, the legislation met with huge resistance, and in many cases led directly to armed rebellions. The conflicts were particularly acute in Peru, where, as I shall describe in Chapter 3, a veritable civil war broke out between defiant colonists and loyal representatives of the monarch. When Charles abdicated in favor of his son Philip, the strife in the New World became a pressing concern for the young sovereign.

It was as Philip's representative that Alonso de Ercilla, courtier and trusted servant, came to America in 1555 to help put down the unrest. Once Andrés Hurtado de Mendoza, viceroy of Peru, managed to quell the colonists' rebellion, he was forced to address the situation in Chile, where the Araucanians were violently resisting conquest and had killed the governor, Pedro de Valdivia. The viceroy named his son, García Hurtado de Mendoza, as the new governor of Chile, and Ercilla departed with him to fight the Araucanians. Thus from the very start the issue of loyalty to the Crown and its imperial authority – an authority often directly conflicting with that of its Spanish subjects in the New World – frames both the formal issues of literary authority in *La Araucana* and the ideological maneuvers of the text.[5]

In its thirty-seven cantos, the poem tells the heroic story of the Araucanians' uprising against the Spaniards and their initial successes under the great leaders Caupolicán and Lautaro.[6] Ercilla comes to Chile with the rescuing Spanish force, and personally witnesses the conquistadors' victories over the rebellious Indians. The first-hand ethnographic knowledge that he obtains in the process, however, exceeds the conventional limits of an epic poem, and changes the material shape of the text. The poet must supplement his cantos with a prose appendix explicating native words and phrases, "porque hay en este libro algunas cosas y vocablos que por ser indios no se dejan entender"[7] [because there are in this book certain things and terms which cannot be understood because they are Indian]. The glossary goes some way towards making the Araucanians readable in European terms: a *palla*, Ercilla tells us, is "what we call a lady"; a *cacique* is "a lord of vassals." When an entry describes how the Spaniards named one city "Imperial," because "they found on all the doors and roofs imperial two-headed eagles, made out of wood in the manner of coats of arms," even ethnographic observation is summarily pressed into imperial service. Yet by its very nature the unusual appendix to the body of the text suggests the incommensurability of the narrator's first-hand observation of New World matters and the formal dimensions of epic.

The poem begins with an ethnographic account of Araucanian culture that portrays the Indians as noble savages, constantly idealizing their courage and strength.[8] The author goes so far as to coin the Latinate term "indómito" – indomitable – to describe the resistance of the natives – as though there were no earlier word in Spanish that would do justice to their courage.[9] Even as he relates the Spaniards' heroism against the Araucanians, the poet betrays his sympathies for the natives. The Spanish victories are qualified: the great leader Caupolicán is finally betrayed by a treacherous turncoat, and the epic ends inconclusively, with a meeting of the chieftains to choose a new leader in the struggle for freedom. So striking is the vision of American resistance in *La Araucana* that the poem was adopted as a symbol for the Creole struggle for independence from Spain over two hundred years after it was written. The real Araucanians, meanwhile, continued to battle the forces of colonialism until their resistance was quelled by the independent Creole state of Chile in the late nineteenth century.

Ercilla's epic account of the Araucanian wars was published in three parts, roughly a decade apart, after the author's return to Spain. The first two volumes end in cliffhangers, with no clear sense of how Spain will fare when – and if – the action resumes. The poetic strategy of interwoven plots and narrative delay stems from Ariosto's *Orlando Furioso*, where authorial interruptions flaunt the narrator's control over his readers and his power to withhold the narrative.[10] But it is not the same to leave a reader hanging for a page, as Ariosto does, as for a decade. What does it mean for an epic – traditionally a triumphalist genre with a victory for "our" side at the end – to come to a premature stop? In a persuasive essay that locates *La Araucana* within the tradition of Christian epic, Ramona Lagos describes the ruptures as the "unfulfillment" of the text's epic program.[11] Quint has suggested that the textual truncation amid bloody warfare gives us "an epic that deliberately falls apart in order to defeat narrative incorporation of a violence that exceeds explanatory or ideological structure."[12] Michael Murrin, in his reading of particularly violent episodes of the poem, goes even further, arguing that, "Ercilla gives us a narrator so upset he can barely tell his story."[13] As these critics all recognize, the fragmented shape of the text corresponds to fractures in its imperial ideology, reflected in turn in the disquieting silences of the narrator.

The ideological fractures are further complicated by the narrator's presence on the scene. Most of the first part of the poem occurs before the narrator gets to Chile, and it is only towards the end of it that he can promise:

> Pues que en autoridad de lo que digo
> vemos que hay tanta sangre derramada,
> prosiguiendo adelante yo me obligo
> que irá la historia más autorizada;
> podré ya discurrir como testigo
> que fui presente a toda la jornada,
> sin cegarme pasión, de la cual huyo,
> ni quitar a ninguno lo que es suyo.

(12.70)

[For if by the authority of what I say we see that there is so much blood spilled, in continuing I vow the story will be more authorized; I will now be able to discourse as a witness, for I was present at the whole journey, without being blinded by passion, which I flee, or taking from anyone what is his.]

Witnessing, the narrator warns, fundamentally changes the nature of the text, introducing, if not a divided consciousness, then at least a distinction between events *seen* and those *imagined*. As Ercilla conflates the narrator and witness functions, the text attains a new level of authority.[14] The passage implicitly sets up a wishful correlation between "la historia más autorizada" and the decrease of violence, but, in fact, things only get worse once Ercilla arrives on the scene. So devastating is the field of battle that the narrator must seek relief elsewhere.

Despite his promise to stick to what he has seen, Ercilla departs most spectacularly from witnessed events to give the reader huge panoramas of imperial conflicts in Europe and the Mediterranean, incorporating the "imperial gaze" within the text.[15] These scenes correspond to the epic tradition of a prophecy which reveals to the unknowing hero visions of his own future greatness and that of his descendants. By simultaneously projecting it into the future and recounting its solemn origins, triumphalist prophecy establishes the legitimacy of the imperial project.[16]

But Ercilla's use of this topos oddly transforms it, introducing a complicated negotiation of authority and sympathy within the text. The first prophecy is provided by Bellona, the goddess of war. She initiates the narrator's epic vision of Philip II's victory over the French at St. Quentin in 1557 (17.52 and following). While the poet sleeps, Reason replaces Bellona as the prophetic agent, and shows Ercilla the events that will lead to the battle of Lepanto. The battle she will not recount, and instead directs the poet to a certain magician Fitón, who will complete the predictions. Meanwhile, Reason turns to most unreasonable topics, abandoning the epic momentum of the prophecy to offer the poet the romance motifs that he has eschewed to that point (18.64). After much struggling with contradictory impulses – to return to his narration of the conquest or to intersperse some romantic relief into so many stories of combat – Ercilla actually wanders off the battleground, like the irrepressible heroes of romance, to find the magician's cave.

Fitón, although his name stems from the Greek *python* (spirit of divination), is no allegorical personification but actually an Araucanian magician.[17] Ercilla's conception of the native as a source of authority in this crucial episode creates a basic dissonance with respect to triumphalist epic models, in which the victims of empire would be the last to provide visions of imperial greatness. The artificer's otherness tangles the threads of evidence, authority, and sympathy that the author has so carefully woven. An Araucanian magician with the power to conjure the triumphs of Philip II in a crystal ball, Fitón possesses a kind of ontological primacy over the Spanish conqueror. The mimesis of prophecy grants the conjurer greater power than the conjured. Ercilla himself foregrounds the vexed question of mimesis and authority in the exordium to Canto 18, before Fitón even appears on the scene, as he ponders the implications of reducing the King to a representation:

> ¿Cuál será el atrevido que presuma
> reducir el valor vuestro y grandeza
> a término pequeño y breve suma,
> y a tan humilde estilo tanta alteza?
> Que aunque por campo próspero la pluma
> corra con fértil vena y ligereza,
> tanto el sujeto y la materia arguye
> que todo lo deshace y disminuye.

[Who will be the daring one who will presume to reduce your valor and greatness to a small extension and scant amount, and so much majesty to such humble style? For even if the pen runs over a rich field with a fertile vein and speed, it so reveals the subject and the matter, that it destroys and diminishes everything.]

This preliminary mea culpa in reducing Philip to text suggests a link between the vatic poet himself – the original visionary artist – and Fitón, a link strengthened by the description of the magician's highly ornate and wrought surroundings.[18]

Fitón's cave is awesome to behold, despite (or perhaps because of) the diabolical substances it contains. The magician's inner lair is so rich and complex that it defies the poet's powers of description: "su fábrica estraña y ornamento/ era de tal labor y tan costosa/ que no sé lengua que contarlo pueda,/ ni habrá imaginación a que no exceda" (23.65) [its strange artistry and ornament/ was of such workmanship and so costly/ that I know not what tongue could tell of it/ nor can there be an imagination unsurpassed by it], although of course he goes on about it for several octaves. This vision of native wealth and power coded in Western imagery functions in several ways: on the one hand, it grants the native magician a level of (European) sophistication and civilization which would greatly enhance his standing in the eyes of the Spanish. On the other hand, it makes his hidden riches available to the narrator who, he tells us, feasts "la codiciosa vista" (23.69) [his greedy sight] on the cave's art and riches. Ercilla's fantasy compresses discovery and consumption into one short scene: imagining these New World marvels, contemplating them greedily, and incorporating them is but the work of a moment.

Although the passage initially calls attention to the limitations of the

Spanish poet's powers of description, it performs a complicated rhetorical appropriation. Part of what the narrator sees in the cave is a reflection of his own poetic labors: the space is full of sculptures of great men surrounded by paintings of their great deeds – "el estremo y excelencia, de armas, letras, virtud y continencia" (23.67, 7–8) [the extreme and excellence of arms, letters, virtue, and continence]. These men, Fitón informs him,

> son los más desta vida ya pasados,
> que por grandes hazañas sus renombres
> han sido y serán siempre celebrados;
> y algunos, que de baja estirpe y nombres
> sobre sus altos hechos levantados,
> los ha puesto su próspera fortuna
> en el más alto cuerno de la luna.

(23.70)

[These are the ones who have passed on from this life; their reputation has been and always will be praised for their great achievements; and some, who have been raised by their great feats above their lowly names and stations, prosperous fortune has placed on the highest horn of the moon.]

Fitón surrounds himself with the images of great heroes – an act of commemoration akin to the labors of the epic poet, who also records heroic feats. Praise for the powerful native magician thus becomes a solipsistic gesture of praise for the narrator, as Ercilla collapses the distance between the two artificers. The reference to "el más alto cuerno de la luna" [the highest horn of the moon], although proverbial, sounds an ironic note, recalling the Ariostan voyage to the moon and St. John's frank appraisal of the compromised nature of poetic truth, discussed in Chapter 1.[19] The passage nonetheless suggests that Fitón's authoritative pronouncements are profoundly intertwined with those of the poet, despite the fact that one is an Araucanian and the other a Spaniard.

The glowing praise of the native magician, and his figuration as the knowing poet's double, introduces an internal contradiction at the very point where *La Araucana* attempts to display Philip II's imperial power most spectacularly. The vision of the powerful and rich Fitón contrasts quite tellingly with Ercilla's earlier appraisal of Araucanian magic. Here is Ercilla's more prosaic, almost ethnographic description in Part I of the poem:

> Usan el falso oficio de hechiceros,
> ciencia a que naturalmente se inclinan,
> en señales mirando y en agüeros
> por las cuales sus cosas determinan;
> veneran a los necios agoreros

que los casos futuros adivinan:
el agüero acrecienta su osadía
y les infunde miedo y cobardía.

Algunos destos son predicadores
tenidos en sagrada reverencia
que sólo se mantienen de loores,
y guardan vida estrecha y abstinencia.
Estos son los que ponen en errores
al liviano común con su elocuencia,
teniendo por tan cierta su locura,
como nos la Evangélica Escritura.

(1. 42–3)

[They have the false profession of wizards, a science towards which they are naturally inclined, paying attention to signs and omens through which they determine their affairs; they venerate the foolish soothsayers who divine the future, and the omen makes them bolder, and instills in them fear and cowardice.

Some of these are preachers who are held in sacred reverence, who subsist only on offerings and lead a straitened life in abstinence. These are the ones who mislead the fickle common people with their eloquence, holding their own madness as true as we do the Sacred Scriptures.]

In a rare moment of relativism, this complex account of native wizards grants them a great deal of authority and force of conviction. But the first stanza unhesitatingly condemns the belief in prophecies and omens as a sign of a primitive, "natural" people. When Ercilla then turns to prophecy himself, in Part II, the text registers the incommensurability of epic convention and the American experience. Although clearly it would never occur to anyone to read the instances of prophecy in the *Aeneid* or *Orlando Furioso* as signs that the protagonists of those texts are primitives, because prophecy is so clearly recognizable as a literary device, the stakes set out by Ercilla's own ethnographic introduction to Araucanian customs color the epic convention with a tinge of the native. And in a text that already suffers from excessive sympathies for the other side, such a connection between native forms of knowledge and Spanish destiny becomes quite fraught.

To complicate matters further, Ercilla's most immediate classical source for the scene of Fitón's cave, Lucan's *Pharsalia*, provides a highly problematic model of prophecy. Ercilla's description of Fitón's pharmacopoeia echoes Lucan's account of the witch Erictho's potent arsenal, which includes "every nastiness that nature conceives and produces."[20] But in the *Pharsalia*, the scene of prophecy is very clearly marked as illicit: not only does Lucan introduce Sextus Pompeius, who seeks out the prophecy, as "Pompey's unworthy son," (VI, 451–54) who will stain with his own shame his father's reputation, he describes the young man's appeal to the witch as a flagrant deviation from authorized sources of prophecy:

> Sextus was not content to approach the tripod of Delos,
> Nor the Pythian cave; he disdained to inquire at Dodona . . .
> . . . Nor did he look for one who could read the future by omens
> Taken from animals' entrails, interpret the secrets of bird lore,
> Watch for the message of lightning, or scan the stars with the famous
> Arts of Assyria, or practice any recondite
> Yet permissible means.
>
> (VI, 458–66)

Instead, Sextus turns to the "filthy practice of witchcraft" (VI, 469), and Erictho decides to satisfy his request by reviving the cadaver of one of the many dead soldiers on the battlefield and making it speak the future.

The resuscitated cadaver offers Sextus no hope for this life, but promises that the undeserving victors in the struggle will suffer in the underworld, while Pompey and his house will soon "trample the ghosts of men made gods by the Romans" (VI, 883). Thus, although Fitón himself is etymologically connected to licit sources – the Pythian cave – Ercilla's detailed description of his magic arsenal refers back to a prophecy which is illicit, demonic, and, furthermore, wholly inauspicious. Moreover, by removing the dead soldier who figures so prominently in the classical model, Ercilla collapses the roles of soothsayer and war victim into one character – the native sorcerer – thereby underscoring the profound ambivalence that colors his vision of Spanish successes. The reference to the *Pharsalia*, unlike the intratextual one of Araucanian ethnography described earlier, does not invalidate epic as a conceptual model for an American encounter, but instead seriously undermines the worth of Fitón's prediction precisely because of the particular epic prophecy it recalls. Thus while Fitón's Araucanian identity confounds a triumphalist epic prophecy in the tradition of the *Aeneid*, the alternative epic precedent of the *Pharsalia*'s hellish prophecy places the native's visionary authority under a distinctly negative light. The layered frame casts Fitón's prediction of Spain's greatest triumph against the Turks, at the battle of Lepanto, as a diabolic utterance.

These contradictions signal the text's deep ambivalence about the fundamental truth of Fitón's prophecies. They are questionable not because they fail to come about (Ercilla obviously writes after the prophesied events have taken place), but because their significance must be evaluated in the context of the events in Chile that *La Araucana* so poignantly describes. Fitón evades the question that Ercilla the conquistador would have found most pressing – what does fate hold for Chile? – and provides instead an answer for Ercilla the writer.[21] The magician explains that he will offer a vision of the Spanish triumph at Lepanto because a sea-battle will nicely round out the story of land-wars that Ercilla is telling (23.73). But by focusing on Lepanto, Fitón avoids showing the Spaniard what will happen locally, stating merely, "dejaré de aclararte algunas cosas" (23.72) [certain things I will not clarify]. Thus the prophecy once again fails to fit the classic epic model, which would lead the reader safely from the time of the narrative to the glorious present of the poet's patron-ruler. Instead, the glorious triumph of the prophecy contrasts violently with the uncertainty of Spain's present position in Chile.[22]

Significantly, because this epic relates contemporary events in their frontier setting, it is not the imperial leader Philip II who wanders off into an American cave to receive reassuring visions, but instead the narrator/witness Ercilla, who has a decidedly more ambivalent attitude towards Spanish conquest than does his sovereign. The poem thus participates in a long tradition of uneasiness vis-à-vis conquest on the part of Spaniards who penetrate deeply into American territory and cultures, and who often give voice to an anti-imperial discourse.[23] Paradoxically, because Ercilla actually participates in the campaigns he recounts, he finds it more difficult to place himself solidly behind Spanish lines. His sympathies, like his narrator, stray into more indeterminate spaces, such as the cave of Fitón.

The ambiguity of Ercilla's frame for the prophecy contrasts most starkly with its purpose: to show Spain's greatest moment of glory in its struggle against the infidel. His description of Lepanto in Cantos 23–24 makes of it a second Actium, carefully locating the later battle by reference to "donde se definió la gran porfía, entre César Augusto y Marco Antonio" (23.77) [where the great struggle was defined between Caesar and Mark Antony]. As Quint has pointed out, the vision creates multiple and incompatible identifications for the Spaniards through its echoes of epic models. Through the lens of the *Aeneid*, the Spanish forces against the Turks become the Romans subduing the Eastern barbarians; through the lens of the *Pharsalia*, however, their battle with the tyrannical forces of the Ottoman empire likens them to the opponents of Caesarism.[24] Quint's brilliantly layered reading shows the profound difficulties that this passage presents for assessing Lepanto in conjunction with the simultaneous campaign against the Araucanians in Chile. In this moment of multiple identifications, is empire ultimately coded positively or negatively? In Ercilla's poem, mimetic reference to an imperial epic tradition becomes a highly treacherous rhetorical weapon.

Although I find Quint's interpretation of this passage crucial for understanding the ideological confusion of Ercilla's epic, it seems to me to disregard Spain's own very real sense of an Islamic threat. Taking into consideration the seriousness of Turkish assaults on Christendom, corsair raids on Spanish coasts, and the 1568–71 rebellion of the Moors within

Spain, the identification of the Spaniards at Lepanto with the resistance against empire registers, I believe, not only *La Araucana*'s ambivalence about imperial expansion but the instability and fragility of the Spanish empire confronting a modern Eastern threat. Spain pursues its imperial ambitions while guarding constantly against the depredations of others. If we take seriously Spain's vulnerability to Islam, we might also modify Quint's assertion that, when the Araucanian leader Caupolicán boasts that the natives will conquer metropolitan Spain itself (8.16), the episode involves primarily a comic or, more profoundly, a satiric reflection on the Spaniards as conquerors.[25] The scene – which features the Indians dressed as Spaniards – also enacts a serious imaginative reversal that recalls Spain's preoccupation with its own territorial vulnerability, if not to Amerindians capturing the metropole, then certainly to Moors and Turks invading from North Africa. The Araucanians conjure a Spain invaded – an empire turned to imperial possession. When the American image is translated to a Mediterranean context – and *La Araucana* constantly shifts from the New World to the Old in precisely this way – it strongly evokes the threat of Islam. And while the reader – then or now – might realize how disproportionate Caupolicán's ambitions are, the narrator and his peers share a fairly tenuous sense of the Spaniards' imperial power at the limits of empire, in the remote reaches of Chile. For the duration of Part I, in which Caupolicán makes his boast, the Araucanians seem to be winning. Furthermore, as the account of Lepanto in Part II makes clear, Spain is not the only empire around. Perhaps at this moment the text poses a most revolutionary question: how much more ludicrous is Chile in Spain than Spain in Chile?

When the narrator visits Fitón a second time in Canto 26, the magician addresses the question of Chile more explicitly. He first voices his reservations about helping a Spaniard, whose kind have killed so many of his own. Then, heeding "the heaven's wish," he announces that the time has come for the natives to be cured of their arrogance. Yet just when it seems that his prophecies will portend Spanish success, he reverts to a non-Christian framework to issue a dire warning:

> y aunque vuestra ventura agora crezca,
> no durará gran tiempo porque os digo
> que, como a los demás, el duro hado
> os tiene su descuento aparejado.
>
> Si la fortuna así a pedir de boca
> os abre el paso próspero a la entrada
> grandes trabajos y ganancia poca
> al cabo sacaréis desta jornada.

                                                           (43–44)

[And even if your good fortune grows now, it will not last long, because I tell you that, as for the others, harsh fate has its diminishment ready for you. Although at the beginning fortune makes way for your prosperous steps exactly as you desire, in the end you will get from this journey great labors and small gains.]

Far from being especially marked for a glorious destiny, the Spaniards are as vulnerable as "the others" to the workings of Fate. Ercilla finds this sinister, yet wants to know more, and follows the magician to his cave. There, in Canto 27, Fitón shows him the whole world in his magic sphere, prefacing his extended enumeration of places with repeated commands to the narrator to "Look" and "See."

But what Fitón shows is quite peculiar – it focuses on the present, with some references to the past, while the future is almost entirely absent. Geographical extension replaces temporal projection, leaving a strange vacuum: what actions will take place in these spaces? Where the reader might expect a strong prophecy of Spanish conquest in the various lands described, Ercilla provides instead a non-committal *list* of place-names, with few verbs attached. The rare moments of action often refer to past empires destroyed or overthrown – as in the case of Carthage (23) – or to past glories of Spain, such as the Spanish defeat of Francis I at Pavia (25) or Ferdinand's symbolic crossing of the Pillars of Hercules to open the way to the New World (37). But of the future of Spain little is said, except that Heaven has good luck in store for the city of Madrid (35, 1–2). The only real prophecies are Philip's victory at St. Quentin – first announced to the narrator in Canto 17 – and his subsequent building of El Escorial. And although Fitón mentions unknown lands, yet to be discovered (52), he does not state to whom God will reveal their secrets, much less mark them for Spain's glorious future. The references to Spain's present in Fitón's panorama are inauspicious: the commercial vibrancy of Seville (36) is overshadowed by violence in the south of Spain. The sorcerer alludes to the 1568 rebellion of the Moors in Granada, eerily showing Ercilla death before the city:

> mira adelante a Córdoba, y la muerte
> que airada amenazando está a Granada,
> esgrimiendo el cuchillo sobre tantas
> principales cabezas y gargantas.

(27.35, 5–8)

[Look ahead to Córdoba, and Death who, irate, is threatening Granada, brandishing the knife over so many noble heads and throats.]

The Chilean present, finally, also bodes ill for Spain: Fitón describes "el pujante Arauco, estado libre y poderoso" (27.50, 1–2) [the vigorous Arauco, free and powerful state] giving no indication that the Indians will be defeated and underscoring instead their political organization and freedom.

The prediction *manquée* in Canto 27 results partly from Ercilla's difficulties in writing an epic of current events; he cannot realistically predict the future of Philip's rather vulnerable empire because he actually enjoys no privileged position, and hesitates to make a "false" prediction of successful conquest in light of the strong resistance encountered in the New World. Fundamentally, the narrator cannot be both witness and prophet. By voicing his inconclusive visions through the mouth of an Araucanian, however, Ercilla makes them both far more resonant and less straightforward. Where the epic tradition leads us to expect a triumphal panorama of soon-to-be-conquered lands and peoples, we instead get a hodgepodge of places in no particular historical relationship: Cairo, Florence, Norway, and so on. More importantly, the imperialist epic itinerary is frustrated by one who should be "conquered," but nonetheless refuses to portray his own people as anything but powerful. Thus at multiple levels the scene of prediction reveals the tensions in Ercilla's relation to the epic tradition and to the imitative imperialist extension of that tradition to the Americas.

Ercilla's first description of the Araucanians' contests of strength, which precedes the much longer account of military games in Canto 10, thematizes the tensions inherent in replicating epic conventions. Although these contests suggest an analogy between the natives and the Greeks or Trojans of epic, they ultimately serve to mark the difference far more strongly. Under the guidance of the old chieftain Colocolo, the Araucanian chiefs decide to hold a lifting contest by which to choose their ruler: whoever can hold up a huge log for the longest time shall lead them (2.35). The test appears so primitive, and the prize so incommensurate, that the episode seems to emphasize at first the chasm of difference between these savage people and Europeans. But just as the reader is ready to ascribe this scene to the condescending imperial gaze of the Spaniards, Ercilla turns the tables. He adds an account of Colocolo's shrewdness in calling for the competition: because Colocolo knows that the right man to lead is the absent Caupolicán, strongest of chieftains, who has not yet arrived at the meeting place (2.61), he uses the contest as a form of delay. By making the test of strength one of duration, he hopes to postpone the decision long enough for his favorite to arrive, participate in the games, and emerge the victor:

> Así propuso astuta y sabiamente
> (para que la elección se dilatase)
> la prueba al parecer impertinente
> en que Caupolicán se señalase,
> y en esta dilación tan conveniente

dándole aviso, a la elección llegase,
trayendo así el negocio por rodeo
a conseguir su fin y buen deseo.

(2.62)

[Thus he shrewdly and wisely proposed (so that the election would be delayed) the apparently inappropriate test in which Caupolicán could distinguish himself, and by this most convenient dilation, being warned, could come to the election, thus bringing the business, in a roundabout way, to his desired end.]

Here, the initial account of brute force is retrospectively recast as the aged chieftain's wily dilatory maneuver to enable the right man to lead the Araucanians. The contest, it turns out, is not just a test for potential leaders but also for hasty readers, too quick to read according to the conventions of epic. By conjuring both parallels with and differences from the epic tradition of martial games, and then exposing those relationships as mere red herrings, Ercilla explodes our readerly expectations. Perhaps, he suggests, reading in an epic key proves misleading when reading of New World conflicts. The Araucanians are not simply like or unlike the Trojans; the very comparison is inappropriate.

Nonetheless, Cantos 10–11 provide a much more extensive description of Araucanian games, this time closely modeled after the *Aeneid*. Perhaps it is not so simple, after all, to renounce the authority of epic imitation. And perhaps, too, representing the Araucanians as a challenge to the expectations of epic ultimately deprives them of the European sympathy the author wishes to evoke. Do the conventional epic games, then, represent a concession to the exigencies of genre? While they rehearse the tropes of epic, they also forcefully recall the earlier scene of epic unreadability. The second games ultimately function to confirm the command of the leader, Caupolicán, over disgruntled warriors. By foregrounding Caupolicán's authority, the epic martial games mark their indebtedness to the previous contest, one unreadable in epic terms – the satisfying resolution of the imitative scene therefore depends logically on what lies beyond the borders of the genre. Thus the apparatus of Ercilla's text leads the reader to the verge of epic time and time again, only to suggest that it might be a dead end where America is concerned.

The mimetic conventions of epic do not travel well to the New World. There, the competing discourse of ethnography and the pressures of contemporary empire-building undermine literary verities with first-hand knowledge of different peoples and their different motivations. The narrator's ambivalent appraisal of Araucanian magic fundamentally compromises the role of triumphalist prophecy in *La Araucana*: while Fitón is individually praised as a powerful magician, the rest of the natives appear merely superstitious. Nor can ethnography replace epic topoi as a satisfying source of poetic authority: the Araucanians' use of heavy lifting is not a cultural ritual but simply the individual strategy of the wily Colocolo. The real challenge to epic conventions seems to lie not in ethnographic insight, but in the first-hand observation that both makes such knowledge possible and also qualifies it. Ercilla's selection of a contemporary event as the subject of his epic poem – a choice Tasso discouraged in his *Discorsi*[26] – and, moreover, of one in which he himself participates, radically alters the quality of textual authority in *La Araucana*. While the poem cannot command the authority of epic, it reveals other, more complicated truths: poetic authority in the service of empire is compromised precisely by the personal experience of empire-building. The problem is not that the poet knows too little of his subject matter to deploy convincingly the conventions of literary tradition – it is that he has seen too much. What he has witnessed so complicates both his literary and his imperial loyalties that he risks betraying an epic cause.

Civil Moors

War, civil war and worse, fought out on the plains of Thessalia
Times when injustice reigned and a crime was legally sanctioned
Times when a powerful race, whose prowess had won it an empire,
Turned its swords on itself, with opposing armies of kinsmen –
This is my theme.   Lucan, *Pharsalia*[27]

While the war against the indomitable Araucanians dragged on in Chile long after Ercilla had returned to Spain in 1563, the metropole faced a more intimate rebellion: the 1568 uprising of the Moriscos in the mountains of the Alpujarra. Unlike the remote civil war in Peru, which posed at most a distant challenge to the Crown's authority, the revolt in the Alpujarras threatened to turn back the clock to a time before the territorial consolidation of Spain. The rebellion was a response to the Crown's severe repression of the Moriscos – the "little Moors" who remained in Spain after the fall of Granada. The guarantees of cultural and religious freedom that Ferdinand and Isabella had offered the Moors when they surrendered in 1492 were deliberately ignored. By the turn of the century, the Church had instituted forced baptisms *en masse*, bringing the Moriscos under the aegis of the Inquisition and provoking a spate of rebellions.[28] Although the new converts were initially able to maintain their own cultural practices simultaneously with Christianity, they came under increasing attack as the century progressed, in a process that Deborah Root has identified as "the production of the Moriscos as an internal other and of Morisco culture as something deviant, to be recognized and rejected by the community."[29] Such persecution would become ever more acute, culminating in the expulsion of the Moriscos – all of whom had by then been baptized – after 1609.

By 1567 the repeated interdiction of Morisco cultural practices had come to a head, with laws that required, as Pérez de Hita relates,

que los Moros de Granada y su Reyno (pues eran baptizados y christianos), para que mejor sirviessen a Dios nuestro Señor, que mudassen el hábito y no hablassen su lengua, ni usassen sus leylas y zambras, ni hiziessen las bodas a su usança, ni en las Navidades y días de Años nuevos sus comidas o sus costumbres, las quales comidas se llamavan mezuamas, y sin eso otras cosas les fueron vedadas que no convenía que las usassen.[30]

[that the Moors of Granada and its Kingdom (for they were baptized and Christians) the better to serve the Lord our God, should change their clothing and not speak their language, nor have their songs and instruments, nor perform their weddings as is their custom, nor have their traditional dishes on Christmas or the New Year, which are called "mezuamas," and beyond these other things were forbidden them which it was not convenient for them to do.]

Although similarly repressive legislation had been passed earlier, these new decrees attacked Morisco culture directly and on every front, forbidding the use of Arabic, annulling all contracts made in that language, forcing the Moriscos to change their Moorish names, demanding that they wear clothes "a la castellana," and generally obliging them to observe Spanish Christian mores.[31]

The devastating legislation, which took some time to implement, directly led to the rebellion in the Alpujarras: goaded by mounting cultural repression, the Moriscos fought one last time for their survival in Spain. From 1568 to 1571 the rebellion raged, until it was finally contained by Don Juan de Austria, Philip's illegitimate brother, who would go on to lead the European forces against the Turks at Lepanto. During the rebellion, there was a real fear in Spain that its own territory would be overrun by outside forces coming to the aid of the Moriscos. The Moorish states of North Africa, the Ottoman Turks themselves, and their allies, the French, were all perceived as imminent dangers. Although it eventually became clear that the Turks were not willing to provide the Moriscos with the necessary military aid, the Spaniards remained anxious about the vulnerability of their empire. The rebellion in the Alpujarras forced Spain to ship its troops back from Naples, where they had been defending that end of the empire, and provided the Turks with an opportunity to reconquer Spanish outposts in North Africa. Thus an ostensibly internal problem not only challenged Spain's domestic *imperium* but rendered it vulnerable to the imperial depredations of others.

The role of the Spanish Moors as internal obstacles to Spain's imperial might becomes particularly interesting when considering Pérez de Hita's

Guerras civiles de Granada, a text whose alternation between romance and epic conventions complicates any location of the "enemy." In the *Guerras civiles*, the lines dividing Christian inside from Moorish outside grow ever fainter, a particularly striking ambiguity given the Counter-Reformation context in which the text was written. Published in 1595, the first volume of the mongrel text – part romance, part historical novel, part collection of ballads – describes wars between several factions in Granada, which, Pérez de Hita suggests, ultimately led to the city's downfall in 1492. Notably, the Moors are presented as highly sympathetic and cultivated figures, making this first part of the *Guerras civiles* a prime example of "Moorophile" literature. The second volume of the text, finished in 1597 but published in 1604, departs dramatically from its predecessor: here, a kind of prose epic chronicles the vicious fight against rebellious Moriscos in the Alpujarras, a cause in which the author himself participated.[32] Thus from one section to the other the Moors are transformed from fantastic chivalrous figures to actual historical enemies. Yet the sympathies of Part I actively haunt Part II, undermining Pérez de Hita's account of achieved *imperium*.

The ideological thrust of Pérez de Hita's work is apparent even in the remarkable – yet largely unremarked – yoking together of Parts I and II of the *Guerras civiles*. I will use the title pages of the two parts of this purported whole as a touchstone for my analysis. The first one reads:

Historia de los vandos de los Zegríes y Abencerrages Cavalleros Moros de Granada, de las Civiles guerras que huvo en ella, y batallas particulares que huvo en la Vega entre Moros y Christianos, hasta que el Rey Don Fernando Quinto la ganó.

Agora nuevamente sacado de un libro Arávigo, cuyo autor de vista fue un Moro llamado Aben Hamin, natural de Granada. Tratando desde su fundación.

Traduzido en castellano por Ginés Pérez de Hita, vezino de la ciudad de Murcia.

[History of the factions of the Zegríes and the Abencerrajes, Moorish Knights of Granada, of the Civil wars within it, and the individual battles in the Valley between Moors and Christians, until King Ferdinand V conquered it.

Now newly taken from an Arabic book, whose author apparently was a Moor named Aben Hamin, native of Granada. From its foundation onward.

Translated into Spanish by Ginés Pérez de Hita, resident of the city of Murcia.]

And for the second part:

Segunda parte de las guerras civiles de Granada y de los crueles vandos entre los convertidos Moros, y vezinos Christianos: con el levantamiento de todo el Reyno y última revelión, sucedida en el año de 1568

Y assí mismo se pone su total ruina, y destierro de los Moros por toda Castilla.

Con el fin de las Granadinas Guerras por el Rey nuestro Señor Don Felipe Segundo deste nombre.

Por Ginés Pérez vecino de Murcia.[33]

[Second part of the civil wars of Granada and of the cruel factions between the converted Moors, and Christian inhabitants: with the uprising of the whole Kingdom and its late rebellion, which took place in the year 1568

And also describing its complete ruin, and exile of the Moors throughout Castile. With the end of the Grenadine Wars by the King our Lord Philip the Second of this name.

By Ginés Pérez resident of Murcia.]

Aside from attempting to profit from the enormous success of Part I by producing an ostensible sequel, the author uses the forced connection between the two parts to defend the Moors. Part II insistently asks the loaded question: where are the descendants of the many virtuous knights and ladies portrayed in Part I? Are they not these same rebellious Moriscos?[34] These titles, with their emphasis on civil war, comprise a very peculiar version of the history of the Spanish Moors from the late fifteenth to the late sixteenth centuries. Pérez de Hita uses the notion of civil war to connect the two texts (and therefore the historical events they relate). Yet clearly "civil" means something very different in each part. In the first, noble families within Granada engage in an internecine struggle, vying for favor at the court of the last Moorish king. The author describes as wars the conflicts that occur within the city, while the external battles with Christians (although they will in fact lead to the downfall of Granada) are mainly discussed as individual chivalric encounters. This corresponds to the general presentation of the court of Granada as the mirror-image of an idealized chivalric Christian court: the Moors joust, pine for Petrarchan ladies, and are generally models of chivalry, courteousness, and devotion. The Zegríes, the villainous faction in the story, are very much the exception to the author's vision of Moorish nobility. The Granada of Part I moves irrevocably towards Christianity; the more sympathetic the characters, the more quickly they reach this implicit goal, and several of the Moorish knights ask to be baptized on their deathbeds. Pérez de Hita's vision of Granada makes it the mimetic equal of an idealized, chivalric Spain.

By the second part of the *Guerras civiles*, however, the situation has become very different. After the conquest of 1492, Granada is portrayed as fully a part of Spain, so that the civil wars recounted are fought between Spaniards. Despite the fact that the text narrates a cruel conflict, the differences between "convertidos Moros" and "vezinos Christianos" are not enough to make them proper enemies; the struggle remains a civil war because they are all part of the same state. The rebellion, of course, was fought over how, precisely, the Moriscos could be incorporated into Spain. Although the transformation of the meaning of "civil" from Part I to Part II might be read as Pérez de Hita's coercive textual incorporation of the Moriscos, the simple grafting of these marginalized figures onto the body politic is in fact a highly sympathetic gesture.

Such rhetorical inclusion allows the author to register the appropriate horror at what "we" are doing to "ourselves" – Christians to other, albeit newly converted, Christians – and counters the othering of the Moriscos in the text. Thus, although Part II begins with an account of violent Moorish resistance to Christians in the period 1492–1568, Pérez de Hita contradicts his own criticism of the Moriscos to bemoan "las civiles guerras que se tuvieron, que ansí se pueden llamar; pues fueron Christianos contra Christianos, y todos dentro de una ciudad y un Reyno" (II, 10) [the civil wars that occurred, for so they may be called, because they were Christians against Christians and all within one city and one Kingdom].[35] Here, cultural mimesis functions to counter the state's marginalizing of the Moriscos, rendering the *same* what the state would make other. Whereas Part I achieved its sympathetic representation of the Moors by portraying them as thinly disguised chivalric knights, Part II insists on locating the Moriscos as part of Spain by deeming their rebellion a civil war.

Pérez de Hita describes the second *guerra civil* from a far more visceral perspective. Although certain sections rely heavily on previous accounts of the uprising, such as Juan Rufo's *Austríada* – an epic poem on Juan de Austria, first published in 1584 – others are clearly based on the author's experience of the war or that of his Morisco sources.[36] The author foregrounds his use of such sources, as though the exigencies of accuracy obviated any question of misplaced sympathy: "Esto escribo assí como fué informado de muchos moriscos haziendo yo diligencia para escribir esta segunda parte, y entiendo que ello sería assí, pues tanto me lo averaron por cosa cierta" (26) [I write this as it was reported by many Moriscos, when I made inquiries in order to write this second part, and I gather that it happened thus, for they so averred it was true]. Yet the question of sympathy becomes more vexing when Pérez de Hita considers his own role, recalling repeatedly not only his first-hand witnessing of certain events, but also his active participation in them. He expresses his horror at a particularly cruel incident, in which Morisco women kill a captured priest by slashing him repeatedly in the shape of the Cross, then notes with satisfaction how an avenging lightning bolt immediately destroys the whole town. After this improbably neat resolution, the author assures us that he will tell his harsh story "tratando verdad como testigo de vista y como quien anduvo tres años y más siguiendo la guerra" (17) [dealing in truth as a first-hand witness, and as one who spent three years and more in the war].

Yet his subsequent account ironizes the earlier tale of Moorish cruelties and swift retribution, lingering on Christian excesses that the narrator either abashedly joins or fruitlessly counters. When all around him plunder, he participates in the "disorderly greed," admitting, "todos en común erán ladrones y yo el primero" (63) [all of us were thieves and I the first among us]. When the Spaniards engage in "terrible cruelties," on the other hand, the narrator denounces them in no uncertain terms and keeps his distance, singling out his own role in saving the child of a butchered mother (79–80). Thus the narrative that stems from Pérez de Hita's participation is hardly a consistent one. Instead, the authority of witnessing – and his use of Moorish sources on the field – allows Pérez de Hita to qualify his denunciations of Morisco excesses by presenting both sides of the story. If he recounts the harsh and unnatural cruelties of the Moriscos – such as the women who make a martyr of the priest – he also decries Christian cruelties, describing his own horror and pity. Much like Ercilla, Pérez de Hita finds any straightforward account immeasurably complicated by the narrator's presence on the scene of the conflict.

Like Ercilla, too, Pérez de Hita attempts to escape the pressures of the battlefield by turning to romance. The idealizing motifs of Part I find their way into Part II, albeit refracted through the historicity of the struggle related in the second "half" of the text. The most memorable character in Part II is the Moor Tuzani, who loved the beautiful Maleha, trapped and killed by a Christian in the brutal siege of Galera. Tuzani – an "aljamiado" or Hispanicized Morisco – is purely Pérez de Hita's invention, and does not appear in any of his sources.[37] Beyond eliciting considerable sympathy for the rebels, the ill-fated Morisco couple challenges any possible racial reading of the difference between Spaniards and Moors. Maleha fits perfectly the whitening Petrarchan model for ideal female beauty. When she is discovered slain, the color of her skin is not obvious, because death leaves her preternaturally pale as the blood drains from her face (II, 293), but when Tuzani finally finds her murderer, the Christian soldier expands upon her description: "verla muerta tendida en el suelo, con aquella camisa labrada y los cabellos rubios como hebras de oro tendidos alrededor de su cuello, no parecía sino un bellísimo ángel" (II, 331) [seeing her there lying on the ground, with that embroidered shirt and her blonde locks like golden threads lying about her neck, she resembled nothing so much as a beautiful angel]. The angelic Moorish beauty is consummately European – the conventions of romance have brought her into Spain's fold, so much so that she is best described in terms of a Christian religious representation. While this equation depends on the aestheticization of Maleha's violent death, it nonetheless brutalizes the "true" Spaniard who killed her, despite her perfect Christian looks, merely because she was a Moor.

Tuzani himself also breaks down the distinctions between Spaniard and Moor in the course of the romance plot. To find his lady's killer he clothes himself "en ábito de Christiano" (notice that Pérez de Hita specifies *Christian*, not *Spanish* attire) and, "confiado en su hablar claro y cortesano" (325) [relying on his clear and courtly speech], infiltrates Juan de Austria's camp as a soldier. Neither his language nor his appearance give him away, as he spends days eliciting stories of murder and plunder from the Christian soldiers by boasting of his own supposed exploits in Galera. While passing, he arranges the escape of the besieged Moriscos of Tíjola under the cover of night, by revealing to them the Spanish password, "Santa María." This single name, significantly, is all that it takes to render them collectively indistinguishable from the Christians.

Furthermore, when Tuzani is finally spotted and betrayed it is by another Moor, a spy who knows him well and who, the text implies, is the only one that can recognize him:

Este, pues, avía tratado mucho al Tuzani y aun entre los dos mediava amistad; por lo qual, aunque andava vestido con uniforme de Christiano, no por esso dexó de conocerle, y mostrando grande alegría se fue en derechura a abrazarle no sabiendo que andava oculto. El Tuzani, sobresaltado, le dixo en algaravía que callasse y no le descubriesse, porque en todo el campo se le tenía en el concepto de Christiano viejo. Dissimuló por entonces el Moro de Purchena, y dixo a algunos que le avían visto abrazar al Tuzani, que le conocía de su tierra por averse criado en ella, y que allí todos los Christianos viejos entienden la algaravía. (334)

[This one had earlier been well acquainted with Tuzani and there was even friendship between them; for which reason, although he wore a Christian uniform, he did not for all that fail to know him, and showing great happiness went directly to embrace him, not knowing that he was hiding. Tuzani, alarmed, told him in Arabic to be quiet and not give him away, because the whole camp considered him an Old Christian. Thus the Moor from Purchena dissembled, and said to some who had seen him embrace Tuzani that he knew him from his land, for he had grown up there, and that all Old Christians there understood Arabic.]

Tuzani is recognized exclusively as an individual, not as a generic Moor; only his old acquaintance can identify him. Furthermore, the Moor from Purchena's ruse reveals the intricate connections between Moors and Spaniards in the south of Spain. Tuzani's successful dissimulation implicates the entire community, both Christian and Moorish, in the proscribed culture. First, his sometime friend attests that Old Christians are perfectly familiar with the "foreign" tongue that the Crown is going to such lengths to eradicate; moreover, he elides the distinction between *knowing* Arabic and *choosing* to speak it in a Christian camp, as though this were the most natural thing in the world for natives of Purchena. Thus Tuzani's absolute ability to pass for a Spaniard confounds the very notion of passing – he is as Spanish as the Spaniards. For if he looks like a Spaniard, loved a fair lady, and speaks "Christian" perfectly, while Old Christians themselves speak Arabic, wherein lies the distinction between them? In this tale, what Root describes as "the problem of dissimulation" is rendered as a mimetization so complete as to negate difference altogether. Pérez de Hita's clear sympathies with Tuzani, moreover, reinforce the sense that Part II of the *Guerras civiles* is a fitting continuation to the idealizing, Moorophile Part I – this Morisco, at least, is an admirable and chivalrous hero, albeit one forced into dissimulation by the extreme violence of the Christians. Yet while the sympathetic portrayal is similar, the stakes are now very different, for the context has changed radically. The Moors are no longer merely engaged in colorful internecine struggles, but in a pitched battle with Christian Spaniards for their cultural survival.

The surprising resolution of Tuzani's story further complicates matters. Betrayed by the spy from Purchena, the Morisco is brought before Don Juan and interrogated. In an amazing speech, he ably refutes all accusations, arguing, first, that avenging his lady was his chivalric duty, and that by helping the Moriscos flee from Tíjola he actually helped the Christians take the fort much sooner. Moreover, he states his determination to die as a Christian and thus rejoin his Christian lady in the afterlife. His resourceful conversion once captured might strike readers as suspicious, but it certainly convinces his audience: Don Juan and his captains are so taken by Tuzani's valor, and by the beauty of the lady in the portrait he wears close to his heart, that they agree to release him. He changes his name to Fernando de Figueroa and joins the Christian forces, fighting at Lepanto and Maastrich and retiring eventually to a quiet life in a small town. It is there that Pérez de Hita finds him and, he stresses, hears the story firsthand. How are we to read this dénouement, in which Morisco other collapses into Christian self? Does it represent the neutralization of the Morisco threat via assimilation, or rather the culmination of Tuzani's career of dissimulation? Perhaps the point is that so complete a mimetization essentially equals authenticity; sympathizing with the valiant Morisco at the beginning of the tale is thus not significantly different from admiring the courageous Christian soldier at the end. In a roundabout romance fashion, Pérez de Hita underlines once more the perfect reproduction of Christian identity by sympathetic Morisco subjects.[38]

Pérez de Hita also attempts to navigate the treacherous waters of affinity and complicit sympathy by replacing the difference between Christians and Moriscos with that between Moriscos and Turks, the better to establish the *Spanish* Moors as part of the Spanish polity. Part II addresses the generalized Spanish perception that the Moriscos operated as a fifth column, rendering Spain highly vulnerable to the Ottoman Turks.[39] Pérez de Hita begins his narrative with a detailed account of how the rebellious Moriscos appealed to the Turks and the North African Moors, and includes as "documents" the purported letters for help: "Carta de los Moros de Granada al Ochalí, Renegado, Rey de Argel" (II, 4–5), "Carta del Ochalí, Rey de Argel, para el Reyecillo de Granada" (II, 34–5). He even includes supposed letters between the sultan Solimán and the king of Algiers. The latter are particularly fascinating, because they show – fairly accurately, in historical terms – the dispassionate approach of the Ottoman Turks to the revolt. Should the rebellion provide the opportunity to invade, Solimán writes, "pediré los puertos necesarios al Francés y yo con gran poder entraré por Italia y daré aviso al de Fez y Marruecos que entre por la parte del poniente" (II, 7) [I will request the necessary ports from the King of France and with great force I will enter through Italy and tell the King of Fez and Morocco to enter through the West]. Yet Pérez de Hita is careful to specify that, given the limited success of the rebellion, the Turk sends the Moriscos of Granada a measly two hundred men as reinforcements.

Towards the end of the revolt, the *Guerras civiles* suggests, tensions between Moors and Turks greatly weaken them in their struggle against the Christians. The author lingers on these tensions in a scene of martial contests and games among those fighting on the side of Islam, which effectively constructs the Turks as the barbaric others of the Moriscos. Where the noble Moors of Granada of Part I had jousted and courted like so many chivalric knights, the foreign Turks who join the revolt perform only brute feats of strength. Whether ethnologically accurate or not, these exoticized displays are certainly not Spanish.[40] In a scene that recalls the Araucanian contests in Ercilla, the Turks lift heavy slabs of marble to see who has the most resistance (II, 177).[41] But unlike Ercilla, who by revealing the contest's true stakes undoes readers' perceptions of the Araucanians as primitives, Pérez de Hita explicitly brutalizes the Turks in order to praise the Moriscos. By establishing a distinction between the two – much as Cervantes distinguishes between harmless Algerians and brutal Turks in "The Captive's Tale" (in *Don Quijote*) – he not only makes the Moriscos seem more "civilized" but challenges the common perception that their allegiance is to the Turks rather than to the Spaniards.

The distinction between civil Moors and uncivil Turks in Part II presents a striking contrast to the romanticized, exotic representation of the Turks as even more dashing than the "native" Moors in Part I. In the earlier volume, Pérez de Hita stages one of the most curious negotiations of religious, ethnic, and national allegiances in the entire text: when the Moorish queen of Granada is accused of adultery, exemplary Christian knights arrive to defend her honor. Even more strangely, they arrive dressed as Turks. The queen chooses Christian knights as her champions because she would not trust Moors with such an important charge; the Christian knights, for their part, come because the queen announces that she will convert to Christianity (210). The general teleological thrust towards Christianity comes to a head here, as the queen herself invites the Christian warriors to invade Granada, so that all Moors who want to become Christians can attain their goal (248). But what is perhaps most curious is the disguise chosen by the four Christian champions, knights of King Ferdinand. In order not to be recognized, the text states, they don Turkish attire:

el audaz y astuto guerrero Alcayde de los Donzeles dió por parecer que todos fuesen vestidos en trage Turquesco, porque en Granada no fuessen conocidos de alguna persona, especialmente aviendo en ella tantos captivos Christianos que los podrían conocer. (221)

[the Alcayde de los Donzeles, that daring and astute warrior, gave his opinion that all should go dressed in Turkish attire, so that they would not be recognized by anyone in Granada, especially as there were so many Christian captives there who might know them.]

Much as the Moor Tuzani could pass in a Christian camp, these Christians can reliably expect to pass for Turks. They even speak the requisite languages: not only Arabic but "the Turkish tongue" (222). Like Tuzani, moreover, if they were recognized, it would be as individuals, and not as members of a particular group.

When the knights present themselves to fight for the queen, they confirm the rumor that she wishes to be championed by Christians. They introduce themselves as "Turcos, Genízaros, de Christianos hijos" [Turks, Janissaries, sons of Christians]. Historically, janissaries were elite Ottoman troops, primarily renegades or young men from conquered territories brought up as Turks, and who had long relinquished Christianity even if they had Christian origins. These hybrid figures, fantastic counter-renegades, bring together the supreme enemies of Spain – the imperialist Ottoman Turks – with its most cherished self-definition: its Christianity. The scene of Spanish knights passing as a paradoxical hybrid of the Spanish self and Spain's other radically disturbs the categories of the text. In the world imagined by Pérez de Hita in Part I, Christian knights who are essentially indistinguishable from both Moors and Turks can pass themselves off as Turks-but-Christians to save a Moorish queen who desperately wants to become Christian herself. Allegiances and camps have become hopelessly mixed: the conventions of the chivalric mode clash repeatedly with the larger conflicts in the offing – Moors vs. Christians in Spain, Turks vs. Spaniards across the whole Mediterranean – while the battle lines of those conflicts in their turn intersect the boundaries of religious identity.

The title page of Part I suggests that these contradictions reflect Pérez de Hita's own complex sympathies. In the first place, the noble Moors of Granada are themselves described as "knights," on a par with the Christian knights whom they engage in individual chivalric contests. More importantly, the author relinquishes his own authority to the apocryphal Aben Hamin, a native chronicler of Granada, and presents himself as a mere translator.[42] This fictitious origin will be ironized by Cervantes in fabricating that most famous of Golden Age Moorish sources: Cide Hamete Benengeli, the "original" author of *Don Quijote*. Cervantes clearly sends up the humanist gesture of founding a text's authority on some previous, recently "discovered" manuscript by ascribing his story to a Moor whose scribblings he has bought at the marketplace. In the case of the *Guerras civiles*, the humanist gesture involves an even more explicit appeal to a marginalized figure, in order to tell the story of a marginalized group. Pérez de Hita privileges a "native" source over an external one, passing his text off as self-representation in an effort to make it more authoritative.[43] In ventriloquizing a Moorish voice, he suggests that a Moor writing about Granada is fundamentally more reliable than a mere observer from Murcia. Given the text's larger goal of defending the Moriscos as part of the Spanish state, such authorial passing reiterates the dissolution of boundaries between Moors and Christians. The mere idea that a Moorish voice could be more authoritative than a Christian one seems quite outrageous – hence the ironic impact of the same gesture in Cervantes.[44] Critics have speculated that Pérez de Hita's sympathy for the Moors stems from the fact that he himself was of Moorish descent;[45] while the possibility is intriguing, his compassion for his "vezinos" the Moors remains a conceivable alternative to more orthodox antipathies to them regardless of his own genealogy.

In a later reference to the Arabic source for Part I, Pérez de Hita imagines a wholly unorthodox trajectory for his history:

Este moro coronista, visto ya todo el Reyno de Granada ganado por los Christianos, se passó en Africa, y se fue a vivir a tierras de Tremecén, llevando todos sus papeles consigo; y allí en Tremecén murió y dexó hijos; y un nieto suyo, de no menos habilidad que el aguelo, llamado Argutaafa, recogió todos los papeles del aguelo, y entre ellos halló este pequeño libro, que no lo estimó en poco, por tratar la materia de Granada; y por grande amistad hizo presente dél a un Judío llamado Rabbi Santo; el cual judío le sacó en hebreo para su contento; y el que estava en Arábigo lo presentó al buen Conde de Baylén, Don Rodrigo Ponze de León. Y por saber bien que el libro contenía de la guerra de Granada porque su padre y aguelo se avían hallado en ella, o su aguelo y visaguelo, le mandó sacar al mismo judío en castellano. Y después el buen Conde me hizo a mí merced de me le dar, no aviéndolo servido. (I, 291)

[This Moorish chronicler, having already seen the whole Kingdom of Granada conquered by the Christians, went over to Africa, and went to live in the land of Tremecén, taking all his papers with him; and there in Tremecén he died and left children, and a grandson of his, no less capable than the grandfather, named Argutaafa, gathered all his grandfather's papers, and among them found this little book, which he regarded highly, since it dealt with the matter of Granada; and because of their great friendship he presented it to a Jew named Rabbi Santo [Saint/Holy]; and this Jew put it in Hebrew for his pleasure; and presented the one in Arabic to the good Count of Baylén, Don Rodrigo Ponze de León. And because he knew well that the book was on the war of Granada because his father and grandfather had been in it, or his grandfather and great-grandfather, he had the same Jew put it in Spanish. And then the good count graced me by giving it to me, for [the first translator] hadn't served him well.]

This retrospective and far more complete account of his text's genealogy establishes for Pérez de Hita a most curious filiation. First, it becomes clear that Aben Hamin is not one of the Moors who were converted and incorporated into Spain. Instead, he fled Spain rather than face the Christian domination of Granada. Presumably, the saintly Spanish-speaking rabbi whom Pérez de Hita's Moor befriends was also forced to leave Spain in 1492, when all Jews were banished. The story becomes rather murkier when the rabbi, in his turn, presents the original to a Spanish nobleman. Where did this exchange take place? And what is the implied relationship between the "translator" Pérez de Hita himself and the Jew whom he replaces in the count's service? The last link in this narrative chain, the Count of Baylén, depended on Moriscos to farm his lands in Granada and therefore requested their exemption from exile.[46] His sympathetic role in affording the author a manuscript highly favorable to the Moors thus makes perfect sense. Yet this still leaves the homologies between Pérez de Hita and the Jew. According to this narrative, the *Guerras civiles* arrives in the hands of its "translator" after passing through those of Spain's banished and marginalized others. Pérez de Hita's foregrounding of this story clearly betrays his sympathies; his belated replacement of the rabbi as the count's translator marks the interdependence of licit identity and licit texts in Counter-Reformation Spain. What does it take to make a history of the Spanish Moors readable? Christian authorship, even if that author effaces himself to foreground the fiction of a Moorish source and a Jewish translator. Simultaneously supplanted and given voice by the proper Christian mouthpiece, the Moor and the rabbi appear as textual remainders of their banished cultures, and of those cultures' paradoxically central place in Spanish identity.

Pérez de Hita further bolsters his reliability while catering to his audience by incorporating popular ballads throughout his ostensibly historical narrative. The ballads fall into two main categories: traditional ballads and *romances fronterizos* that had long been recited about the Moriscos and the Reconquista, and the more sophisticated *romances nuevos* that both Pérez de Hita and his contemporaries were writing towards the end of the sixteenth century.[47] Although I will not analyze individual ballads, I do want to reflect on the structural role that they occupy in the *Guerras civiles*. Again, the comparison between Parts I and II problematizes the author's literary construction of a "reliable" account.

Part I, especially, has always been noted for its incorporation of *romances* – indeed, its double valence as chivalric "history" and ballad anthology seems to have accounted for its great popularity. Each chapter ends with one such ballad, as a reprise of the episode recounted in the chapter. In a feat of historical legerdemain, Pérez de Hita claims the popular ballads as proof that his own stories of Granada are true, when in fact the former are the *pre*-texts for the latter. Thus a fictional narrative drawn largely from the ballad tradition will be presented as the inspiration for that same tradition: "Y por esto se hizo un galán romance, que dize . . ." (I, 6) [And because of this a gallant ballad was made, that goes . . .], "Por esta manga se dixo aquel romance, que tan agradable ha sido a todos" (I, 9) [Because of this [embroidered tournament] sleeve that ballad was recited, which has proved so agreeable for all . . .].[48] The repeated tag before all these ballads typically invokes a strong causal relationship between historical narration and popular poem – it is because of what I just narrated that this ballad was sung – and an indeterminate, collective author – "se hizo" or "se dijo" – for the ballad itself. Moreover, the preposterous construction of historical truth from popular ballads continues even when the author turns to his own poems or those of his contemporaries as proof. The formulas for introducing the ballads remain consistent, even when the novelty of the poems must be explained away: "Y por esto se dixo aquel romance que agora nuevamente ha salido, que dize ansí:" (I, 1) [And that is why that ballad used to be recited, which has now come out again, and goes like this:].

Pérez de Hita in fact often tampers with both traditional and new *romances*, mixing and matching them to meet the needs of his plot.[49] Thus even when he incorporates historical ballads, his text is often his own doing and saying, and not that of the broader culture. Yet the formal structure of the chapters serves to subject the popular or anonymous truth of the *romances* to the authorized truth of Pérez de Hita's own account. The importance of this strategy becomes evident in Part II, where Pérez de Hita, as narrator-witness, has no conceivable need of a ballad to support his truth-claims. Nonetheless, he is reluctant to abandon the validation that the ballads supply, so that he announces, after narrating the beginning of the Moors' rebellion: "Y ansí desto passado diremos un romance, por no quebrar el estilo de la primera parte" (II, 1) [And so we will recite a ballad on what occurred, so as not to break with the style of the first part].

The tags that introduce the ballads in Part II are very different. Here, Pérez de Hita is much more explicitly the author, or at least the transmitter, of the ballad at hand, and the poems exist in the future rather than the past: "de lo ya dicho diremos el que sigue" (II, 2) [Of what has just been said we'll say the following]. Although the author's witnessing of the events in the Alpujarras should sufficiently validate his account, he turns once more to the literary guarantors of authenticity from Part I – the popular ballads. Apparently, the "real" cannot be merely one man's opinion; it requires the sanction of custom. Pérez de Hita here introduces an ontological contradiction reminiscent of Fitón's crystal ball in *La Araucana*: the validation of a vexed history paradoxically depends on its convincing imitation – its re-presentation – within the text. Yet the fracture that the Alpujarras rebellion represents within Spain seems reflected in the fracture of the heretofore close relationship between history and popular literature – their connection is no longer seamless, although Pérez de Hita tirelessly weaves his unraveled cloth with an undistinguished series of ballads in Part II. When he writes about the rebellion, Hita can no longer reconstruct "history" from popular romance; instead, the brutality of recent history severs any meaningful ties to the ballad tradition of noble Moors and their fair ladies. Whereas in Part I the recourse to literary precursors conferred upon the author historical authenticity, his grasping to make new poetry of recent events in Part II underscores the fundamental loneliness of his voice as a chronicler of noble Moriscos. Hardly any popular ballads were written about the Rebellion in the Alpujarras – the events, like the unfulfilled conquest in Chile – were too close, too raw, too unresolved to be written comfortably.

In their depiction of contemporary struggles for the consolidation of Spain's dominion, *Las guerras civiles de Granada* and *La Araucana* betray fractures of sympathy within the ostensibly homogeneous "home" camp of empire, be it the metropole, the "true" Christian Spaniards, or the single-minded conquistadors. The texts seek to dissimulate these fractures through a constant thematization of literary authority, which instead only calls into question their rhetorical loyalties to Spain. When an imperial narrative is paradoxically authorized by the empire's supposed enemy – whether an Araucanian magician, an exiled Moor, or a saintly Jew – or by the narrator's ambivalent presence on the battlefield, it suggests the impossibility of recounting the conquest without imaginatively, at least, changing sides. Moreover, these texts not only write themselves into the camp of the other, they confuse the boundaries between the camps. By exploiting the possibilities of different modes of telling – ethnographic observation, epic prophecy, romance dilation – they construct a game of mirrors in which difference disappears in a flash of resemblance. Relentless in their depiction of Spanish greed and barbarity, the texts carefully limn the romantic heroism of Araucanians and Moriscos, their love of freedom and inalienable sense of honor, until these others appear to achieve the Spanish ideal. By thus erasing the distinctions between conquerors and conquered, *La Araucana* and *Las guerras civiles de Granada* suggest the fragility of imperial goals and expansionist justifications that depend on ethnic or religious difference. At the same time, they insist on the global context for Spanish empire, a context that includes Spain's very real sense of itself as a target for Ottoman imperialism, and hardly the only contender for universal dominion. Thus these two texts adumbrate the common perception of a firm teleology guiding Spanish conquest. In its place, they posit a far murkier image of contradictory impulses and imperial vulnerability.

3   Lettered subjects

I have the impression – I may be wrong – that there is a certain tendency
to present the relationship between writing and the narrative of the self as
a phenomenon particular to European modernity. Now, I would not
deny it is modern, but it was also one of the first uses of writing.

Foucault, "On the Genealogy of Ethics"[1]

The life of Inca Garcilaso de la Vega is emblematic of the many dimensions
of Spanish empire in the sixteenth century. Born Gómez Suárez de
Figueroa in 1539 to Sebastián Garcilaso de la Vega, a noble conquistador,
and the Inca princess Chimpu Ocllo, Garcilaso led an intellectual as well as
an historical existence that straddled the two very different worlds he
inherited. Although the elder Garcilaso never legally recognized the young
mestizo as his son, thus withholding from him the blessings of legitimacy,
he did develop a strong attachment to the young man, leaving him a small
inheritance for traveling to Spain and continuing his education in the
metropole.[2] It was in Spain that the younger Garcilaso adopted his *nom de
plume* and effectively became a mestizo writer.

This chapter explores how Garcilaso's massive two-part *Comentarios
reales de los Incas* – his highly influential contribution to Spanish historiography of the New World – positions the writer within an imperial structure while challenging the nature of Spanish rule with concerted rhetorical
attacks. I pair Garcilaso and his negotiation of the realities of the Conquista with the Amerindian writer Felipe Guaman Poma de Ayala, whose
Nueva corónica i buen gobierno (written ca. 1615) explicitly denounces the
Spanish presence in southern Huamanga, Peru. Whereas Garcilaso actually publishes his writings in Spain, Poma's unpublished text is intended as a
direct missive to Philip III. Poma, who was probably born shortly after the
Spanish reached Peru in 1535, inflates the details of his biography in order
to achieve the necessary voice for this direct address. Thus he claims that
his father had been an ambassador for the Inca Huáscar and saved a
Spaniard's life in battle, and that his mother was the daughter of the Inca
Tupac Yupanqui. What is clear is that early in his life Poma had worked as
an interpreter between the Spaniards and native peoples, and collaborated

in early campaigns against native resistance. Yet by the time he wrote the *Nueva corónica* he had become completely disillusioned with the Spanish conquest, and spoke out bitterly against its abuses.

Poma and Garcilaso's respective self-fashioning – although quite original – is based on the mimetic appropriation of imperial ideologies. Whereas Ercilla and Pérez de Hita challenge imperial certainties through their highly self-conscious refraction of literary conventions, Garcilaso and Guaman Poma articulate autobiography, translation, historiography, and religious ideology in order to write themselves as contentious imperial subjects. As in Chapter 2, Spain's confrontation with Islam – both in the late medieval Reconquista of the Peninsula and in the sixteenth-century persecutions of the defeated Moriscos – functions as a crucial context.

The writings of Garcilaso and Guaman Poma require a reading along both the diachronic and the synchronic axes of Foucault's formulation above. The focus here is on the writing of the self at a very early point in "European modernity"; to explore how such writing functions for those located *outside* Europe. Can it afford them a place within? Does it make them legible to the imperial state? A textualized subjectivity, I suggest, may strategically incorporate the colonizing ideologies of Catholicism and expansionism to create a hybrid identity that poses a challenge to the colonizers. The texts' staging of resistance thus depends on the transformation of the writers into subjects of the empire, albeit contentious subjects.

The key to this transformation lies at an intersection between Garcilaso and Guaman Poma's own agency and their scripting by the imperial state. Foucault's insistence on the subject's own role in his or her "subjectification" thus provides a more persuasive model than Althusser's account of more passive interpellations of the subject by the state.[3] The Althusserian model fails to account for how both Garcilaso and Guaman Poma talk back to the Spain that interpellates them as colonial subjects, constructing alternative identities through their writing, and developing specific forms of address to the Crown. They articulate their subjectivity both by writing a history of the New World that confounds Spanish imperial aims and by reproducing Spain as an idealized interlocutor, precisely suited to hearing, and validating, their claims.

Like Don Pablo Nazareo de Xalcotán, whose letters to Philip II are discussed in Chapter 1, these authors imitate the rhetoric of Spanish identity for their own ends. Their texts call attention to mechanisms by which an "original" discourse – literary, religious, historical – shapes national identities, and show also how an individual agency can intervene by mimicking such a discourse. Garcilaso challenges the validity of the Spanish empire not as a simple mestizo, but as the epitome of Spanish *hidalguía*, his nobility guaranteed as much by his forays against the

Moriscos as by his learned histories of Spanish conquest. His transformation through both arms and letters renders his critique of Spain all the more powerful, insofar as it comes from a paradigmatic Spaniard. Guaman Poma's even harsher criticism of Spanish empire is spoken by a devout Christian convert decrying colonial abuses in the name of the Church. He replicates the logic of Spanish imperial ideology, ventriloquizing not only Spanish voices but their very arguments for colonization, the better to expose the abuses they lead to. In both cases, the construction of the authors as composite subjects, imitating Spanish ideologies yet combining them with a heterogeneous perspective, enables their radical critique of Spain. This chapter delineates the parameters of such mimetic self-creation and its rhetorical import.

The empire of insurrection

> Comenzaron los bandos entre Pizarro y Almagro por ambición y sobre quien gobernaría el Cuzco; empero crecieron por avaricia y llegaron a mucha crueldad por ira y envidia; y quiera Dios que no duren como en Italia güelfos y gibelinos. Siguieron a Diego de Almagro porque daba, y a Francisco Pizarro porque podía dar. Después de muertos ambos, han seguido siempre al que pensaban que les daría más y más pronto. Muchos han dejado al Rey porque no les tenía qué dar, y pocos son los que fueron siempre reales, pues el oro ciega el sentido, y es tanto el del Perú, que causa admiración. Pues así como han seguido a diferentes partes, han tenido doblados corazones y aun lenguas, por lo cual nunca decían la verdad sino cuando hallaban malicia.
>
> – Gómara, *Historia general de las Indias*[4]

The conquest of Peru and its bloody aftermath posed an enormous challenge for the Spanish Crown. Whereas Mexico was relatively close to the Spanish bases in the Caribbean and easy to access from elsewhere in the New World, Peru was remote, almost as difficult to reach by land as by sea, and consequently difficult to control. In his *Tesoro de la lengua castellana* (1611), Sebastián de Covarrubias offers several etymologies for the name Peru; the two most striking ones address precisely its remoteness and riches:

Otros quieren que sea nombre hebreo, quasi pere . . . parad, partiri, dividere, separare, por ser tierra tan apartada y dividida de las demas. Y muchos autores graves dizen ser esta tierra Ophir, de la cual se hace mención en muchos lugares de la Escritura, particularmente 3 Regum, capite 9, ibi: Qui cum venissent at Ophir, sumptum inde aurum quadrigentorum viginti talentorum detelerunt ad Regem Salomonem, etc.[5]

[Others consider it a Hebrew name, quasi pere . . . parad, partiri, dividere, separare, because this land is so remote and separate from the rest. And many wise authors say that this is the land of Ophir, mentioned in many places in Scripture, particularly 3 Kings, ch. 9, thus: They came then to Ophir and fetched from thence gold, four hundred and twenty talents, and brought it to King Solomon, etc.]

Though a difficult prize, Peru was worth the effort. Like so many latter-day Solomons, the kings of Spain received from its mines a flow of wealth greater than anything they could have imagined. The wealth the colonizers extracted from Peru financed Spain's constant wars elsewhere, as Garcilaso himself points out: "pues gozan de sus trabajos y ganancias los cristianos, gentiles, judíos, moros, turcos y herejes, que por todos ellos se derraman las riquezas que cada año vienen de [Perú]"[6] [since those who profit from their labors include Christians, gentiles, Jews, Moors, Turks, and heretics, for all of whom these realms pour forth their riches every year].

Yet all the riches in Peru were not enough to satisfy wave upon wave of conquistadors, or to recompense them as they saw fit for services rendered the Crown. The primary cause of civil strife in the colony can readily be identified as the struggle to defend a very large pie from the newest arrivals at the table, or conversely, to ensure that there was a piece for every worthy guest. Lope de Aguirre, one of the most spectacular rebels against the Crown, who led a hallucinatory expedition down the Amazon, murdering most of its members, wrote the king a letter explaining his behavior, signing himself, "Hijo de fieles vasallos tuyos vascongados, y yo rebelde hasta la muerte por tu ingratitud, Lope de Aguirre, el Peregrino"[7] [Son of your loyal Basque vassals, and myself a rebel unto death because of your ingratitude, Lope de Aguirre, the Pilgrim]. The son of loyal subjects in Spain, Aguirre turns against his king in the New World for the latter's failure to recognize – and recompense – his achievements as a conquistador.

The greatest challenge that the Spanish empire faced in keeping control of what had been the Tawantinsuyu, or Inca empire, came not from the natives but from Spaniards rebelling against the Crown. Civil strife in Peru significantly hampered the pursuit of empire by exposing the cupidity of the Spaniards and contradicting their carefully deployed justifications for conquest. The rationale of a "just war" against the natives, whom the Spaniards were supposedly freeing from the servility of their previous polity and from the monstrosity of such practices as cannibalism, sodomy, and incest, was significantly compromised by the Spaniards' own violence.[8] When the peace the Spaniards were ostensibly bringing to the Andes was broken again and again by their own infighting, and the conquerors themselves could not seem to agree on precisely what form of government they were bestowing upon the natives, any justification of "civility" threatened to disappear among so many civil struggles.

The civil wars in Peru began as early as 1537, with Francisco Pizarro and Diego de Almagro, two of the first conquistadors, fighting for control of the Inca capital of Cuzco. No sooner had the first wave of unrest died down than a more virulent spate of rebellions broke out against the Crown. To an even greater extent than in Mexico, the Spaniards in Peru had fashioned themselves into a kind of instant feudal aristocracy, assigning themselves entire villages of natives. The *encomienda* had rapidly become a thinly disguised form of serfdom. The Spaniards who were ostensibly entitled to command tribute and labor from the Indians in return for providing them with spiritual guidance instead treated them as their property. Moreover, they looked upon their feudal privileges as the proper compensation for their exertions on behalf of the Crown.[9]

The Crown, however, was not oblivious to the threat posed by such a colonial aristocracy: in 1542, and at the urging of Bartolomé de Las Casas, renowned defender of the Indians, Charles V passed the New Laws against the *encomiendas*. The decrees conveniently reined in the authority of the conquistadors while attempting to improve the lot of the natives. By abolishing slavery, severely limiting the numbers of *encomiendas*, and claiming these for the Crown after the death of the person to whom they had been awarded, the laws shattered whatever hopes the conquistadors might have had of retaining their wealth and status and bequeathing them in perpetuity. Furthermore, the decrees strengthened the Crown's authority in Peru by establishing the office of viceroy and dissolving the *encomiendas* of any Spaniard who had been involved in the earlier civil wars. (According to which source one consulted, this last category could include most of the Spaniards in Peru.)[10]

The catch, however, was the implementation of such laws in the distant colony. Blasco Núñez Vela, named first viceroy of Peru, insisted on enforcing the New Laws immediately, without waiting for the *encomenderos* to appeal to the king. This provoked Gonzalo Pizarro, Francisco's brother and presumptive heir to his power in Peru, to mount a military challenge to the viceroy. This particular wave of rebellion would play a decisive role in the Inca Garcilaso's future. Doubtful of the elder Garcilaso's loyalty to him, Gonzalo Pizarro kept him a privileged prisoner during the many months that he fought the Crown. Sebastián Garcilaso de la Vega's own allegiance to the Crown could subsequently be proved only by stressing the compulsory nature of his prolonged association with Pizarro. As his son ruefully explained in his history of the conquest, the Crown accused the elder Garcilaso of treachery for having offered his horse to the traitor Pizarro at the battle of Huarina, in his struggle against loyal forces, yet Captain Garcilaso himself had never actually fought against the Crown.

The prolonged internal conflicts that framed Ercilla's account of the

Spanish campaigns in distant Chile, discussed in Chapter 2, were central to Garcilaso's experience, and occupy a proportional place in his intellectual production. The repeated waves of civil war among Spaniards reveal fundamental rifts in their colonial goals – the Crown vs. the conquistadors, the imperial bureaucracy vs. the feudal fiefdom – which in turn enable Garcilaso's rhetorical intervention. His own history calls attention to certain cracks in the armature of colonial administration, while dissimulating others where it suits him. At one level the author seems preoccupied mostly with clearing his father's name and with fashioning himself into a subject worthy of the king's material recognition. At another level, however, his detailed analysis of the workings of two empires – the Incan and the Spanish – often proves a harsh indictment of the latter.

The *Comentarios reales* serve as the culmination of a literary-historiographical career in which Garcilaso variously explored the workings of the imperial state. His first and most frankly literary work was a translation of the exiled Spanish Jew León Hebreo's neo-Platonic *Dialoghi di amore* from Tuscan to Castilian. Garcilaso entitled his work *La traducción del indio de los tres diálogos de amor de León Hebreo* (published 1590), and signed it "Garcilaso Inca." This first recorded use of "Inca" as part of Garcilaso's name[11] suggests a connection between the author's own perceived place as a mestizo and his reintroduction of the exiled – yet consummately European – Jew into Spanish letters. Garcilaso's labor of translation counters the contemporary madness of blood purity and makes Spanish culture more inclusive in spite of itself, repatriating the Jew's dialogues via a mestizo translation.[12] The translator's role as a kind of intimate outsider is clearly reflected in the Spanish humanist Francisco Murillo's acerbic comment on the translation, a comment which Garcilaso proudly includes in the preface to the second part of his history of Peru: "Un antártico nacido en el Nuevo Mundo, allá debajo de nuestro hemisferio y que en la leche mamó la lengua general de los indios del Perú, qué tiene que ver con hacerse intérprete entre italianos y españoles" [An Antarctic, who was born in the New World, there below our hemisphere, and suckled with the general tongue of the Indians of Peru – what business does he have becoming an interpreter between Italians and Spaniards].[13] The "Antarctic" outsider has become the go-between.

Garcilaso's next project was *La Florida del Inca*, his account of De Soto's early expedition to Florida (published 1605). While it bears a topical similarity to the author's later history of Peru, *La Florida* approximates neither its scope nor its ambition. The *Comentarios reales de los Incas*, Garcilaso's historiographical masterpiece, would occupy him almost until his death in 1616, with the second part published posthumously that same year. The author presents his extensive account of both the Inca world before the arrival of the Spaniards, and of the Conquista itself, as "commentary" on previous chronicles and histories, yet his combined roles as transcriber, editor, and critic – in addition to the autobiographical dimensions of the text – paradoxically afford his *Comentarios* a certain primacy over their sources.[14] Garcilaso presents to the reader a subtle reinterpretation of what the Spaniards have written about Peru, complete with corrections and not so subtle rebukes for their linguistic and imaginative limitations.[15]

The first part of the *Comentarios* relates the history of the Inca empire from its mythical beginnings, constantly presenting the Incas, in their purported belief in a single god and peaceful acquisition of empire, as a prefiguration of the Spaniards and their conquest. In this text, Garcilaso no longer translates between Europeans, as Murillo testily complained about the *Diálogos*, but functions as a conduit for indigenous accounts of the Incas, which he had, he claims, from his mother's family when he was growing up in Cuzco. The second part narrates the vicissitudes of the Conquista, in a lengthy and detailed account of the conflicts between Spaniards. By retelling the complex history of the conquest of Peru – a history narrated by several Spanish chroniclers before him – Garcilaso ensures his place in that history, writing himself beyond the initial conquest and into the unsettled colonial realm he describes.[16]

In closing his *chef-d'oeuvre*, Garcilaso himself describes the relationship between the two parts in autobiographical and familial terms. With the first, he explains, he discharged his obligation to his country and his mother's family. The second fulfills in part his obligation to his father and *his* countrymen (II, 8.21). Yet even this distinction threatens to break down, for Peru is Garcilaso's *patria* [fatherland], even if it corresponds to his mother's family. The exact correlation between the two parts of the texts and the two sides of the author cannot hold.

This tension between the separate parts and their tendency to collapse into a single body of text is nicely recapitulated in the vicissitudes of the work(s) title: although the second part is now usually known as the *Historia general del Perú,* Garcilaso intended the two halves to bear the same name. Because the second was published posthumously, however, the title was changed and the two parts severed. The change – which actually provides Part II with a fitting title – begs the question of why the author planned to present both parts as the *Comentarios reales de los Incas*. Was it to insist on the continuity of Peruvian existence – a continuity which he himself embodied – rather than on the huge rift that the conquest represented? Or was it the better to compare and contrast the imperial exploits of the Incas with those of the subsequent imperial power in the Tawantinsuyu? No doubt these were good reasons for presenting a

seamless history, under one title. More importantly, however, the
unifying device of the common title allowed Garcilaso to claim the same
special authority for Part II as he had for Part I, even though the narrative of Part II is far less dependent on the author's unique access to
sources. The extensive authority earned and documented in Part I supplements the more dubious authority of Part II, where Garcilaso narrates a
recent and hotly contested history in order to present his urgent personal
claims.

The first part of the *Comentarios reales* is read more often and associated
more closely with the Inca Garcilaso, but it is the second part that directly
addresses the author's most pressing concerns in his own lifetime.[17] The
text's central moment – a kind of *mise-en-abîme* for the whole question of
historiographical authority – is the refutation of other historians' claims
about the treachery of Sebastián Garcilaso de la Vega. Garcilaso tries to
explain why they might have gotten the story wrong, and concludes:

De manera que no sin causa escribieron los historiadores lo que dicen, y yo escribo
lo que fue, no por abonar a mi padre, ni por esperar mercedes, ni con pretension de
pedirlas, sino por decir verdad de lo que pasó, porque de este delito que aplican a
Garcilaso, mi señor, yo tengo la penitencia sin haber precedido culpa; porque
pidiendo yo mercedes a Su Majestad por los servicios de mi padre y por la
restitución patrimonial de mi madre, que por haber muerto en breve tiempo la
segunda vida de mi padre quedamos los demas hermanos desamparados y viéndose
en el consejo real de las Indias las probanzas que de lo uno y de lo otro presenté,
hallándose convencidos aquellos señores con mis probanzas, el licenciado Lope
García de Castro, que después fue por presidente al Perú, estando en su tribunal,
me dijo: "¿Qué merced queréis que os haga Su Majestad, habiendo hecho vuestro
padre con Gonzalo Pizarro lo que hizo en la batalla de Huarina y dádole aquella
tan gran victoria?" Y aunque yo repliqué que había sido testimonio falso que le
habían levantado, me dijo: "Tiénenlo escrito los historiadores ¿y queréislo vos
negar?" (5.23)

[The historians therefore did not write as they did without cause; and I write what
passed, not to justify my father, or in hope of reward or with any idea of claiming
one, but merely to tell the truth about what happened. For this crime has been
imputed to my lord Garcilaso, and I have done penance for it without any guilt or
blame. I asked His Majesty to reward my father's services and restore my mother's
property – for as my father's [legal descendants] died so soon after him, we brothers
and sisters were all impoverished. But when the Royal Council of the Indies studied
the evidence I presented about all this, and they were convinced of the solidity of
my case, a member of the court, Licenciate Lope García de Castro, who was after
president of Peru, said to me: "What reward do you expect your majesty to grant
you when your father did as he did at the battle of Huarina and gave Gonzalo
Pizarro that great victory?" And although I replied that this was false witness that
had been brought against him, he said: "The historians have written it: and you are
going to deny it?"]

This humiliating story carries the seeds of Garcilaso's own historiographical production and makes clear the financial, as well as moral, stakes in rehabilitating his father's reputation. The *occupatio* – "I am not seeking mercies" – illuminates the fraught nature of historical "truth" when it is reconstructed soon after the events in question. Denying what other historians have written, or at least sifting through the evidence, becomes a huge part of Garcilaso's enterprise to recuperate the true story of his father's loyalty, and with it the material rewards due him. These rewards include the *encomienda* that reverted to the Crown when Sebastián Garcilaso's legal descendants died in childhood – thus effectively locating the author as one more disgruntled Spaniard fighting the Crown for his "due." Yet instead of rebelling, Garcilaso addresses the legal apparatus of the state, carefully observing historiographical conventions, and refuting competing accounts. His originality lies not only in how he manipulates those conventions for his own goals, but in the way he uses his carefully constructed and honed *in-betweenness* to buttress his own claims.

While I agree with Roberto González Echevarría's canny characterization of the *Comentarios reales* as a *relación*, a legal appeal to have the elder Garcilaso's name cleared of treachery by the Council of the Indies, I disagree with his assertion that it seeks to exculpate "Garcilaso's father and the Spaniards as a whole, to make good the Inca's pretensions in Spanish society."[18] The dynamics of the Inca's writerly inclusion in Spanish society are more complex than might at first appear. The Inca longs for a version of Spain in which his father's chivalric gesture would not register as a betrayal of the Crown, but as a noble knight's duty when appealed to by a peer in danger. This is not to say that the elder Garcilaso was not in fact thoroughly modern, attempting to preserve good relations with all sides in a devilishly complicated political situation – it is just to suggest that his *son* chooses to read him as the epitome of an anachronistic model of chivalry particularly dear to the Spanish heart.[19] Garcilaso's sense of Spain, derived mainly from the family lineage, involves a profound nostalgia for the Spain of the Reconquista, where fighting the Moors was an accepted path to glory.

The conquest of the faithful

Critics have often remarked upon Garcilaso's utopian description of his mother's people as benign conquerors and enlightened civilizers.[20] Yet the author romanticizes the Spaniards, too, albeit in a different way. Too close to the squabbles for power in Peru to idealize the contemporary Conquista, he instead attaches himself to a feudal idea of Spain, in which single combat and military heroism against the Moors led to glory. This anachronistic romanticization partly underlies Garcilaso's self-fashioning: when he changes his name from Gómez Suárez de Figueroa to Garcilaso de la Vega in late 1563, he is not only taking the name of his calumnied father, and of the famous poet of the same name, but also casting himself as the scion of ancestors who had played distinguished roles in the Reconquista.[21] So famous were these knights that their history even found its way into popular ballads. The "de la Vega," one of these ballads explained, had first been added to Garcilaso's ancestor's name after he defeated a Moor who had profaned the Virgin:

> Garcilaso de la Vega
> desde allí se ha intitulado
> porque en la Vega hiciera
> campo con aquel pagano.[22]

[Garcilaso de la Vega [of the Valley] he has since been called, for in the Valley he fought that pagan.]

By changing his name, the former Suárez de Figueroa from the Indies establishes an onomastic claim to a Peninsular history of chivalric exploits. It is particularly significant, I believe, that Garcilaso does not take his new name upon arriving in Spain (Old World, new name) but only after unsuccessfully petitioning the Crown for the rewards due for his father's services as a conquistador. Rudely rebuffed by the Council of Indies because of the infamous loaned horse, the conquistador's son takes the name of not only his wronged father but also his knightly ancestors, whose chivalry had never conflicted with their loyalty to Spain and whose exploits had been enshrined in popular balladry instead of being maligned by historians.[23]

Once a bureaucratic resolution to his claims appeared impossible, then, Garcilaso turned to both arms and letters. He first took up arms by association, proudly adopting the name of the famous knights. A few years later, however, the rebellion in the Alpujarras provided the mestizo scion of the Garcilasos with the opportunity to reenact his forebears' exploits, by joining the king's forces against the Moriscos – diminished descendants of the gallant Moors. Garcilaso was not only the first Peruvian to serve in the king's forces in Spain, as a captain, he also commanded native Spaniards.[24] Varner speculates about Garcilaso's possible "modicum of sympathy" for the Moriscos as "a people who, though tainted with ancestral theologies, had accepted, like his own people, the outward semblances of Christianity and Christian culture."[25] This seems to me counterintuitive: Garcilaso probably perceived no connection between himself and the Moriscos, and the fact that *others* might make such a connection made it even more imperative that he distance himself from them. If fighting the Moors was, as his family's august tradition had proved, the quintessential way to prove oneself as a Spaniard, then Garcilaso must refuse any analogy between himself and these domestic others. As Varner himself notes, Garcilaso apparently owned Morisco slaves obtained as plunder in the Alpujarras revolt, which suggests that his regard for these victims of Spanish consolidation was not particularly strong.

How did Garcilaso come about this particular sense of Spain? He was evidently fascinated by the role of his ancestors as Spanish heroes, a topic he explored further in a short work of genealogy, the *Descendencia de Garci Pérez*, in which he traced those family connections in order to woo a wealthy relative as a patron.[26] But the recent experience of the American conquest would also have provided ample opportunities for the mestizo to associate Spanish glory with the conquest of Islam, for the Spaniards recycled the imagery of the Peninsular Reconquista when they encountered the great civilizations of the Americas. Just as Cortés' *relaciones* had described the great "mosques" of Tenochtitlan, early accounts of Peru described how the Incas "in each town build their mosques to the sun."[27] As Pagden observes, "ideologically the struggle against Islam offered a descriptive language which allowed the generally shabby ventures in America to be vested with a seemingly eschatological significance."[28] Thus in America as in Spain the core of Spanishness was associated with the constantly redeployed images of the fight against Islam, images revived by the rebellion of the Moriscos in the Peninsula in the late 1560s.

These images make their appearance in actual New World performances as well as in the *relaciones*. When Viceroy Francisco de Toledo made his formal entrance into Cuzco in 1570, he was greeted with a pageant and games that clearly represented the metonymical substitution of one Conquista for the other: in the main square where the Incas had once held their festivals, the Spaniards had produced a Moorish castle and enchanted wood. There was also a fountain where young women came for water, only to be carried off by the "Moors" who emerged from the castle. Then the tournament was on, with the Christian knights engaging in fierce mock combats with the mock-Moors to free the women.[29] What the natives thought of this spectacle one can only conjecture, but the choice of such a representation for an occasion of great civic importance in the colony indicates the privileged place that the mythology of the Reconquista occupied in the minds of the Spaniards.[30]

Given this context, it is easy to see how the 1568 rebellion in the Alpujarras – raging in full force even as Toledo presided over chivalric games against "Moorish" opponents in Cuzco – might have appeared to Garcilaso as the perfect opportunity to prove his Spanishness, in the service of a militantly Christian Spain. Yet what is particularly striking in the author's embrace of anti-Islamic ideology is his refusal to countenance the Spaniards' translation of such imagery to the Americas. In his much annotated copy of Gómara's *Historia general de las Indias*, Garcilaso refutes the author's claims that a Spaniard had found Indians who practiced sodomy, looked like Jews and spoke like Moors, writing, "Of course they are not Jews or Moors but gentiles, in spite of the author and the one who told him this."[31] Thus he counters Gómara's famous claim – that the conquest of the Indians followed hard upon that of the Moors so that Spaniards would ever fight for Christianity – by insisting that the Indians are *not* the enemies of the Church. He clearly accepts the notion of a Spanish identity constructed around the struggle against Islam, but resists transposing that struggle to the Americas, where the Indians would stand in for the Moors.

The delicate balance between Garcilaso's idealization of a chivalric Spain and his defense of the Indians is nicely encapsulated by his treatment of Reconquista-style miracles in the conquest of Peru. Christian miracles – those useful hybrids which had provided Tasso with a provisional solution to the problem of the marvelous vs. the verisimilar – here allow Garcilaso to erase the differences between Indians and conquistadors. When engaged in battle, the Spaniards often invoked the aid of holy figures such as the Virgin Mary or St. James, patron saint of Spain against the Moors.[32] Garcilaso recounts how these divine messengers performed miracles on behalf of the conquistadors during a dramatic battle in Cuzco in 1535, during the earliest days of the conquest. The Indians try to burn down the building that houses the Spaniards, but cannot make it catch fire. After days of siege, the Spaniards finally decide to face the Indians:

Con la misma ferocidad y ánimo salieron los españoles, para morir como españoles, sin mostrar flaqueza. Arremetieron a los indios, llamando a grandes voces el nombre de la Virgen y el de su defensor apóstol Santiago. (II, 2.24)

[But the Spaniards attacked the Indians with the same courage and ferocity [to die like Spaniards, without showing weakness], calling aloud on the name of the Virgin and that of their defender the apostle St. James.]

The Spaniards do not make their appeal in vain: their suicidal courage in deciding to die "like Spaniards" is rewarded by the intercession of those divine allies who had so often fought on the side of Spain against Islam:

A esta hora y en su necesidad, fue nuestro Señor servido favorecer a sus fieles con la presencia del bienventurado apóstol Santiago, patrón de España, que apareció visiblemente delante de los españoles, que lo vieron ellos y los indios encima de un hermoso caballo blanco, embrazada una adarga y en ella su divisa de la orden militar y en la mano derecha una espada que parecía relámpago, según el resplandor que echaba de sí. Los indios se espantaron de ver el nuevo caballero, y unos a otros decían: "¿Quién es aquel *viracocha* que tiene la *illapa* en la mano?" (que significa relámpago, trueno y rayo).

[In this hour of need our Lord was pleased to favor His faithful with the presence of the blessed apostle St. James, the patron of Spain, who appeared to the Spaniards. Both they and the Indians saw him mounted on a splendid white horse, bearing a shield showing the arms of his military order and carrying in his right hand a sword that seemed like a flash of lightning, so brightly did it shine. The Indians were terrified at the sight of this new knight and asked one another: "Who is the Viracocha with the *illapa* in his hand?" [meaning lightning, thunder, and thunderbolt].]

Garcilaso weaves the miraculous tradition of divine appearances in the fight against Islam with careful details that locate the story firmly in the Andes. There is, for example, the irony of the Indians referring to St. James as "Viracocha" – a Quechua term that had originally designated a divine messenger from the Sun but that was applied to the Spaniards because the Incas first considered them such messengers. Calling St. James a *viracocha* represents an odd kind of truth in this situation: as a saintly apparition, he *is* a messenger from the Spaniards' (and Garcilaso's) God, even if the conquistadors themselves are far from holy. Garcilaso's use of a second Quechua term, *illapa*, and his amplification of his own metaphor (lightning) into a tripartite translation (lightning, thunder, and thunderbolt) not only establishes the consistency of both sides' version of what they saw but makes him, as translator, the privileged guarantor of that consistency. The rhetorical congruence of the explication belies the battle between the two sides; as translator, Garcilaso is performing miracles of his own.

The episode continues with the blinding apparition of the Virgin Mary, bearing the baby Jesus, as the Indians attempt to renew the attack. Garcilaso compares the momentary blindness she produces to the more obdurate blindness of the infidel ("pero como la infidelidad sea tan ciega . . ."), but then interrupts his narrative of the siege to argue that the Spaniards could never have survived without the help of the "domestic Indians," who not only brought them food but served as spies:

[los indios domésticos] les servían de espías y atalayas[33] para avisarles de día y de noche con señas y contraseñas de la determinación de los enemigos. Todo lo cual atribuían también a milagro de Dios, viendo que aquellos indios en su misma tierra y contra los suyos propios se mostrasen tan en favor y servicio de los españoles. Demás de la Providencia divina, también es prueba del amor y lealtad que atrás dijimos, que aquellos indios tienen a los que les rinden en la guerra. (II, 2.24)

[[the friendly Indians] served them as spies and watchmen, warning the Spaniards day and night of their enemies' intentions by secret signs. It was also regarded as a miracle of God that the Indians should do so much on behalf of the Spaniards in their own country and in opposition to their own people. In addition to divine providence, it is also a proof of the love and loyalty which, as we have already mentioned, these Indians show toward those who have conquered them in war.]

These other native translators, with their signs and countersigns, literalize the connection Garcilaso had established previously: the Indians and the Spaniards are in fact miraculously compatible. While some Indians might be blind to the faith, others do see the light of the miracle.

Garcilaso's textual conversion of the Indians from foes to faithful friends occurs through language, as he provides extensive linguistic evidence of their transformation. He carefully records the new converts' multiple names for the Virgin Mary, sure proof of their piety, and details the Spanish or Latin source for each one. Once again, Garcilaso's bilingualism provides the ultimate authority for his claims:

[los indios], no contentos con oir a los sacerdotes los nombres y renombres que a la virgen la dan en la lengua latina y en la castellana, han procurado traducirlos en su lengua general y añadir los que han podido por hablarle y llamarle en la propia y no en la extranjera cuando la adorasen y pidiesen sus favores y mercedes. De los nombres pondremos algunos para que se vea la traducción y la interpretación de los indios:

Dicen *Mamanchic*, que es señora y madre nuestra. *Coya*, reina. *Ñusta*, princesa de sangre real. *Zapay*, única. *Yurac amancay*, azucena blanca. *Chasca*, lucero del alba. *Citoccoyllor*, estrella resplandeciente. *Huarcarpaña*, sin mancilla. *Huc hanac*, sin pecado. *Mana chancasca*, no tocada, que es lo mismo que inviolata. *Tazque*, virgen pura. *Diospa maman*, madre de Dios. También dicen *Pachacamacpa maman*, que es madre del hacedor y sustentador del universo. Dicen *Huac chacuyac*, que es amadora y bienhechora de pobres, por decir madre de misericordia, abogada nuestra, que no teniendo estos vocablos con las significaciones al propio, se valen de los asonantes y semejantes. (II, 2.25)

[[The Indians], not satisfied with learning from the priests the titles given to the Virgin in Latin and Spanish, have tried to render them in the general language of Peru and add others so as to be able to address Her in their own tongue and not in a foreign language when they adore Her and seek favors and mercies of Her. We shall now give some of these names so as to show how the Indians translate and interpret them.

They say *Mamánchic*, "our Lady and mother"; *Coya*, "queen"; *Ñusta*, "princess of the royal blood"; *Sapay*, "unique"; *Yurac Amáncay*, "white lily"; *Chasca*, "morning star"; *Citoc Coillor*, "shining star"; *Huarcarpaña*, "immaculate"; *Huo Hánac*, "without sin"; *Mana chancasca*, "untouched," which is the same as "inviolata"; *Tazque*, "pure virgin"; *Diospa Maman*, "mother of God." They also say *Pachacamacpa Maman*, "mother of the creator and sustainer of the universe"; and *Huacchacuyac*, "lover and benefactor of the poor," or "mother of pity," "our advocate" – having no words with these meanings in their own language, they use what is nearest.]

Through the intercession of the Virgin, Garcilaso has transformed the Indians from potential stand-ins for the recalcitrant Moors into willing Christian converts. With his rhetorical work of translation, akin to the Indians' going-between, he distinguishes between the two discourses or modes for conceptualizing a battle: one the Peninsular model for fighting fierce infidels, the other a Peruvian model for winning over potential lambs of God. Of course, the translation is never complete: witness the linguistic sediment of Inca culture in the translated names of the Virgin that Garcilaso lists. The name "Pachacamacpa maman" seems particularly significant in this respect, since it recalls the Inca deity that Garcilaso – very much imposing his own Europeanizing reading on the local culture – presents in Part I as the native version of the Christian God (2.2). The rather suspicious inclusion of such a name within this list calls attention to the cultural (as opposed to "merely" linguistic) work of the translator, as he attempts to bring the natives into the fold. Whereas – at the most superficial level – the linguistic translation aims at transparency, the cultural work of the in-between includes the preservation of such residues of Inca lore in all their opacity.

In translating the Indians from infidels – New World "Moors" – to pious converts, Garcilaso repeats the Spaniards' Reconquista/Conquista analogy while stressing the difference in that repetition. The slippage of the New World natives from eternal opponents – the obdurate Moors – to probable allies recalls, I would suggest, a glaring aporia of Spanish racial/religious ideology in the sixteenth century: although the Spaniards were ostensibly converting Indians to Christianity as fast as they could in the New World, Jews and Moors who had converted in Spain were still persecuted as "New Christians." While in the New World the creation of such new converts remained one of the main justifications for conquest, in Spain being called a New Christian not only constituted a grave insult but could lead to persecution from the Inquisition.

Garcilaso's own search for an appropriate basis for a Spanish identity in the myth of the Reconquista and the demonization of the Moors brings him face to face with an intractable problem: how exactly are new subjects to be incorporated into a Christian Spain? While his attachment to an idealized chivalric Spain characterizes the mestizo writer's self-construction, his effort to problematize the translation of that fabled warring Spain to the actual battlefields of the Americas accounts for the many contradictions in his oeuvre. It helps to explain his intermittent support for Spanish empire, his glowing description of the Incas' own conquests, and his fervent account of the miraculous apparitions of the Virgin and St. James to ensure the triumph of the Christians – new and old.

A lettered empire

I will turn now to Garcilaso's complex account of empire, in order to show how his position as exemplary knight and expert translator affords him the authority for a subtle critique. Zamora has shown how Garcilaso's description of Inca conquests, in Part I of the *Comentarios reales*, effectively divides Peruvian civilization into two stages: a barbaric age of unreason prior to the Incas and an enlightened age in which the Incas, throughout their own empire, essentially laid the groundwork for the Spaniards' conquest and Christianization of the natives.[34] Zamora's account of the Inca Garcilaso's irony is highly persuasive; she stresses his ambiguous use of passages that criticize the Inca empire, such as "con el título de su idolatría encubrían su ambición y codicia de ensanchar su reino"[35] [they used their idolatry as a cover for their ambition and desire to extend their realms], *after* the analogy between the Inca and Spanish empires has been established. Garcilaso's extensive amplification of the topic of empire in Part II might itself be read as an ironic commentary on Part I: the reason there is so much to say about the Spanish empire in Peru over a relatively short period of time is that the conquistadors fought themselves in endless waves of civil war.

Garcilaso's use of irony, I would argue, is just one of the powerful strategies of indirection in his oblique comparison of the two imperial powers in Peru. What makes it so complicated to trace these moves is Garcilaso's own ambivalence towards empire. The various distancings and rapprochements in his text are not only between Incas and Spaniards, but between the author himself and the utopias or realities of empire, as he variously imagines and records them.

I will attempt to chart this movement by examining Garcilaso's account of the role of language in the Conquista. The author traces its function ab initio: in Part I, he famously exposes the Spanish ignorance that leads to the name "Peru." In interpreting a native's answer to their question, "what land is this and what is its name?" Garcilaso explains, "Los cristianos entendieron conforme a su deseo, imaginando que el indio les había entendido y respondido a propósito, como si él y ellos hubieran hablado en castellano" (1.4) [The Christians understood what they wanted to understand, supposing the Indian had understood them and had replied as pat as if they had been conversing in Spanish]. The Spaniards' ignorance does not prevent them from naming the new territory, however, and the power of their naming is such that the incorrect name sticks.

Even more powerful than naming, Garcilaso suggests, is the magic of writing. The Spaniards confound the natives with their ability to communicate across great distances and monitor the Indians' behavior. In a celebrated anecdote, Garcilaso underscores the peculiar magic of the letter as a long-distance instrument of control. The story tells of two Indians who were sent by a rural overseer with ten melons for the owner of the farm, who lived in the city. The overseer also gave the bearers a letter for the owner, and warned them against eating any of the melons, for the letter would tell on them. When the Indians got thirsty on their way, they decided to eat a couple of melons, but only after throwing the letter behind a fence, so that it would not see them doing so. They then proceeded on their way with the "ignorant" letter, which, to their great dismay, nonetheless managed to give them away upon their arrival. The author's commentary on the episode is quite revealing:

Los indios, en aquellos principios, como no sabían qué eran letras, entendían que las cartas que los españoles se escribían unos a otros eran como mensajeros que decían de palabra lo que el español les mandaba, y que eran como espías que también decían lo que veían por el camino. (I, 9.29)

[In those early days the Indians did not know what writing was, and thought that the letters Spaniards wrote to one another were like spies who might report what they saw on the way.]

Garcilaso's explanation emphasizes the efficacy of writing in the conquest – as indefatigable messenger or wily spy, writing serves as a precious weapon for the Spaniards. This understanding of writing in fact corresponds quite closely to the role that letters and other documents played in the metropole's control of the Indies, and the way officers at every level controlled their subordinates.[36]

But within the immense scope of the *Comentarios*, there are multiple stories of the *inefficacy* of rhetoric, stories in which, paradoxically, Garcilaso narrates the breakdown of what has become his own weapon in establishing a place for himself in Spanish society. Garcilaso's critique of the Spaniards in Part II charts the failure of written communication, in counternarratives that show rhetoric as a less well-honed weapon. These narratives abound in Part II, suggesting that the Spanish superiority set up in Part I is undermined by the misguided letters of the second half. Amid the civil wars and confused factions that Garcilaso painstakingly reconstructs in his own text, Spanish writing often turns against Spanish masters.

Recounting the history of the Conquista, Garcilaso records the dangers writing posed for the Spaniards from the very earliest days, when the enterprise seemed most risky and ill-advised. When the conquistadors decide that Pizarro should press on while Almagro returns to Panama for more men (II, 1.8), the latter refuses to take any of the troops back with him, lest they communicate their discouragement to the possible recruits "y difamasen su empresa" [and defame his enterprise]. He even refuses to take any letters, since they would suffice to discredit the expedition. But writing nonetheless worms its way into the story, in a spool of cotton thread:

Por mucho que los capitanes procuraron que sus soldados no escribieran a Panamá, no pudieron estorbarles la pretensión, porque la necesidad aviva los ingenios. Un fulano de Saravia, natural de Trujillo, negó a su capitán Francisco Pizarro, siendo obligado a servirle más que otro por ser de su patria; envió a Panamá en un ovillo de hilo de algodón (en achaque de que le hiciesen unas medias de aguja) una petición a un amigo, firmada de muchos compañeros en que daba cuenta de las muertes y trabajos pasados y de la opresión y cautiverio presente; y que no les dejaban en su libertad para volverse a Panamá. Al pie de la petición en cuatro versos sumaron los trabajos, diciendo:

> Pues, señor gobernador,
> mírelo bien por entero,
> que allá va el recogedor
> y acá queda el carnicero.

(II, 1.8)

[Although the leaders tried to prevent the soldiers from writing to Panama, they could not stop them from doing so, for necessity sharpens the wits. A certain Saravia, a native of Trujillo, repudiated his captain Francisco Pizarro, though as he came from the same town his obligation was to follow him more loyally than the rest. He sent to Panama a ball of cotton on the pretext that they should knit him some socks with it. It contained a petition to a friend signed by many of his companions, in which they described their hardships and the death of their comrades, and their present captivity and oppression, declaring that they were deprived of the liberty of returning to Panama. The petition ended with a verse summarizing their plight as follows:

> So my lord governor
> bear this in mind:
> the scrounger's gone to Panama
> and the butcher's stayed behind.]

The damning letter concealed in the thread effectively ruins the expedition; the coerced men are freed on a judge's orders and the conquistadors are left without troops. Thus the witnessing power of the letter – even when carefully hidden, in this case, not behind a fence but inside a spool of thread – winds its way from the remote reaches of the "discovered" lands to uncover the myths and lies that fuel expansion. In a cross-cultural game of mirrors, the signifying thread recalls, too, the *quipus* or colored knots that the Incas used for record-keeping and to which Garcilaso refers as an authenticating source for his own story (I, 6.9).[37]

At times even the Spaniards' "official" letters dissemble, carrying not truth but dangerous lies. When Garcilaso recounts the later wars between

Gonzalo Pizarro and the various representatives of the Crown, he describes how such conspiratorial letters functioned as offensive weapons:

Echaron cartas a la ventura, enviándolas con indios para las personas principales del real del visorrey, con grandes promesas de perdón y mercedes a los que le matasen, las cuales causaron escándalo y sospecha para que adelante, como se dirá, hubiese muertes de gran lástima, porque no fueron justificadas, que como eran guerras civiles, los que tenían particulares pasiones y enemistades enviaban del un bando a otro cartas echadizas en nombre ajeno para que el visorrey sospechase mal de los que consigo tenía, que Gonzalo Pizarro nunca escribió cartas para que matasen al visorrey, ni los del visorrey las escribieron a Pizarro, como dicen los autores, sino que las traiciones encubiertas causaron muchos males en aquella guerra. (4.25)

[They sent off letters at a venture, dispatching them by Indians to the chief persons in the viceroy's camp and offering great promises of pardons and rewards to anyone who killed him. This caused great scandal and sowed suspicion, so that later there were some very regrettable killings without any justification. As these were civil wars, those who had private passions and enmities sent letters to one another under false signatures. Gonzalo Pizarro never wrote letters to try to have the viceroy killed, nor did the viceroy's followers write to Pizarro, as these authors say: hidden treachery caused many evils in this war.]

Like Discord itself traveling between the enemy camps, the treacherous letters create confusion and suspicion, blurring the lines between friend and foe.[38] As false messengers, they usurp the authority of the leaders and seriously threaten the unity within any one camp, a unity, moreover, which is already fragile given the civil nature of the conflict. There is no way to tell a false letter from a real one, just as there is no way to distinguish between true subjects and traitors, for the letters condemn their recipients regardless of whether they follow the treacherous advice contained therein.

This perilous lack of difference between friend and foe, loyalist and traitor, appears at crucial moments as the insurmountable condition of civil war. On the one hand, the situation is so unstable that battles sometimes simply dissolve: opportunists on the losing side break ranks and mingle with the victors, from whom they are indistinguishable. At the battle of Sacsahuana, Gonzalo Pizarro's men defect en masse and blend into the royalist camp: they leave their side as fierce warriors on the offensive, but quickly *become* the enemy themselves as they mingle with the loyalist troops. Garcilaso remarks upon the peculiar nature of this encounter: "Esta fue la batalla de Sacsahuana (si se puede llamar batalla), en la que no hubo golpe de espada ni encuentro de lanza, ni tiro de arcabuz de enemigo a enemigo" (5.36) [Such was the battle of Sacsahuana, if it can be called a battle, for there was not a sword thrust, nor a clash with lances, nor an arquebus shot between the two sides]. On the other hand, Garcilaso records a peculiarly Peruvian confusion of terms that corresponds to the same annulment of difference in the context of civil war. In Peru, he explains, the term "tyrant" is used to mean "traitor" (6.23). This usage makes sense if one considers the vertiginous speed with which leaders come and go in this part of the empire – when it is not clear who is betraying and who is being betrayed, the term "traitor" makes little sense. The non-relational "tyrant" has the added advantage of providing an Aristotelian justification for the inevitable fall of the rebel in question. The sheer proliferation of these tyrants – both petty and not so petty – in Garcilaso's narrative eventually raises doubts about the possibility of any legitimate government in Spanish Peru.

Such legitimate government would depend upon writing – in a territory as large and as sparsely populated by Spaniards as Peru, political representation necessarily comes to rely on textual representation. But for every instance when Garcilaso's text shows the Spaniards trying to govern by letter (calling back conquistadors from remote provinces for a military emergency, conveying the king's wishes, and so forth), it tells also of letters willfully unread, unopened, or simply gone astray. Licenciate Gasca, one of the many representatives of the king to fight the rebel Gonzalo Pizarro, burns the latter's missive "por no oír alguna libertad si se la escribía" (5.7) [so as not to hear any impertinence it might contain]. And of course the rebels at each particular juncture disregard the written orders they receive from the authorities.[39]

These moments of rhetorical insubordination in Garcilaso's text problematize González Echevarría's notion of it as one extensive *relación* in the name of the father. Garcilaso's ostensible aim may well be to set the record straight by correcting those historians who have done a disservice to the cause of truth, but his own accounts of the failures of written communication in Part II challenge not only the civility of Spanish empire (which writing should guarantee) but also the possibility of relaying a historical truth. The two preoccupations come together in an episode where the supposed arrogance of the natives results in a breakdown of rhetoric. Garcilaso ambivalently presents this anecdote, but ultimately discounts it as an interested lie.

The tale he explicitly refutes – of the Inca lord Atahualpa's purported rejection of Christianity – matches the famous episode of the melons from Part I. As the apologists of empire would have it, when this lord was handed a Bible by a priest at his first encounter with the Spaniards, he failed to hear it "speaking" to him, and threw it violently to the ground, thereby providing the Spaniards with ample justification to attack him. Denouncing the tale as a calumny, Garcilaso underscores the unreliability of those who tell stories "quitando lo que fue en contra y añadiendo lo que fue en favor por no condenarse ellos mismos, pues enviaban a pedir mercedes por aquellas hazañas que habían hecho, y es cierto que las habían de dorar y esmaltar lo mejor que pudiesen" (II, 1.26) [suppressing whatever was unfavorable and adding what seemed favorable, so as not to condemn themselves. They were writing to ask for rewards for the deeds they had done, so they obviously gilded them and varnished them as best they could]. Instead, Garcilaso quotes his own sources, who – at least in the selections the author presents – write abundantly of the incivility of the Spaniards who slaughtered the Indians even when their leader Atahualpa ordered them not to fight back. In Garcilaso's version, such conduct is not merely immoral but sacrilegious, for it ignores the miracle of God's mercy interceding for the Spaniards.

Yet although Garcilaso here mobilizes the discourse of religious teleology to justify his own version of events, his previous claim about the relative nature of historical truth necessarily colors his narrative. If, as Garcilaso suggests, writing with an end in view produces redoubtable truths, then his own text must answer to the same charges, for he himself is seeking favors from the king by reconstructing a favorable history. The author's compositional mode, in fact, would give any suspicious reader pause: his constant cutting and pasting from previous historians' versions to improve them leaves his text vulnerable to the same kind of interested recombinatory appropriations. Garcilaso himself seems to suggest that historical texts are fundamentally relational; they are "trustworthy" only in context, when dismembered and quoted in the service of a particular truth. Thus his own authority as a mestizo historian – combining his native and his Spanish learning to recompose previous versions of American history – is in a sense achieved at the expense of the integrity of Spanish letters.

In a poignant coda to the competing claims of interested histories, Garcilaso admits that his own project has interfered with a last set of letters, which he ruefully confesses to having ignored. He describes how the descendants of the Inca rulers sent him a suit for favors to be presented to the king, letters which he was not able to shepherd properly "por estar ocupado en escribir esta historia, que espero no haber servido menos en ella a los españoles que ganaron aquel imperio que a los Incas que lo poseyeron" (II, 8.21) [as I have been engaged in writing this history, which I hope will have been as great a service to the Spaniards who won the empire as to the Incas who formerly possessed it]. Despite his own text's abundant evidence of the slipperiness of writing, Garcilaso closes with a claim for its larger import, which transcends that of a specific petition. His writing attempts to do justice to both empires, and the lettered self he creates in the process bears all the contradictions of such a double allegiance. Thus, while writing affords Garcilaso the "subjectification" that

Foucault describes, it registers also the contradictions and fractures of the self. The author's strategic translation of imperial ideologies to his own experience of the Conquista renders him both an exemplary and an exceptional subject of the empire.

Poste restante: letter to an imper(v)ious king

There is a certain tragic irony in the fate of Felipe Guaman Poma de Ayala's *Nueva corónica i buen gobierno*, a letter probably undelivered – and perhaps undeliverable – for centuries. In his extensive missive, the author engages in a complex set of discursive negotiations with an imagined addressee, Philip III of Spain. Not content merely to present his vision of things, Guaman Poma actually imagines the king's responses and anticipates his objections. Thus, one of the most poignant sections of the text, the "Capítulo de la pregunta" consists of him ventriloquizing the king – who asks all the right questions – as though the writer almost suspected that the text might never be read by its addressee.

The text has several parts, some of which correspond to Garcilaso's "before and after" model for the history of Peru. There is an introduction to the figure of the author, a history of the Andean people before the Spaniards, the less distant history of the "Conquista deste reino," and, most original of all, an extended discussion of contemporary conditions in the Andes with recommendations for "Buen gobierno y justicia." Unlike Garcilaso's *Comentarios reales*, which were read widely and considered an authoritative text on Peru until the late eighteenth century,[40] Guaman Poma's urgent program of reform probably had no contemporary readers. The voluminous letter never seems to have reached its destination, but instead sat unread in a Copenhagen archive until it was "discovered" in 1908. Yet even as an undelivered missive it is a fascinating document, evincing the rhetorical and discursive strategies through which a native author could interrogate the structure of Spanish empire in Peru.

The *Nueva corónica i buen gobierno* is thoroughly steeped in the literary, religious, and political debates of its time. As Rolena Adorno has brilliantly shown, Poma draws on the traditions of sixteenth-century historical writing (the *crónica* and the *relación*), on the "heroic conception" of both epic and exemplary biography, and on contemporary recommendations for religious or moral persuasion in sermons to construct his own text, which itself resists classification as any one genre. Adorno lucidly renders the text readable from the perspective of European letters, and demonstrates how the incorporation of colonialist ideas can itself function as a tool for resistance.[41] Yet the *Nueva corónica* is not merely an imitation of European forms: it exhibits instead a fascinating hybridity, bringing

together European and Andean conventions of representation, both linguistic and pictorial, and interspersing Quechua with the Spanish.[42] As
Mary Louise Pratt has pointed out, it is an autoethnographic text, involv-
ing "a selective collaboration with and appropriation of idioms of the
metropolis or the conqueror."[43]

Spanish racial and religious ideologies take on a peculiar force within
Guaman Poma's rhetorical arsenal. In particular, he ably translates the
Spanish preoccupation with class, honor, and "clean" blood to an Andean
context. His account of himself as a subject adapts Spanish notions of
racial purity to the New World, first, to enhance his own authority and,
second, to argue for a radical separation of the colonizer from the colonized. The logical conclusion of Spain's emphasis on difference, in Poma's
forceful argument, is the containment of colonial expansion. Thus this
native of Peru challenges the Spaniards on their own ground, transforming
the very logic of empire into an argument for colonial reform.

What's in a name?

Guaman Poma begins by establishing his own rank and authority. He
presents himself as "señor y príncipe" and then repeats the claim in his
father's voice. He describes his father, don Martín Guaman Mallque de
Ayala, as "segunda persona del Ynga deste rreyno del Pirú" [second
person to the Inca of this kingdom of Peru].[44] This "second person" writes
a second, abbreviated letter to the king, recommending the much larger
letter within which it is embedded. In this related letter the author Guaman
Poma is again described as "*capac*, ques préncipe, y gobernador mayor de
los indios" (4) [*capac*, which means prince, and chief governor of the
Indians]. The secondariness of this validation recurs in the material in-
scription of the author's rank in the text: there is evidence that Guaman
Poma went back over his manuscript a second time to replace "cacique
principal" [principal lord] with "capac, ques préncipe" [*capac*, which
means "prince"], and to add "prince" to his name in a number of different
places.[45] Through this multilevel textual maneuvering, the author ascribes
to himself a noble status that makes him commensurate with, if not equal
to, his royal addressee.

Perhaps the single most important gesture Guaman Poma makes to
place himself within the confines of Spanish letters is to declare himself an
honorary Spaniard. He recounts how a Spanish captain bestows his name
upon the author's father – knighting him after a fashion – to thank him for
saving his life in battle. The scene has strong chivalric overtones:

Y estando en esto, [Don Martín de Ayala] fue serbiendo a un cauallero, capitán
general, muy gran servidor de su Magestad, llamado capitán Luys de Aualos de

Ayala, padre de dicho santo hermitaño Martín de Ayala, mestizo, de quien se hace mención. Estando en la batalla, rreniendo en el Collao, en Uarina Pampa, peleando en el servicio de su Magestad, en el encuentro cayó del cauallo de una lansada al suelo el padre de este santo hombre, Luys de Aualos de Ayala, contrando con el dicho traydor Gonzalo Pizarro. Y de su capitán defendió y le salbó de la muerte y le mató al dicho traydor Martín de Olmos contrario, le xarretó y le mató el dicho don Martín de Ayala. Y ancí se salbó el dicho Luys de Aualos de Ayala y se levantó y dio bozes diziendo, "¡O señor deste rreyno, don Martín de Ayala, seruidor de Dios y de nuestro muy alto enperador don Carlos de la gloriosa memoria! Aunque a yndio, tendrá cuydado de dalle su encomienda su Magestad."

Y ací, por este dicho seruicio, ganó onrra y mérito como señor y cauallero del rreyno y se llamó Ayala, segunda del emperador en este rreyno, don Martín de Ayala. (11–12)

[And meanwhile [Don Martín de Ayala] was serving a knight, captain general, great servant of His Majesty, called Captain Luis de Aualos de Ayala, father of the said holy hermit Martín de Ayala, mestizo, whom we mention. In the middle of the battle, fighting in the Collao, in Huarina Pampa, fighting for his majesty, in the middle of the fray the said Luis de Avalos de Ayala, father of this holy man, was thrown from his horse by a spear-blow, while fighting the traitor Gonzalo Pizarro. And he defended his captain and saved him from death and killed the enemy traitor Martín de Olmos, lanced him and killed him, did Don Martín de Ayala. And thus was saved Luis de Avalos de Ayala, who got up and shouted, "Oh lord of this kingdom, Don Martín de Ayala, servant of God and of our great emperor Charles of glorious memory! Although you are an Indian, His Majesty will make sure to give you your *encomienda*."

And so for this service he won honor and merit as a lord and knight of the kingdom, and he was called Ayala, second to the emperor in this kingdom, Don Martín de Ayala.]

The mixed-up temporality of Guaman Poma's account gives us kaleidoscopic prefigurations of the author's honorary Spanishness: his father seems to possess the Spanish name even before the conquistador really grants it to him. To make things even more confusing, the passage mentions another Martín de Ayala: the mestizo son of the conquistador Luis de Ayala, who, unlike Poma's father, got *his* name from his physical parentage and his mixed blood. This homonymous mestizo functions as a foil for both the author and his father; his is the other, far less heroic route toward a Spanish identity.

Given the disdain for mestizos that Poma will voice throughout his text it is particularly interesting that he praises this particular mestizo as the one who taught both his father and himself Christian doctrine, thus fleshing out their Spanish identities (11). The drawing that illustrates this relationship echoes the praise: a large figure of the "Padre Martín de Ayala, Santo de Dios amado" [Father Martín de Ayala, Saint beloved of

God] towers over the young Guaman Poma and his most Christian father and mother (13). The mestizo both represents an exemplary model for the clergy in Peru, which is a particular target of Poma's critique, and completes the "shadow" family of Spaniards and model Christians with which the author surrounds himself even as he maintains his own racial purity.

The familial relationship between these homonymous but unrelated Ayalas comes to the fore when the mestizo is described as teaching Christian doctrine "a su padrastro don Martín de Ayala, segunda persona del Ynga, y a su madre y a sus ermanos," (12) [to his stepfather Don Martín de Ayala, second to the Inca, to his mother, and to his brothers]. While Poma carefully distinguishes the mestizo "brother" from his onomastically Spanish father, the connection between the two pervades these early pages of the text: Christianity comes to Poma via this "familiar" mestizo, and the phrase "segunda persona del Ynga," with which he describes his father, recalls also that other "second person," Martín de Ayala, spiritual father-figure to the author. In this autobiographical passage, Poma juggles various kinds of Spanish identity, privileging the scene of naming but recognizing also the importance of his Christianization in making him what he is. Yet his claim of a special bond with the holy mestizo ironically reveals a darker side to the constitution of his extended family. Luis de Avalos de Ayala has marked them in more than one way: by conferring his name on Don Martín, but also by saddling them with his illegitimate son, born to Poma's mother. The colonial violence implicit in this arrangement qualifies the heroic account of Don Martín's chivalric induction into Spanish identity. Poma's emphasis on the power of naming in a martial setting elides other, far more abusive domestic transactions.

How exactly does the honorific "de Ayala" transform Poma's father? The name functions as a double-edged signifier, recognizing the conquistador's obligation – "you are now one of us" – while making the recipient grammatically the property *of* the Ayalas – "you belong to us."[46] This peculiarity of the Spanish name would not bear remarking upon were it not for Luis de Ayala's grateful assurance in the passage that Don Martín's deed will make him worthy of an *encomienda* (that is, of owning Indians) from the king even though he is an Indian himself.[47] Perhaps this claim accounts too for the honorific *don*, which locates Martín in an exalted position in the Spanish hierarchy. The bewildering scene of naming thus conjures the very real appropriation of Indians' persons and labor in the *encomienda* even as it grants Poma's father a metaphorical identity which makes him "belong" to his Spanish benefactor. The end of the passage makes Don Martín's position in the colonial order even more uncertain: the slippage in his description from "segunda persona del Ynga" to "segunda del emperador en este rreyno" ambiguously transfers his loyalty to the Spanish ruler, while suggesting sotto voce that the new master should respect previous hierarchies and offices.

Despite its convoluted dynamics, this metaphoric self-transformation ultimately allows Guaman Poma to voice Spanish ideology with greater confidence without forsaking the prerogatives of his "pure" Andean birth. He mimics the attributes of a Spanish identity without ever adopting it fully. Adroitly, he skirts the pitfalls of actual *mestizaje*, inventing instead a scene of chivalric obligation that magically baptizes his father and, by extension, himself as Spaniards. The tutelary efforts of a mestizo lead them towards Christianity, but they themselves remain pure Indians. The episode of the name-giving battle bears fascinating parallels to the "primal scene" of the Inca Garcilaso's father's honoring the principles of chivalry over the Crown's authority to loan his horse to Pizarro. Whereas in that case the son takes the name of the father to rescue his reputation, but finds his entire position within Spanish culture compromised by the father's act, here the Indian son is granted an onomastic key to Spanish identity by the name bequeathed on his father for his courage.

The scene makes Don Martín not just an ordinary Spaniard but one who bears his name as a sign of chivalric achievement.[48] Moreover, the writer presents his father's entire career as an accommodation of Spanish power, and a model of loyalty. Yet what may seem like a betrayal of the Andean cause to support the Crown is actually a subtle refutation of Spanish justifications for conquest. For the career Poma imagines for his father, as official ambassador of the Inca, includes a crucial revision of the original meeting between Spaniards and Indians. Poma tells of his father greeting the first conquistadors with open arms when they first land at Tumbes. This description of the landing as a friendly encounter, which the author expands upon when he actually recounts the story of the Conquista (349), is not simple nostalgia for what might have been but a calculated jab at Spanish consciences. Given such a willing reception as Poma describes, the Spaniards could never justify their war against the natives. In the author's version of the scene, the Indians offer nothing but friendship to the conquistadors, leaving them with nothing that they might legitimately conquer.

As Adorno has pointed out, the epigraph to Poma's history of the conquest might paradoxically be the "y no ubo conquista," that Poma repeats as he stresses over and over again that the Indians did not fight back.[49] The accounts of Indians fighting Spaniards are instead transformed into stories of the natives' loyalty in fighting always on the side of the Crown, as in the famous illustration where the (rebel) Spaniards are shown literally turning tail before the loyal Indians' attack. The caption reads: "CONQUISTA. Batalla que hizo en seruicio de su Magestad el excelentísimo señor *capac apo* Don Martín de Ayala, padre del autor, Chinchaysuyo, y *apo Uasco, apo Guaman Uachaca*, Hanan, Lurin Chanca, con cien soldados y Francisco Hernandes, trescientos soldados. Fue vencido y se huyó" (401) [CONQUEST. Battle fought for His Majesty by the most excellent lord capac apo Don Martín de Ayala, father of the author ... with one hundred soldiers against Francisco Hernández, three hundred soldiers. [Hernández] was defeated and fled].[50] Given the speed with which civil conflicts developed in Peru, it is easy to see how the author might rewrite the Indians' struggle against any and all Spaniards as an attack on Spanish rebels, in order to appeal to the good will of the Crown.

Poma's account of the Spaniards' unopposed landing recalls the "civil" battle of Sacsahuana described by Garcilaso in II, 5. 36 – the battle which never actually took place because the rebel Spaniards all saw the wisdom of recognizing the Crown. In that scene, loyalty wins the day without a struggle; here, Christianity decides a similar non-battle. Poma's version of the earliest encounter thus introduces the motif of the natives' willing reception of Christianity, which the author, a new Christian himself, particularly underscores. But whereas Garcilaso had stressed the Indians' willingness to become Christians *after* being dazzled in battle by divine messengers, Poma suggests that the Spaniards' attacks were unjustified, because, with the saints fighting on their behalf (373–77), Christianity was already as good as established.[51] Guaman Poma's own proleptic account transforms the miracles from cause to consequence of the Indians' conversion: "En ese tiempo era señal de Dios questaua ya fixa la Santa Yglecia en el rreyno" (373) [At that time it was the sign from God that the Holy Church was already established in the kingdom].

Particularly interesting in this context is Poma's description of the apparition of St. James and its aftermath. He tells the story of the saint's appearance bearing a great sword and bringing death and destruction for the Indians, an image we have already encountered in Garcilaso. But the connection between St. James and the *yllapa* or lightning bolt here takes a fascinating linguistic turn:

Y desde entonses los yndios al rrayo les llama y le dice Sanctiago porque el sancto cayó en tierra como rrayo, yllapa, Santiago como los cristianos dauan boses, deziendo "Santiago." Y ací lo oyeron los yndios ynfieles y lo uieron al santo caer en tierra como rrayo. Y ancí los yndios son testigos de uista del señor Sanctiago y se deue guardarse esta dicha fiesta del señor Santiago en este rreyno como pascua porque del milagro de Dios y del señor Santiago se ganó. (377)

[And from that time the Indians have called the lightning bolt Santiago because the saint fell to earth like a lightning bolt, yllapa, St. James, for the Christians shouted "St. James." And so the infidel Indians heard it and saw the saint fall to Earth like a lightning bolt. And so the Indians are eyewitnesses to St. James and his day must be observed as a holiday in this kingdom because it was won through God's and St. James' miracle.]

By taking the name of the saint for the lightning bolt, the Indians reintroduce the pantheistic worship of Andean religion despite James' miraculous intervention on behalf of a Christian God (notice that the episode occurs while the Indians are still infidels). The passage depicts a cultural synthesis whereby the Indians add Christian names to their naturalistic pantheon; it certainly does not stress their conversion to Christianity. The pious admonition to observe the saint's day in order to commemorate the Conquista sounds less than authentic. Like Garcilaso listing Andean names for the Virgin, Guaman Poma describes a conversion that preserves much of local beliefs while imitating the guise of Christianity. Without speculating about the sincerity of Poma's own conversion, it seems safe to say that he depicts Christianization in Peru as a syncretic process, which preserves much of Andean culture.

Christians, Jews, and Moors

As a firm convert to Christianity, the author can voice his criticism of Church abuses with authority. Recently inculcated with the principles of the Church, he is quick to spot deviations. Guaman Poma's denunciation of the abuses of the Church in Peru is one of the text's most constant themes. He returns to its failings again and again, stressing in particular the abuse of native women by priests who deflower them "con color de la dotrina" (54 and passim) [with the excuse of teaching doctrine]. The women who have been seduced by priests, Poma suggests, are tainted thereafter, and lose all sexual continence: "Y estas yndias paren mestizos y se hazen uellacas, putas en este rreyno" (534) [And these Indian women give birth to mestizos and become tramps, whores in this kingdom]. The direst consequence of such sinister ministrations, however, is the birth of an increasing number of mestizos who dilute and weaken the Andean stock:

Como los dichos padres de las dotrinas no quieren guardar ni ciguir lo que manda el Santo Concilio y hordenansas y prouiciones rreales de su Magestad, aunque se la a mandado que no tenga solteras ni casadas ni biudas ni bieja ni muchacha ni niña en sus casas y cocina. Ni con color de la dotrina no lo ajunte por los daños y pleytos y no multiplicar, acauarse los yndios y acauarse la hazienda del servicio de Dios y de su Magestad . . .

   Y ancí multiplica muchos mestizos y cholos en este reino. (536)

[The said preachers refuse to abide by the Holy Council or the royal ordinances and stipulations of his Majesty, although they have been told they are not to have single

women or married women or widows or old women or young women or girls in
their houses and kitchens. Nor with the excuse of teaching doctrine should they get
close to them, for all the harm and disputes it causes, and the Indians do not
multiply and they disappear and the servants who are the wealth of God and His
Majesty disappear . . .
And so the mestizos and *cholos* multiply in this kingdom.]

Poma reinforces his moral argument against *mestizaje* with an economic
and political one: the multiplication of mestizos leads to the gradual
depopulation of the Indian towns, thus threatening to leave the King
without any subjects: "Y ací se uan acauando los yndios deste rreyno y se
acauarán y perderá su Magestad su rreyno" (550) [And so all the Indians
of this kingdom will disappear and His Majesty will lose his kingdom].

Yet Poma's most complicated strategy for protesting the adulteration of
Andean blood, I would argue, is his use of the Spanish ideology of racial
purity, as he cannily transforms the Spaniards themselves into the outsiders in the Americas, akin to the Moors or the Jews vilified in Spain. On
the one hand, he notes the implicit equivalence between these groups from
an Andean perspective – a foreigner is a foreigner. As Guaman Poma
explains, "Como dicen *uira cocha* le llaman en común al castellano es-
trangero, judío, moro, turco, ynglés y francés, que todos son españoles *uira
cochas*" (96) [The name *viracocha* they use generally for the Spanish
"foreigner," Jew, Moor, Turk, Englishman, and Frenchman, for all are
Spanish *viracochas*]. On the other hand, Poma raises a concern for racial
purity that would recall for the Spaniards the nagging problem of domestic
others within Spain, a preoccupation that would culminate with the decree
banishing the Moriscos from Spain in 1609.

In Peru, Poma suggests, the Spanish conquest has upset all traditional
hierarchies: the lowly Indians go around calling themselves "Don" and
"Doña," as do the lowliest Spaniards (recall that the author calls his own
father "Don Martín"). Even Jews and Moors "tienen 'don', mundo al
revés" (380) [take "Don," world upside down]. For the topos of the
world-upside-down to have full force, the consummate outsiders of Spanish society must be described in positions of power. The emphasis on Jews
and Moors makes Poma's complaint ring louder in Spanish ears, although
it implicitly equates the Spanish interlopers themselves with the European
outsiders. The disorder that oppresses the Indians, Poma suggests, debases
the Spaniards as well:

Que los dichos coregidores y padres o españoles y caualleros y los dichos caciques
prencipales, ciendo señor de título desde sus antepasados, se acienta en su mesa a
comer y a conbidar y conuersar y beuer, jugar con personas figones y rrufianes y
salteadores, ladrones, mentirosos, ganapanes y borrachos, judíos y moros y con

gente baja, yndios *mitayos*. Y a estos dichos descubren sus secretos y tienen conuersación con estos mestizos y mulatos y negros.

Y ancí hay en esta uida muy muchos dones y doñas de calauasas. (468–70)

[For the magistrates and priests or Spaniards and knights and the principal Indian lords, legitimate lords since the time of their ancestors, sit down to eat and entertain and talk and drink and game with riffraff, ruffians, highwaymen, robbers, liars, laborers and drunkards, Jews and Moors and lowly persons, Indian menials. And they tell these people their secrets and converse with these mestizos and mulattos and blacks.

And so there are in this life many lords and ladies not worth a fig.]

In bringing together the lowly and the high, the disorder of the conquest threatens the Spaniards' traditional hierarchies. In this passage, Poma shifts the focus from his own main complaint – the dissolution of native hierarchies – to focus on the general disappearance of *distinction* in Peru. The chapter quickly moves to racial distinctions and purity of blood, addressing the Spaniards' obsession with clean lineages, i.e., those that were free of Jewish or Moorish blood. Here the uncleanliness is expanded to include mestizos:

El hombre tiene la culpa hazer hijo judío o mestizo y sus parientes tiene la culpa. Y ci fue el hombre gente baja o judío y la muger fue de la casa de caualleros y de cristiano biejo, de todo se echa a perder, parientes y linages y sus hijos, son de rruyn casta, peor que mestizo. Aunque sea negro o español o yndio, tiene que le honrre ci es caballero de título desde sus antepasados y linajes. (470)

[It is a man's fault if he has a Jewish or mestizo son, and it is his relatives' fault. And even if the man was lowly or a Jew and the woman was of a noble house and an Old Christian, everything is lost, relatives and lineages and their children are of the lowliest class, worse than mestizos. Whether he is Black, or Spanish, or Indian, he should be honored if he is a legitimate lord since the time of his ancestors and lineages.]

While the passage initially reinscribes the Spanish conceptions of pure blood, the last sentence betrays the difference between the author and the Spaniards he addresses: he believes in *purity*, but not in European superiority. His aim is to separate what has come together with such unfortunate results in the Conquista, to return Blacks, and Spaniards, and Indians to their proper spheres where they can all be honored as is their due. This surprising moment contradicts the logic of Spanish racial ideology, by which Moors or Jews taint Spanish blood because they are inherently inferior. It thus anticipates Guaman Poma's often contradictory use of these outsider figures in his texts, as he seeks a delicate equilibrium between representing their foreignness and arguing for their rights.

This equilibrium becomes most fraught in the latter part of the text, the chapter "De conzederación," where the author urges Christians to a moral reflection on their behavior. As Adorno has argued, the author recirculates in this section the highly controversial ideas of Las Casas, who not only argued for a restitution of the Incas but insisted on the rights of different peoples to sovereignty over their own territories.[52] This source accounts in part for Guaman Poma's claim that, "todo el mundo es de Dios y ancí Castilla es de los españoles y las Yndias es de los yndios y Guenea es de los negros" (857) [all the world belongs to God and so Castile belongs to the Spaniards and the Indies to the Indians and Guinea to the Blacks]. The Jews and Moors must paradoxically become Spaniards in order to fall under Spanish law: "Que uien puede ser esta ley porque un español al otro español, aunque sea judío o moro, son españoles, que no se entremete a otra nación cino que son españoles de Castilla" [For this law may well exist, for a Spaniard [rules] another Spaniard – even if a Jew or a Moor, they are Spaniards, for he is not intruding into another nation for they are Spaniards from Castile]. This forcible inclusion of Jews and Moors within the Spanish polity is a commonsense gambit on Poma's part: instead of following Las Casas, who argues for the legality of the Reconquista of the Peninsula from the Moors even while he denounces the conquest of the Americas, the Andean author sensibly points out that the Jews and Moors *are* Spaniards. Therefore, he suggests, it is legal to subject them to Spanish laws (even when the laws explicitly repress these groups). Andeans, meanwhile, most certainly do not come under those laws' jurisdiction. In a move to establish his own people's foreignness – the Andeans are not of Spain – Guaman Poma challenges a carefully constructed, if fragile, Spanish identity, one very much based on the *exclusion* of Moors and Jews.

He returns to this topic to consider the difficulty of knowing who is really free of the taint of bad blood, "que cómo se ha de sauer ci tiene mancha de un poco de judío o moro u turco, englés" (878) [for how is one to know if he is stained with a bit of the Jew or Moor or Turk or Englishman]. Having relied on the ideology of blood purity to make his argument against *mestizaje*, Poma now ridicules the possibility of racial certainty in the mixed-up world of the colonies. The solution, he states ironically, is simply to proclaim one's status: "Harto mejor es dezir que soy cristiano biejo" [Much better to say I am an Old Christian]. Certainty, such as it might be, comes from Spain: "La buena prouansa es uálido traer de su casa y patria de España y firmado de su Magestad o de su consejo rreal, es cauallero fino" [Valid proof must be brought from his home and fatherland of Spain, signed by His Majesty or the Royal Council, then he is a fine knight]. The Spanish obsession with origins, Guaman Poma observes, is ill served by the colonial venture, where all distinctions disappear and both Indians and Spanish can remake themselves into nobles. As a space of disorder, Peru urgently needs reform through separation, which Poma himself advocates.

The often contradictory references to the Spaniards' others thus reflect Poma's strategic manipulation of racial sameness versus difference – enough sameness that the Andean peoples can appear civilized on Spanish terms, with the same concerns about purity, hierarchy, and order; enough difference that the disorder of the Spanish presence in the Americas becomes obvious. The more urgent the author's denunciation of the Spaniards becomes, the more likely he seems to equate them with Jews and Moors. In his strongest refutation of the supposed Semitic origin of the Amerindians, Poma highlights instead, for Christians' "conzederación," the common origins of both Jews and Spaniards:

Conzedera que la nació de español fue judío: Aunque tubieron otro ley y tubieron letra y trage, áuito y rrostro, barbas, cudicia, aunque fueron gentiles deferencia en el sacrificio, los judíos conocieron muy de ueras a Dios y tubieron ley de Muyzén y mandamiento. Lo qual no las tubieron los yndios su ley ni áuito ni rrostro ni letra. (882)

[Consider that the Spaniards' nation was once Jewish: even though they had another law, they had letters and costume and appearance, beards and cupidity; although they had a different ritual, the Jews knew God very well and had Moses' law and commandments. Which the Indians did not have, neither the law nor the costume, nor the appearance nor the letters.]

In this formulation, very different from his earlier emphasis on prehispanic "Christianity" in the Andes, Guaman Poma stresses the basic difference of the Indian peoples from what he correctly describes as a Judeo-Christian continuum. By the end of the text, the favorable inclusion of the Indians in a Spanish world-view no longer seems a plausible solution; Poma argues instead for a radical separation. He is pushed towards this stance by Spanish cruelties so extreme that they surpass those of non-Christians: "Jamás se ha oydo en Roma, Castilla, en toda la cristiandad, cino son los moros, turcos y judíos. Con ser ellos tales, tubiera alguna piedad y misericordia a su prógimo" (995) [Such things have never been heard of in Rome, Castile, or all of Christendom, if not from the Moors, Turks, and Jews. And even if they were thus, they had some pity and mercy for their neighbors].

The solution that Guaman Poma proposes to the king for the terrible disorder of Peru reflects the Lascasista ideologies of restitution of the Incas, while recalling also much older models of coexistence between

Moors and Spaniards within Spain. Poma suggests to Philip III that he should be monarch of the whole world, with native rulers for each of the four parts of the globe. This proposal ably harnesses the Hapsburgs' self-presentation as universal rulers to a plan for colonial reform.[53] Whereas Charles V, as Holy Roman Emperor, and the Spanish Hapsburgs after him, relied heavily on apocalyptic myths of the "four world monarchies," and on prophecies of universal rule as preparation for Christ's second coming, Poma imitates these constructs to suit his urgent purposes. He proposes his own son, descendant of the Incas, to rule over Peru, and suggests a "Black prince of Guinea," the "King of the Christians in Rome," and the "Great Turk, King of the Moors," for their respective lands.[54] To reassure Philip, he specifies the protocol and distinction that would protect the monarch's rank over mere kings (889).

This radical solution, Adorno argues, is actually far from utopian: it recalls earlier attempts by Las Casas and his followers to restore Andean rule and offer the king of Spain an annual sum as compensation for his Christianization of the natives.[55] In Las Casas, the solution is compared to the king of Tunis' presentation of a jewel to the Spanish sovereign every year, as a sign of vassalage, and to the tribute once paid by the kings of Granada to those of Castile.[56] This comparison reinforces MacCormack's suggestion that until the 1560s it had been possible to imagine for Peru a kind of *convivencia* or coexistence of cultures such as had characterized interactions between Jews, Moors, and Christians in Medieval Spain.[57] At that time, the *convivencia* might have been based on the fragile residual Inca state of Vilcabamba, to which the Inca descendants had retreated after the initial stage of the Conquista. As MacCormack points out, the existence of this parallel state, "left open an interpretation of the conquest according to which the king of Spain did indeed rule over Spaniards and their descendants in Peru, but the indigenous people – which might include the ever-growing number of mestizos – had their own sovereign, the Inca."[58] Many years after the execution of the Inca Tupac Amaru by Viceroy Toledo in 1572 and the subsequent disappearance of Vilcabamba, Poma gives new currency to the idea of peaceful coexistence of cultures. His final proposal, with its multiple filiations from American and European models, seems a fitting culmination to his constant imitation of Spanish racial ideologies throughout the text. The model of coexistence – separate but tolerated – ensures the order that Poma seems to want so desperately, while enabling the separation advocated again and again through pointed references to Moors and Jews. In Guaman Poma's proposal, the strategic use of racial and religious difference reaches a fruition of sorts, in a powerful model for both harmony and non-interference.

Speaking the Spaniards

It is striking that Guaman Poma's proposal for a world monarchy should immediately precede his most direct address to the king in the famous "Capítulo de la pregunta," a question-and-answer session with the king himself. The chapter is accompanied by an illustration that shows the direct communication between the two, with the caption: "Pregunta su Magestad, Responde el autor/Don Phelipe el Terzero, rrey monarca del mundo/Ayala el autor/Presenta personalmente el autor la Corónica a su Magestad" (897) [His Majesty asks, the Author answers/Don Philip III, King Monarch of the world/Ayala the author/The author personally presents the Chronicle to His Majesty]. The caption suggests that Poma's authorial power to impersonate the king stems from his earlier proposal, for the king he ventriloquizes bears the title that the author has bestowed upon him, of "Monarch of the World." Guaman Poma, meanwhile, refers to himself by his Spanish name – Ayala – to underscore his closeness to the king. Thus he achieves his greatest proximity to Philip III, and the exalted role of royal counselor, based on the radical proposal he has just presented.[59]

The stronger address that ventriloquism affords Guaman Poma in this chapter stems from his ability to incorporate and reformulate Spanish ideology to argue his case. Ventriloquism in Spanish, furthermore, seems far more daring as a metaphorical appropriation of the Spanish voice than earlier instances in the text, when the author "reproduces" the sermons of corrupt priests in Quechua (576–82). In those instances, he forgoes the role of translator and leaves the damning evidence in what must be an opaque form for Spanish readers, although he presents abundant proof of the priests' corruption when not quoting them directly. In ventriloquizing the king, on the other hand, Poma argues for his own intelligibility in Spanish, carefully articulated through strategic reformulations of Spanish ideology and his own self-construction. He thus moves from *correspondent* to *respondent*, metaphorically eliminating the distance between himself and the king that was to doom his appeal for reform.

The enduring irony of *el autor Ayala*'s trajectory to his strongest position of enunciation is that his self-construction depends largely on the disorder he decries: his persona is based on literal or literary "mixtures" of Spaniards and Indians, on the imposition of Christianity on an unchristian people, and on his often painful education in Spanish ideology. Yet his subjectification through writing stands as a model for the negotiation of imperial ideologies in the creation of a resistant self. Ultimately, the author advocates separation from the Spaniards over reform in the colony, yet in constructing his case he ably voices the ideologies of empire insofar as he needs them to be audible to his audience. Unlike the Inca Garcilaso, whose literary career seems largely devoted to achieving a Spanish subjectivity that accommodates his differences, Guaman Poma only assumes a Spanish self insofar as he must in order to argue for the radical separation of the Andes from Spain.

4 Virtual Spaniards

La mayor leyenda de la historia de España es la de su propia existencia política.

Pedro Córdoba[1]

Chapter 3 analyzed how Inca Garcilaso and Guaman Poma, as New World writers, negotiate their way into Spanish discussions about the nature of empire or the proper government of the colonies by invoking and often manipulating Spain's racialized religious ideology. Garcilaso constructs himself as a true Spaniard by aligning himself with Christian Spain against Islam, and establishes careful distinctions between the American Indians – willing converts to the Faith – and recalcitrant Moors. Guaman Poma, on the other hand, invokes the Spanish hysteria over the improper mixing of bloods – Christian versus Jew or Moor – to argue for the survival of the Indian population of Peru and against increasing *mestizaje*. For these authors who are outsiders, able manipulation of Spanish exclusionary rules paradoxically provides a way in, even if, at least in the case of Guaman Poma, the historical results suggest the limitations of rhetorical strategies. Yet while it may not succeed in stopping the abuses they decry, their ability to identify, imitate, and indeed translate the ideology of Spanish identity affords them their own resistant subjectivity.

The question then arises of how the Moriscos, a group consistently targeted and indeed demonized by a racialized religious ideology within Spain itself, were able to intervene in that ideology. These "little Moors" experienced increasing persecution and ostracism over the course of the sixteenth century, and repeatedly faced the challenge of countering or deflecting the legal assaults on their culture. As I suggested in Chapter 2, the very presence of the Moriscos challenges the notion of a homogeneous Spain; even as they are persecuted and repressed, they approximate "Spanishness" in a way that undermines the ostensible transparency of the category. The similarity of the Moriscos forces the Spanish state, via the Inquisition, to keep raising the bar of national identity, from conversion to Christianity, to adoption of "Christian" cultural practices, to genealogical purity.[2]

The case of the Moriscos' effect on Spanish culture and identity is especially complicated, because this was a minority completely neutralized and largely destroyed. The expulsion decrees of 1609 and the years following attempted nothing less than to cleanse Spain finally and completely of the Moorish taint. As Root has argued:

> The indeterminability of faith apparent in the Inquisition's inability to determine dissimulation, and its effort to circumvent this by continually increasing its demands for proof of orthodoxy, meant the definition of orthodoxy could migrate to genealogy: Moriscos were not and could not be "truly" Christian because of their ancestry, and they were by definition reduced to impenitent heretics and dangerous outsiders. A polarity had been constructed that became impossible to deal with except by "amputation" and the "casting out" of the deviants.[3]

Given the ruthless nature of these "solutions," my reading of Morisco interventions into the culture that ostracized them cannot aim at a heroic recuperation of agency. The historical record of the suffering and loss surrounding the expulsions is too blatant to disregard in such a fashion. Instead, I want to explore precisely the issue of "dissimulation": how the Moriscos essay various strategies of cultural mimesis, or pointed imitation of hegemonic Spanish culture, achieving, if not the survival of their own culture, a kind of enabling syncretism. They undo the easy oppositions between Christian and Moor, to suggest that the binary Spaniard/Morisco in fact functions as a dyad. Despite their powerless role as the internal colonized, the Moriscos crucially affect the debates over Spanish identity, primarily by blurring the neat distinctions on which such a hegemonic identity seems to depend.

This chapter examines two principal Morisco interventions into the debates over Spanish history and identity, in order to show how their rhetorical arguments for inclusion actually render them an intrinsic part of the Spanish self. These interventions must be read in the double context of the Crown's attempts over the course of the sixteenth century to commission a definitive history of Spain that would uphold the role of the monarchy, and of the writing of chorography, or local histories, that countered such general and centralized versions.[4] The highly self-conscious and often liberally embroidered genre of Renaissance historiography, which included such creative practitioners as the famous Annius of Viterbo, made possible the writing of multiple versions of Spain. Whereas influential and widespread accounts such as Annius' made liberal use of myth to glorify the role of the monarch, others spun particular tales to serve particular constituencies, arguing for the preeminence of a city or for its central role in Spain's Christian past.[5] Histories could serve to argue for the importance of a particular city or region within Spain, as well as to defend that city's prerogatives against the monarch.[6] These multiple representations of Spain's past suggest the active debates throughout the sixteenth century over, on the one hand, the particular shape that Spanish identity would take after unification and, on the other, just how the emerging nation would resolve the conflicts between local and national allegiances.[7] Morisco interventions into this debate are, I will argue, of particular interest for three reasons: first, the Moriscos were writing themselves into a culture that increasingly attempted to define them as an irreducible Other. Second, they addressed the problem of the internal history of Islam in Spain, which most Christian chroniclers ignored to devote themselves to the Reconquista. Third, they often wrote in and about Granada, which, as the last city to fall to the Catholic kings, represented both the glorious completion of Spain's territorial unification and the challenges posed to that unification by a highly divergent culture. The first intervention that I analyze in this chapter is precisely a secular argument for the inclusion of Grenadine customs in the plurality of Spanish cultural forms; the second a set of religious forgeries in Granada that "miraculously" Arabize the early Christianization of Spain. I begin with Francisco Núñez Muley, longtime advocate of the rights of, as he calls them, the *naturales*, or natives, of Granada.

Spanish Grenadines or Morisco Spaniards?

Part of what makes Núñez Muley such a fascinating figure is the protracted span of his advocacy. He was probably born soon after the fall of Granada, and lived through the various stages of state policy towards the Moriscos, from the initial tolerance and compliance with the terms of the capitulation of Granada, to the forced baptisms of the turn of the century, to the much more severely repressive royal ordinances against Moorish cultural practices as the century progressed.[8] The text I will analyze here is Núñez Muley's petition to Don Pedro de Deza, head of the Audiencia or provincial court of Granada, against the 1567 decrees prohibiting Morisco cultural practices.[9] The petition is a last-minute attempt to hold back the tide of increasing repression, against which the Moriscos would eventually rebel in late 1568. Chapter 2 suggested some ways in which Ginés Pérez de Hita, as a historian of that rebellion (or *guerra civil*, as he significantly termed it), domesticated the difference of the Moriscos. Here I hope to show how, before the rebellion that exacerbated the widespread mistrust of the Moriscos, Núñez Muley himself argues for the Spanishness of his people.

Although the actual manuscript of Núñez Muley's petition was discovered in the Biblioteca Nacional in Madrid only in our own century, an abridged version of his arguments had been reproduced as a speech in an early history of the rebellion, Luis del Mármol Carvajal's *Historia del rebelión y castigo do los Moriscos del reyno de Granada* (1600). Mármol Carvajal foregrounds the direct connection between the new ordinances, the failure of Núñez Muley's plea for tolerance, and the desperate revolt of the Moriscos the following year – the written petition can thus be seen to occupy an important space as a formal, final plea for the survival of Morisco culture. When that avenue had been exhausted, rebellion appeared to be the only alternative.

The arguments Núñez Muley puts forth in this document were not new; they had been used by him before with relative success, as he managed over the years to postpone or minimize increasingly repressive measures. Núñez Muley seems to have been less successful in this instance due to two historical factors: first, the increased concern about Islamic threats to Spain, whether from Turks in the Eastern Mediterranean or corsairs off the coast of Spain, and, second, the increased intolerance for heterodoxy in the context of the Counter-Reformation.[10] It was clearly more difficult to sway the authorities on matters concerning the Moriscos in 1568 than it had been earlier in the century. Yet while Núñez Muley does not succeed in suspending the terrible laws against his people, he manages to promote a hybrid identity which writers such as Pérez de Hita take seriously, and which many Moriscos would later invoke in their attempts to resist expulsion.[11] The rhetorical negotiation of sameness and difference in this text, I would argue, resolves the paradox of a "Morisco Spaniard" by introducing pluralistic standards for national identity that enable many different ways of being Spanish.

Núñez Muley begins by tracing the history of attempts to legislate against Moorish dress in Granada, specifying the treaties ignored, tributes forgotten, and other abuses involved in the proposed reinstatement of such legislation. He appeals to the Crown's own interests, much as Guaman Poma does when decrying abuses in colonial Peru, suggesting that the arbitrary legislation will so impoverish the Morisco population that there will be "muncho perjuycio a las rentas reales y a las cosas tocantes al serbiçio de la Corona rreal"[12] [great harm done to the royal income and to the things regarding tributes to the Crown]. But his most profoundly challenging argument comes when he contests the very notion that the proscribed dress is "de moros":

. . . porque el ábito y traxe y calçado no se puede dezir de moros, ny es de moros. Puédese dezir ques traxe del rreyno y prouinçia, como en todos los rreynos de Castilla y los otros rreynos y prouinçias tienen los traxes diferentes unos de otros, y todos cristianos; y ansi el dicho áuito y traxe deste rreyno [es] muy diferente de los traxes de los moros de aliende y Berbería y allá, también en muy grandes diferen-

cias de un rreyno a otro – lo que traen en Fez no lo traen en Estremeçen por el todo,
y en la Turquía muy diferentes del todo, y todos moros; de manera que no se puede
afundar ny dezir que el traxe de los nueuamente conuertidos es traxe de moros; ni
se puede afundar, pues los cristianos de la santa casa de Jeresulon y todo ese rreyno
de cristianos y dotores della, como se an bisto en esta çibdad que se vinieron a ella
en ábitos y tocados como los de aliende, y no en castellano, y son cristianos; y no la
saben la lengua castellana, y son xrisptianos católicos. (211)

. . . because this dress and costume and footwear cannot be said to be of Moors, nor
is it of the Moors. It can be said to be the costume of this kingdom and province –
as in all the kingdoms of Castile and the other kingdoms and provinces they have
different costumes, ones differing from the others, and all of them Christians; and
so the said dress and costume of this kingdom is very different from the costume of
the Moors from over there and from the Barbary Coast; and there, also, there are
very great differences from one kingdom to the next – what they wear in Fez is not
exactly what they wear in Estremeçen, and in Turkey it is completely different, and
all of them are Moors; so that one cannot prove or say that the costume of the
newly converted ones is Moorish costume; nor can it be proved, for the Christians
of the holy house of Jerusalem and all that Christian kingdom and its learned men,
who have been seen in this city, came in dress and headdress like those from over
there, and not in Castilian dress, and they are Christians; and they do not know the
Castilian tongue, and yet they are Catholic Christians.

Núñez Muley's analysis of the categories of dress effectively dissociates
culture and religion, while complicating the idea of a national identity. His
radical taxonomy suggests that Grenadines (as he generally refers to "the
newly converted") and their culture are just as *Christian* as the Castilians
or the inhabitants of any other kingdom in Spain. By implication, one
might imagine, the Grenadines are as *Spanish* as anyone else, but Núñez
Muley does not specifically speak of Spain. The somewhat anachronistic
use of the term "kingdom" to describe Granada is especially interesting in
this context: even as he describes a Spain homogenized by Christianity, the
author recalls a time when the province of Granada actually was a separate
kingdom, under the Nasrid dynasty.[13] Granada is sui generis: while it
obviously does not have the same customs as other parts of Spain, it
cannot be assimilated to the Barbary Coast, or to Islam in general, Núñez
Muley suggests, because it has its own, separate culture. The question of
self versus other has been reformulated as a matter of disparate parts
versus the whole, all within a Spanish context. Thus the threatening
otherness of the Moors is recast as the geographical peculiarity of a region
chafing under the increasing control of a centralized state. By focusing on
what is licit in and for Granada, Núñez Muley's argument recontextualizes
the persecution of the Moriscos as an instance of monarchical abuse of
local prerogatives.[14]
    Once he has established the singularity of Granada, Núñez Muley

attacks the problem from a different angle, arguing that even those who seem to be Moors can be perfect Christians. Neither the language nor the dress of Castile, he suggests, is necessary to Christianity; moreover, the accidental trappings of the Christian religion might well include the use of Arabic and Moorish dress.[15] This second attempt to dissociate culture and religion is, I would argue, even more profoundly radical than the first, for it suggests that those who appear most foreign by virtue of their language, culture, and geographical provenance may in fact be "the same" where it matters most to Christian Spain, i.e., in their profession of Christianity.[16] If these exotic others can be brought into the fold, so to speak, the domestic others whose apparently contradictory presence provokes such vicious persecution should certainly be recognized as part of Spain. Thus Núñez Muley resolves the apparent contradiction of the Morisco Spaniard, suggesting, first, that all Grenadines – and not just recently converted ones – participate in the kingdom of Granada's cultural forms, and second, that an unfamiliar or non-Castilian culture in no way impedes the practice of Christianity.[17]

Having set up the lineaments of the theoretical argument for the preservation of Morisco, or, as Núñez Muley would have it, Grenadine, dress, the author then proceeds to more practical considerations. What happens when Moriscos, under pressure from the authorities, actually adopt Castilian dress? Núñez Muley bitterly points out that capitulating has not afforded them the benefits of inclusion; they are still treated "como los nueuamente conuertidos en todo" (212) [as the newly converted in all things]. Thus he exposes the inherent treacherousness of the Crown's demands: the more the Moriscos comply with the directives to erase all outward signs of their culture, the more those signs will be internalized, until the discourse of difference becomes an explicitly genealogical one. Essentially, Núñez Muley is calling the Crown's bluff: if adopting Castilian forms will make such a difference, why not prove it by treating those Moriscos who have already complied more fairly?[18] Moreover, as Núñez Muley cannot fail to point out, fidelity to Spain is not only a matter of dress: the real test of Morisco loyalty came when they did not join the popular revolt of the Comuneros (213), but remained faithful to the Crown.[19] The current mild protest against cultural repression is implicitly contrasted favorably to such serious disruptions of the polity. Hindsight makes this particular claim bitterly ironic, for Núñez Muley's failure to soften the repression would soon be followed by the bloody rebellion of the Moriscos in the Alpujarras.

Núñez Muley moves from dress to musical instruments, another category of culture explicitly repressed in the new legislation. Here, he not only repeats his arguments about the singularity of Granada's culture (i.e.

these are not Moorish but Grenadine peculiarities) but refines the argument to suggest that there *are* essential elements to religion. If, as is the
case, the instruments and songs of Granada are different than those of Fez
or Turkey, Núñez Muley suggests, then they cannot be central to Islam:
"Y si fuese çirimonia o rretos de Moros auían de ser toda una ygual, por
cunplir su seta, lo cual no se auerigua, ni se puede aueriguar" (215) [And if
this were a Moorish ceremony or ritual they should all be the same, to
comply with their religion, which is not what we find, nor can such a thing
be found]. Núñez Muley takes the implicit argument of the Crown – only
certain very specific, invariable cultural signs can guarantee Christianity –
and turns it on its head: if the instruments and songs of Granada vary from
those of the African Moors, then they cannot be the essential marks of
Islam, because they are not consistent with those of avowed Muslims.
Thus Núñez Muley suggests that the cultural specificity of Granada – a
serious obstacle for a homogenizing centralized State – may in fact signal
its dissociation from Islam.

Beyond offering conceptual models for the tolerance of difference within
Spain, Núñez Muley hints at methods for achieving the gradual erasure of
that difference without repression. He notes, for example, that the benign
Hernando de Talavera, first archbishop of Granada, allowed the Moors to
keep their instruments and songs, which they used, Núñez Muley avers, to
praise the Holy Sacraments in the festival of Corpus Christi. In fact,
Talavera's syncretism extended to the use of Arabic during the mass, and
he encouraged clerics and priests to learn the language.[20] Although this
pragmatism might seem inconceivable when considering the subsequent
fierce repression of Moorish culture in Granada, it mirrors evangelical
practices in the New World, especially in New Spain, where friars devoted
incredible energy to learning multiple native languages, the better to
convert the Indians.[21] Thus the syncretism – or at the very least accommodation of a native culture – that Núñez Muley nostalgically advocates is by
no means a fond fantasy, but rather a model that the Spanish Church had
found appropriate, at other times or in other places.[22]

The central problem with Núñez Muley's plea is that he assumes an
audience sympathetic to claims that the new legislation will erase Moorish
culture from Spain, while ignoring the fact that such was precisely the aim
of the repressive measures. His description of the confusion that will ensue
if the state erases such crucial markers as Moorish clan names and
documents in Arabic anticipates precisely the desired goal – an acculturation that leaves no traces of Moorish culture, but subsumes it within Spain:
"Perderse an las personas y los linajes moriscos; no sabrán con quién
tratan ni compran ni casan, no conociendo el linaje" (219) [All the Moorish persons and lineages will be lost; they will not know whom they deal

with or buy from or marry, not knowing the lineage]. Yet the argument takes an interesting turn as it invokes the preservation of history as a central goal for Spain:

Pues, ¿qué se sirue querer perderse tales memorias, ansy los ávitos y traxes, como en los sobrenombres, como en todo lo susodicho? ¿No le paresçe a V.S.R. que [en] quedar estas memorias ay grandes ensalzamientos de los Reyes que ganaron estos rreynos, de ver las diuersas maneras que ganaron? Y ésta fue la yntinción de los Reyes Católicos en anparar este rreyno en la manera que lo anparon y los arçobispos pasados; y esta yntención e voluntad tuvieron los Enperadores e Reyes Católicos en anparar las memorias de las casas rreales del Alhambra y otras memorias, tales que quedasen en la mysma forma que heran en el tiempo de los rreyes moros, para que se manyfestase lo que ganaron sus Altezas y se paresçería más claro. (219–20)

[For what is the point of wanting to lose such remembrances,[23] or the costume and dress, or the last names, or all that I have mentioned? Do you not think that in the preservation of these remembrances there is great honor done to the Kings who won these kingdoms, in seeing the diverse ways in which they won them? And this was the Catholic Kings' intention in protecting this kingdom in the way they did, as did prior archbishops; and this was the intention and will of the Emperors and Catholic Kings in protecting the memory of the royal houses of the Alhambra and other memories, so that they would remain as they had been in the time of the Moorish kings, in order that what their Highnesses won should show and appear more clearly.]

Núñez Muley insists upon the fact that the history of the Moors *is* the history of Spain. The erasure of Moorish culture would not only wreak havoc with the Crown's efforts to police and tax the Morisco population, it would also erase the memory of the Reconquista and the glorious feats of the Catholic kings. While Christians have no qualms about forgetting treaties or prior guarantees offered to the Moriscos, as Núñez Muley bitterly points out (204), they should not obliterate the signs of their own victory, but instead memorialize it. The unstated premise, of course, is that such memory depends on the living presence of a culture, and cannot be guaranteed by the mere preservation of monuments. (One could argue that romantic Moorophile literature, which I discuss in Chapter 2, functions as one such fetishized monument to the Reconquista, without enabling or preserving the actual culture of the Moriscos.) Nonetheless, Núñez Muley's argument for the importance of memory and memorialization as conditions for national history brings up certain pressing questions for Spain: how is a Spanish history of al-Andalus to be written? Can the Moors be incorporated into the historical narrative of a Christian Spain? Does their erasure imply the erasure of the heroic Reconquista? How, after all, is Spanish history to reconcile more than 700 years of Islamic presence?

In posing these questions, Núñez Muley has put his finger on a very sore spot in the emerging national imaginary. What to him is an urgent and local problem – how to extend the Catholic kings' protection of monuments and signs of Moorish culture to the actual meager remnants of that culture in the 1560s – represents a much larger problem for the Spanish Crown as a whole, as it attempts to achieve centralized control in the century after the fall of Granada. The second part of this chapter suggests how both Moriscos and Christian Spaniards address the problem of reproducing history, in a way that mirrors each camp's ideals for sixteenth-century Spain. These mimetic histories function as attempts to legitimate a certain vision of Spain by rewriting its past, reinterpreting events, and even reproducing its central historical artifacts. In this game of mirrors, fidelity to an idea of Spain becomes far more important than adhering to "truth," as different groups attempt to harness cultural mimesis to their own goals. The consequent proliferation of truths destabilizes the project of a national history, opening up the space for multiple Spains in the same contested historical terrain.

Saints and sources

Historians have identified a variety of pseudo-historiographic phenomena in late sixteenth-century Spain that seem to have one common theme: the creation of a licit, Christian history for Spain. The motivation for these mimetic endeavors seems clear: after the completion of the territorial Reconquista of southern Spain, the newly unified state faced the additional challenge of redressing its historical status. Once the present had been taken care of, the past demanded urgent attention. How, as Núñez Muley anticipates, would Spain deal with the fact that its history was largely the history of Islamic occupation? How could it rewrite its past into something more befitting the nation that championed Catholicism against heretics, Protestants, the infidel, and the vast hordes of pagans in the New World? To answer such questions, a cluster of hugely creative historiographic enterprises in the late sixteenth century attempted to supply an authorized, Christian history where none existed.

The term "falsos cronicones" has been frequently used to describe several of the phenomena I will discuss.[24] I will retain it advisedly and provisionally, without echoing its positivist disapproval, because it is useful on two counts: first, it underscores the interrelatedness of historiographic events that might at first glance appear unconnected, and, second, it reminds us of the ways in which those events have been read and dismissed by critics. The standard account is José Godoy Alcántara's *Historia crítica de los falsos cronicones* (1868). Of the many apocryphal histories that he describes, I will discuss three central ones, all making their appearances in the 1590s: the "medieval" chronicles of Spain written by the Toledan Jesuit Ramón de la Higuera; the so-called "true story" of King Rodrigo, who lost Spain to the Moors, written by the Morisco Miguel de Luna; and the spectacular discoveries of religious "relics" and "gospels" in Granada. All of these mimetic endeavors are fundamentally concerned with the question of *origin*, in its double sense of beginning and ancestry, while necessarily masking their own suspect originality.

In order to unpack my quotation marks, I would like to consider here the problem of agency and truth as it relates to these *cronicones*. To what extent can we apply contemporary notions of the fraudulent and the apocryphal to the texts at hand? How do their various contexts and authorship belie the relevance of positivistic *truth*? The interesting problem is not really whether they are true, but rather what truth-effects they had and why Spaniards believed – often quite passionately – in their veracity.[25] Although, as Godoy Alcántara abundantly shows, the *cronicones* did not lack for critics in their own time, these critics were often overruled by popular support for the stories, suggesting how slippery indeed was their "truth." This suggests that the "truth-problem" is somewhat of a red herring; the real question here is not how the authors of these works got away with fraud – for in fact they did not – but rather why the *cronicones* survived early criticisms of their textual accuracy or feasibility to proclaim a different kind of truth. As I argued in my discussion of the Spanish censorship of chivalric romances in New Spain in Chapter 1, a culture can proclaim its faith in the absolute truth of certain stories even as it acknowledges their contingency. Thus while in New Spain the Spaniards had worried about the contagion of fictionality from romances of chivalry to the "true" stories of the Bible, in Spain they themselves enthusiastically supported doubtful stories that recreated Spain as a heroically Christian nation.

The central problem that the *cronicones* addressed was the ancient history of Christian Spain, and its evangelization. The most pressing question was whether St. James – the patron saint of Spain invoked so often in the New World battles chronicled by Garcilaso and Guaman Poma – had ever actually led a mission to Spain. St. James, or Santiago, as he is known in Spanish, was a crucial figure in Spanish culture. Often referred to as "Santiago Matamoros," or "killer of Moors," he stood for a militant Spain ready to take on the infidel, and occupied a central place in the national pantheon. The fact that the territorial Reconquista was essentially completed with the fall of Granada by no means diminished his importance; as I suggested in Chapter 3, the apparition of St. James to aid the Spaniards in battles in the New World was one way to code the conquest of the Americas as a new version of the Reconquista.

Yet perhaps the final consolidation of Spanish territory in 1492 did make it possible to challenge the cult of St. James as it had never been challenged before. As T. D. Kendrick has shown, there was much at stake in the controversy over St. James, beyond the purportedly glorious early Christian history of Spain.[26] Because the saint had helped Spain win a crucial battle against the Moors in the ninth century, Spaniards owed him eternal gratitude. To fulfill this obligation, the Church of St. James in Compostela, where James was supposedly buried, claimed an annual tax on harvests – the *Voto de Santiago*. In recognition of St. James' support in the conquest of Granada, the Catholic kings specified that the newly "liberated" kingdom would be subject to this tax. The novel law emboldened the Church in Compostela to demand that *all* Spain should pay the tax – a demand that made a certain amount of sense, given the newly unified polity, but that nonetheless met with enormous resistance from many fronts. Efforts to discredit Compostela's version of the saint's life in order to avoid the tax and challenge that city's religious primacy had the dangerous potential to raise doubts about the entire St. James creed, as indeed happened when powerful legal challenges were mounted against the onerous Voto de Santiago. The challenges culminated in the *Colección de Concilios* (Toledo, 1593) – an account of the medieval councils of the Spanish Church suggesting that the mission of St. James to Spain had never occurred. This conviction found its way into the official Vatican Breviary, setting off a diplomatic crisis between Spain and the Vatican. The crisis was only partly resolved when St. James' mission was acknowledged in the revised Breviary, but described as a "traditional belief" of the Spanish Church.[27]

The incident led to great consternation, and to a generalized longing for evidence of James' presence in Spain. This dire context led some writers to lend their support to false claims, or at least look the other way, all for the greater good of Spain. When it was a question of backing Spanish claims, Godoy Alcántara tells us:

Ends justified means; pious frauds – the *dolo pío* – were admitted in the ethics of the time when they aimed to edify, and there was no lack of writers of repute who defended faking history when the honor or reputation of the fatherland demanded it.[28]

This context of acceptance for pious inventions ensured that the acute longing for proofs of St. James' mission would soon be satisfied. The aspersions cast on St. James and the doubts about Compostela's primacy provided a perfect setting for the "Dextro-Máximo-Eutrando" chronicle, crafted by the Toledan Jesuit Ramón de la Higuera. As a Toledan, Higuera was not about to justify the city of Compostela's claim to primacy, but in his mimetic histories he did provide ample reassurance to other cities all over Spain that St. James had founded their bishoprics. Higuera's method was simple: he would begin with an obscure figure mentioned in medieval Church histories, and transform him into a chronicler in his own right. Thus "Dextro" had supposedly written a history of the world, of which only two fragments survived. Luckily for Spain, the first fragment covered the crucial years 36–348, and recounted not only James' arrival in Spain, but also that of St. Peter and St. Paul! The chronicle continues with the accounts of Máximo and Eutrando, both of whom give copious details about the antiquity and importance of the Toledan Church.[29] As Godoy Alcántara points out, although they were supposedly written in different centuries, all three fragments evince the same formal qualities and writing style.

It would be over-simplifying matters to suggest that Higuera's forgeries were unquestioningly accepted because of the great desire for proofs of Santiago. In fact, the author's first attempts to circulate the *cronicones* in the mid-1590s stopped abruptly when the learned bishop of Segorbe, Juan Bautista Pérez, made it clear that he could see right through Higuera's fictions.[30] Higuera then put away his *cronicones* for a few years, to await a more propitious audience. In the meantime, he concocted an elaborate fraud to suggest that one St. Thyrsus, a third-century martyr from Phrygia, was actually a Toledan. This fraud, too, was challenged, since a new contender for patron saint of Toledo upset many devotees of older patrons; nonetheless, the case for Thyrsus garnered enormous popular support. The exchanges between Higuera and his critics reflect beautifully the relative status of truth in these controversies. Higuera holds that no harm stems from his claims: "¿Qué inconveniente se sigue [de] que San Tirso sea de Toledo, o qué daño se sigue a la fe, ni qué perjuicio a las buenas costumbres?"[31] [What inconvenience follows from St. Thyrsus' being from Toledo? What harm to the faith, or damage to good customs?]

The response to this rhetorical question comes, interestingly, in a lay document, a report to the king from the civic authorities of Toledo, who explained that:

se opusieron a que no passasse adelante este enredo y fábula, por la injuria que se hacía a los verdaderos patronos naturales desta ciudad: porque en tiempos venideros, como se viesse ser mentira que el señor San Tirso era natural de Toledo, no se pensasse que con la misma liviandad se tenían por naturales y patronos los que verdaderamente lo son.[32]

[they were opposed to this intrigue and fable continuing unchecked, because of the offense done to the real patrons of this city; lest, in times to come, when people realized that it was a lie that St. Thyrsus was a native of Toledo, they should think that others were lightly taken as natives and patrons when in truth they were not.]

Once again, the problem seems to be the contagion of fictionality from the faked to the true. Whereas Higuera seems to think that, when it comes to local patrons and other incentives for the faithful, the more the merrier, his critics fear that all truths about patrons will be cast into doubt because of one bad apple. Although the temptation to keep adding to a city's pantheon may be great, it is possible to have too much of a good thing, including local saints. Despite – or perhaps because of – Higuera's best efforts, the multiplication of authorized sources paradoxically vitiates all authority, casting into doubt past saints and present histories.

Gothic and Anti-Gothic

Están tan confusas nuestras historias (discreto lector) que a ninguno de quantos hasta hoy las han leydo han dado satisfación de la verdad. . .
Miguel de Luna, *Verdadera historia*[33]

Whereas Higuera and his multiple forgeries can at least be explained away as the over-zealous endeavors of a misguided defender of the faith, historiographic mimesis becomes more complex in the hands of recently converted Christians, whose allegiance to the Church is always suspect. Such is the case of the Morisco translator Miguel de Luna, who undertook a "new and improved" version of the fall of Spain to the Moors, in his *La verdadera historia del Rey Don Rodrigo*.[34] This text rewrites the fifteenth-century *Crónica sarracina* of Pedro de Corral, which itself embroiders the medieval legends about the fall of Spain with the motifs of chivalric romance.[35] Like Pérez de Hita in the first part of his *Guerras civiles*, Luna claims to be merely the translator of the work, in this case supposedly written in Arabic by one wise Moorish *alcaide*, Abulcacim Tarif Abentarique. As this particular invention goes, Abentarique wrote an eyewitness account of the events at hand, which Luna then found in a manuscript in the library of Philip II's Escorial, the very seat of Spanish royal power. The author's elaborate philological hoax includes detailed marginalia which translate Spanish words back into the Arabic, as though to prove both the text's origin in that language and the translator's competence: "*Inuención llama el arábigo muzah*"[36] [Invention in Arabic is muzah.] As in the case of Pérez de Hita, however, the historical context significantly changes the import of the humanistic pseudo-historiographical device, for Luna's fiction both suggests the importance of considering Arabic points of view and (somewhat tongue-in-cheek) foregrounds Arabic itself – which the Crown had proscribed – as a worthy object of philological study.

Luna's history undoes the myth of a heroic, Visigothic Spain tragically falling to Islam, and replaces it with a providential account of the Muslim invasion.[37] Whereas traditional accounts emphasize the individual, fatal flaw of King Rodrigo, who single-handedly lost Spain to the Moors through his implacable lust for Florinda, the *Verdadera historia* counters such myths with a general indictment of the corrupt monarchy of the Visigoths as the reason for Spain's fall.[38] Far from being a model worthy of sixteenth-century nostalgia, the early Spain that Luna describes is rotten through and through. Not only are things amiss at the top, but the king's moral turpitude corrupts his subjects: "Del mal ejemplo de vida y costumbres deste Rey nacieron tantos vicios, maldades y trayciones entre sus súbditos, que no se tratava verdad ni podían vivir, sino con gran trabajo"[39] [From the bad example this King set in his life and behavior there sprang so many vices, evils, and betrayals among his subjects, that there were no honest dealings, nor could they survive, except with great effort]. Rodrigo's noxious influence upon his people is literalized when, fleeing from battle, he exchanges clothes with a lowly shepherd, in order to go undetected.[40] With this chiasmic class transvestism, Luna spreads Rodrigo's moral taint to peasants far from the corrupt court – precisely the group that sixteenth-century Spain glorified as being most unsullied by the urban contagion of Semitic blood.[41] All ostensibly pure peasants, Luna's image suggests, participate in the wickedness of Rodrigo.

In the aftermath of the Reconquista, Luna's project involves a radical redefinition of the hysteria about "miscegenation" of Moors and Christians; he forcefully recasts the Spain of mixed bloods that follows the Muslim conquest as an improvement on the purity of the Goths. Most significantly for Luna's contemporary audience, those characters who have "clean" blood, because they predate the Muslim invasion, are presented as morally corrupt. Far from contaminating Spain, the arrival of the Moors cleanses and redeems it. And, as one might expect, the Moors are magnanimous to the conquered, offering them full access to the privileges of the conquerors if only they agree to convert. The Goths are quick to take the conquering Moors up on their offer, and "infinite numbers" of men convert, while the women marry Moorish warriors.[42] Moors and Christians, it turns out, have been indistinguishable for centuries.

By placing the work in its historical context, critics such as Márquez Villanueva have highlighted the willful blindness of earlier readers, who focused on the "scandalous" nature of Luna's "fraud," without interrogating their own notions of historiographic truth, or the official wisdom of an effectively re-Christianized Spain.[43] My own account of Luna's historical fiction suggests how, among the proliferation of creative histories of Spain, Moriscos could find opportunities to intervene in the retrospective imagining of Spanish origins. In imitating the medieval legends of Rodrigo via the deployment of a complicated apparatus of translation and philology, Luna subverts the singularity of more orthodox accounts, suggesting that there is no single, original source on origins.

"Found" syncretism

Este monte de cruces coronado,
cuya siempre dichosa excelsa cumbre
espira luz y no vomita lumbre,
Etna glorioso, Mongibel sagrado,

trofeo es dulcemente levantado
no ponderosa grave pesadumbre,
para oprimir sacrílega costumbre
de bando contra el cielo conjurado.

Gigantes miden sus ocultas faldas,
que a los cielos hicieron fuerza: aquella
que los cielos padecen fuerza santa.

Sus miembros cubre y sus reliquias sella
la bien pisada tierra. Veneraldas
con tiernos ojos, con devota planta.

                         Góngora, "Al Monte Santo de Granada"[44]

If sixteenth-century Spain as a whole experienced an acute need to find for itself a glorious Christian past, the situation was far more desperate in Granada, which, as the last holdout of Islam in Spain, had spent the longest time under Moorish domination, and had the largest Morisco population. As critics have pointed out, Granada's need to prove itself wholeheartedly Christian and Spanish was even more pressing in the aftermath of the Morisco rebellion in the Alpujarras (1568–71).[45] In 1588, as the minaret of the mosque of Granada, commonly known as "Turpin's Tower," was being demolished in order to build the third nave of the triumphant new cathedral, workers found a peculiar leaden box in the rubble.[46] The box contained a parchment written in Arabic and some fragrant relics. Two Arabists were called in to study the mysterious document: the Moriscos Miguel de Luna, whose historiographic efforts I have described above, and Alonso del Castillo.[47] As official translators to Philip II, both these Moriscos held a very special status in the eyes of the authorities – nonetheless, they were required to come up with independent translations in order to ensure their probity.

When they finally deciphered the parchment, they found an apocalyptic prophecy by St. John translated into Castilian by one St. Cecilius, first bishop of Granada, whose own commentary in Arabic followed. The prophecy had been hidden to protect it from infidel Moors, until such a time as the Christian Arabs of Spain could decode it.[48] The find thus provided something for everyone: it supplied Granada's lack of a Christian past by proving that there had been a bishop there very early in the Christian era, while suggesting that there was no contradiction between matters Christian and Arabic, since both had coexisted in Granada since the evangelization of the city.

Whereas Miguel de Luna's *Verdadera historia* attempted to rewrite the medieval history of Spain, the Grenadine apocrypha harked back to the very beginnings of Christianity in southern Spain, the better to suggest the essential conflation of Christian and Arabic elements in the history of the region. Critics were quick to point out that Castillo himself had been spreading the word that a great discovery would be made when the minaret was torn down, and that the ink, handwriting, and, most crucially, the language of the parchment were not ancient but "antiqued."[49] While skeptics such as the historian Mármol Carvajal suggested in no uncertain terms that Castillo himself must be behind the hoax, before these criticisms could have any effect, a far more spectacular discovery was made.

In 1595, the caves of Valparaíso, just outside Granada, yielded some incredible finds. Whereas Turpin's Tower had merely contained one parchment and a few relics, the site quickly rebaptized as the "Sacromonte" produced a fantastic series of religious treasures. First, some workmen at the site found an engraved lead tablet that announced the martyrdom of St. Mesitón; soon ashes and human remains followed. Another tablet announced that one St. Tesifón, disciple of St. James and contemporary of St. Cecilius, had also been martyred on the spot, after writing a book called *Fundamentum Ecclesiae*, or the essential doctrines of the Church. Amazingly enough, the lead book itself appeared a few days later. Soon other tablets appeared, cross-referencing the earlier discoveries in Turpin's Tower in a most convincing way. The parchment in the tower may be read as a rehearsal for the much more spectacular hoax of the Sacromonte, as the forgers carefully planted the "finds" gradually, so that they would be able to assess the city's reaction and create a "blessed expectation" of further developments.[50]

The discoveries led to incredible excitement and religious fervor in Granada. Here, finally, was what the city had been hoping for: Christian antiquities in abundance, martyrs, relics, and even – in a real embarrassment of riches – gospels in Arabic written by the disciples of James himself. What exactly was in the leaden books that led to such excitement? In the first place, their authorship not only confirmed the existence of St. Cecilius but proved, once and for all, St. James' mission to Spain. Saints Cecilius and Tesifón, two Arabs who had been converted to Christianity and chosen by James as his personal secretaries, followed him on that mission and authored the leaden books. These nineteen texts, with such titles as "Of the History of the Truth of the Gospels" or "Of the Essence of God," focus on the sayings of St. James and the Virgin Mary, as taken down by the two brothers. The books establish the central role of Arabs and Arabic in the history of Christian Spain, and present a syncretic version of Christianity and Islam, authorized by early Christian martyrs. As L. P. Harvey puts it: "The texts were indubitably Christian, but the Christianity contained in them was a sort of Lowest Common Denominator, those aspects of Christianity least likely to give offense to Islamic sensibilities."[51] From the vision of Jesus as a prophet to the insistence on the propriety of veils for women, these texts attempt to rescue as much Muslim doctrine as possible, while maintaining a studious silence with respect to certain crucial differences between the two religions, such as polygamy and the adoration of images.[52] More importantly, they prophesy the central role of Arabs in revealing the books themselves – "God's rightful law" – at a future, apocalyptic moment. The "Book of the History of the Truth of the Gospels" states that at that time the Arabs will be "the most excellent of God's creatures in the lineage of Adam." Moreover, the real triumph of the word of God will come when an "Eastern king" – clearly the Ottoman emperor – strikes fear into the hearts of Western peoples.[53] General reconciliation will come with a religious council in Cyprus – recently fallen to the Turks.

It is amazing that these somewhat transparent claims for what was at the time a cruelly persecuted minority did not in and of themselves discredit the books. Instead, the miraculous gospels found staunch supporters in Granada, who defended them against all critics as crucial evidence for local history. Grenadine chorography, as I have stressed, was an especially difficult enterprise, given the fact that the city remained on the wrong side of the Reconquista until that process was essentially over. Thus the imitation gospels had an extremely positive reception (so positive, in fact, that it emboldened Ramón de la Higuera, for example, to recirculate his dormant *cronicones*). It was only reluctantly that the books were finally sent to the royal authorities in Madrid. There they remained for some time until the Vatican finally managed to have them sent to Rome, whence, needless to say, they never returned.[54] Each of these much-debated stages took the gospels further from the context in which their message rang loudest and found the most attentive audience. Such was precisely the purpose of their detractors in removing them from Granada, for although they were a powerful tonic for the faithful in that city, they were an embarrassment both to Madrid and to the Vatican.

In the city, the leaden books were fiercely defended by church authorities and dignitaries as well as by ordinary citizens. Góngora's sonnet to the Sacromonte – the epigraph to this section – recommends an attitude of devout veneration towards this "sacred volcano," which erupts with Christian light instead of fire. One firm defender of the gospels' authenticity was Adán Centurión, Marquess of Estepa, who in the 1620s took lessons in Arabic specifically to translate them, although by 1631 they had become so controversial that the Inquisitor General of Spain actually banned all translations.[55] Estepa's prologue to his translation provides some clues to the incredible power of the books to confound all critics: part of what convinces the Marquess that they are authentic is their very real effect: "Vi la venerable y grandiosa fundación de la Iglesia Colegial y Colegio de Sacromonte. Vi sus cavernas y sus reliquias decentísimamente colocadas y veneradas con general aplauso y devoción" [I saw the venerable and grand foundation of the Collegiate Church and the College of Sacromonte. I saw its caves and its relics most decently placed and revered with general applause and devotion].[56] Thus the gospels' authenticity is a self-fulfilling prophecy: because they make marvelous claims, they are revered; the physical manifestation of this reverence in turn appears to confirm the truth of the books.

The books' strong argument for the rehabilitation of Arabic itself cannot be overlooked. Years after the expulsion of the Moriscos, Estepa echoes the very arguments that Núñez Muley had proffered for the preservation of his language. He dismisses those critics who would find heresy in the books because they are written in Arabic, "as though Mohammed had invented the language." Arabic, he argues, serves just as well to praise God as any other language; moreover, the three "kings of the Arabs" who announced Christ's coming and will do so again did not forget their own language in order to fulfill their role: "Lo mismo sería condenar la lengua latina porque escribieron en ella Lutero y Calvino siendo la culpa de ellos y no de la lengua" [That would be like condemning the Latin tongue because Luther and Calvin wrote in it, when the fault is theirs and not the language's].[57] In a fascinating twist, this most Christian devotee of the books rehearses the powerful arguments that the Morisco advocate had used to attempt to save his culture: religion does not depend on language; the accidentals of culture do not signal Christianity or the lack thereof. When Estepa unwittingly repeats the arguments of an advocate for Morisco culture, he is indirectly rehearsing that earlier call for tolerance and syncretism.

In this most improbable concurrence of the Morisco and the Marquess we can see how powerfully the apocrypha of the Sacromonte intervened in Spanish culture. Although the Moriscos themselves largely disappeared from Spain, their late interventions into – or on behalf of – local culture profoundly affected Granada's sense of itself, the city's relationship to the centralized state, and, more generally, Spain's own increasingly suspicious attitude towards constructions of its early Christian history. The deliberate mimetic production of a Christian history for Granada – the *facsimile* of gospels and martyrs – effected real changes in the city's sense of itself and in the nation's sense of a Christian identity, even if it ultimately did not ensure a place for the Moriscos within Spain.

Critics from Godoy Alcántara on have convincingly identified Luna and Castillo as the authors of the magnificent hoax of the leaden books. What seems particularly striking is how the devoutly desired truths of the books took on a life of their own: no matter how many times critics expose the fraud, no matter that the Vatican has explicitly condemned it, Granada today continues to celebrate the feast of St. Cecilius at the Sacromonte every first day of February.[58] The Abbey of the Sacromonte is a functioning church with a devout congregation – a symbol, as the plaque for tourists has it, of the "historical truth" of the presence of Christianity in Andalucía for two thousand years. Thus the powerful effects of the Moriscos' constructed history live on, as Granada implicitly rehearses the account they so astutely fabricated. In an odd, subterranean fashion, this Morisco intervention paradoxically managed to project a vision of syncretism far into the future of Granada, even as the Moriscos themselves were cruelly expelled. Perhaps because, in the end, these ostracized others imitated the Spanish self so well and addressed its religious needs so completely, they could never be completely disentangled from that self.

5   Faithless empires: pirates, renegadoes, and the English nation

I thought the diuell was turnde Merchant, theres so many Pirates at Sea.
Dekker, *If This Be Not a Good Play, the Devil Is in It*[1]

The English experience of piracy has usually been glorified as the proleptic wanderings of a future imperial power – pirates as the vanguard of the Empire. Under Elizabeth, England pursued a highly aggressive para-naval policy towards Spain; in the 1570s and 80s, piracy became England's belated answer to Spain's imperial expansion. Long before war became open in 1588, the queen was giving her not-so-tacit approval to privateering expeditions that ostensibly sought new channels for English trade but in fact consisted mainly of attacks on Spanish colonies in the New World.[2] Elizabeth espoused piracy as a kind of imperial mimesis – if England had not yet managed to acquire its own empire, it could at least imitate Spain in exploiting the riches of the New World. Glorified with the name of "privateers," Englishmen such as Francis Drake plundered Spanish colonies and enriched England's treasury. I would like to complicate this narrative of heroic exploits by analyzing how piracy proves a constant source of tension and embarrassment for the Jacobean state as it focuses on trade as a means to empire. As piracy grows uncontrollably, mimicking the English state in "ruling the seas," it poses a challenge to the very powers who had authorized it. Moreover, the frequent alliances between English pirates and Barbary corsairs force England to confront its dangerous proximity to Islam in pursuing its imperial aspirations.

Early on, pirates were recognized as a naval resource for England. John Dee, the magician and mathematician who advised Queen Elizabeth on the constitution of her navy, strongly recommended that the Crown rein in the pirates and profit from their ability. In his *General and Rare Memorials Pertaining to the Perfect Art of Navigation* (1577), Dee stressed the advantages of thus establishing a navy:

By this navy also, all pirates – our own countrymen, and they be no small number – would be called, or constrained to come home. And then (upon good assurance

118

taken of the reformable and men of choice, for their good bearing from henceforth) all such to be bestowed here and there in the aforesaid Navy. For good account is to be made of their bodies, already hardened to the seas; and chiefly of their courage and skill for good service to be done at the sea.[3]

Of course, the problem lies in the elision between "men of choice" and "choice men." Too much independence might make the pirates less than ideal for state service, regardless of how much "good assurance" they gave of being reformed.

Given the strategic value of piracy, the state accorded it different valences at different points: if one attacked ships of a hostile nation for supposedly private purposes but with a mandate from one's government, one counted as a privateer, authorized and fully justified by the state and its pressing needs. Without such a mandate, one remained a pirate, even though the attacks carried out might be directed at the same ships, in the same manner, and with the same concrete results. While the privateer lent the currency of his private quarrel with foreigners to the state for the purpose of its larger aims, payment for this loan of legitimacy was forcibly exacted by those pirates who represented themselves as agents of the state even when they no longer embodied any such authority. When in Thomas Heywood's *The Fair Maid of the West* the apprentice Clem calls them "spirats," he addresses precisely the difficulty of reining in these unruly, often invisible, and apparently omnipresent figures. And, as John Dee's recommendation so patently shows, the trajectory from privateer to pirate is somewhat of a state fantasy in the first place – the pirates are always already there, before the state uses them, and also once it no longer has any use for them.

Pirates constitute a particularly interesting case of the relations between dominant and subordinate elements in early modern England, precisely because of their sometime incarnation as government agents. Their varying roles serve to chart the changes in England's attitude towards imperial expansion, from a rather desperate willingness to attack Spain in the Elizabethan years to a more restrained focus on the expansion of commerce during the reign of James. Piracy also points to the problems with defining Englishness in terms of a particular group or set of social practices. Which classes or agents are to be privileged as representatives of the emerging commercial state, and how does piracy undermine those privileged actors? If, as Richard Helgerson has convincingly argued, the age of discovery saw a mercantile ideology assert itself against an aristocratic one in England, then the figure of the wealthy pirate, enriched and often even ennobled by his pillaging, somewhat complicates this transition.[4] Because piracy in the period after the war with Spain threatens the possibility of trade yet often results in an accumulation of riches, it increasingly interferes with England's conception of itself as a merchant state. The glorification of the pirate Francis Drake into an epic figure of warfare counters the general socioeconomic trend of the period, by which the landed gentry and aristocracy became increasingly involved in commerce through joint-stock ventures and other mercantile excursions.[5] Piracy seems an embarrassing throwback to an epic time of *ad*ventures rather than ventures, when the niceties of trade were disregarded. Yet in a dark way it mimics the incredible accumulation that was the goal of all mercantile (ad)ventures. The taming of pirates into merchants is thus an enterprise fraught with difficulty: how to construct the national self as a mercantile one without losing the epic potency associated with pirates such as Drake?

A pirate by any other name

Sir Francis Drake was the most famous of the privateers, circumnavigating the globe in 1577 and returning home rich with plunder from Spanish settlements and ships. The narrative of Drake's fabulously successful voyage was included in Richard Hakluyt's *Principal Navigations* – a collection of narratives of exploration, accounts of the new worlds, and catalogues of merchandise assembled by its editor as an incentive for English voyages of discovery and trade.[6] The chronicler presents the voyage as an exemplary instance of English courage and enterprising spirit, and Drake's depredations are suitably couched as revenge for Spanish attacks. Drake does not call a halt to his own attacks, the narrator tells us, until he thinks himself "both in respect of his private injuries received from the Spaniards, as also of their contempts and indignities offered to our country and prince in general, sufficiently satisfied and revenged."[7] The elision between private and public injuries reflects exactly the state's appropriation of the "private" in privateer for its own expansionist ends.

Spain suffered English attacks closer to home as well: Drake raided the Spanish port of Cádiz in 1587, and Essex repeated the attack in 1596. Heywood's *The Fair Maid of the West* is set immediately after this second attack and during Essex's Islands Voyage to the Azores, an attempt to intercept the Spanish fleet making its way home from the Indies laden with gold. Yet even during the years when English ships had a legitimate target in the coasts of Spain, a nation with which England was formally at war, English pirates ventured into the Mediterranean to attack what prey might appear, regardless of international allegiances.[8] There the English passed as merchants until they spotted a likely target, which suggests that the differences between English merchants and English pirates were not as clear as it might have appeared at first. The latter understood that often all that was required to operate freely was the *performance* of legitimacy when not actually engaged in piratical activities.[9] The theatricality of piracy was often quite elaborate: the reformed pirate Henry Mainwaring even admitted staging false kidnappings to allow respectable folk to join him in piracy; should they later wish to return to respectability, they could point to their forced captivity as an excuse.[10]

Once the state had withdrawn from piratical activities, as England did when the peace was finally signed with Spain in 1604, the continued depredations carried out by its formerly authorized agents became a source of acute embarrassment, interfering with its quest for sovereignty. James I issued repeated proclamations against pirates; their very repetition suggests how difficult it was to contain the unruly agents that the state had once employed.[11] The pervasiveness of piracy fundamentally challenged state sovereignty at the margins, both on the coasts of England and in those territories, such as Ireland, even more tenuously under its control. The state's turn away from waging war at sea after signing the peace left thousands of unemployed seamen in the port towns, "masterless men" who posed a significant challenge to the Jacobean state, intent on establishing complete authority and controlling disruptive subjects.[12]

The state's imperial sovereignty was further challenged by pirates operating close to home. These not only raided small ships on the coasts, but traded with the local population in the south-west of England, even with those officers who were instructed to suppress piracy.[13] In Ireland, where the English imperfectly controlled a colonial territory, the pirates flourished, making the coastal coves their bases of operations. In his *Of the Beginnings, Practices, and Suppression of Pirates*, Mainwaring describes Ireland as "that Nursery and Storehouse of Pirates," an image that curiously recalls precisely the kind of licit trade and increase that piracy threatened.[14] Whole towns subsisted by trading with the pirates, buying their stolen goods and selling them provisions. Because such trade was obviously illegal,[15] the pirates and their suppliers creatively staged a *non*-exchange: the pirates pretended to "steal" goods for which they were in fact paying double, to compensate the sellers for their risk in dealing with pirates, or they "found" goods conveniently placed by the locals on some desolate shore.[16] While the pirates staged the absence of trade, their English suppliers even mimed empire, in some cases relocating to Ireland to trade with the pirates "under the colour of planting."[17] England's imperial hold on Ireland was thus undermined by the same mercantile instincts on which the nation was counting for its imperial expansion; in this case trade literally supplied the pirates – the very scourge of trade.

Because piracy requires a constant performance of the more orthodox negotiations of commerce, empire, and expansion, it threatens the legitimacy of the original transactions. This imitative staginess marks piracy as an ideal site on which to study the cultural anxieties attendant upon the representation of a merchant nation and the development of an English empire based on commerce. By examining a selection of plays about pirates from the period 1600–1623, I will show how the multiple transactions in the texts involve a traffic not only in merchandise, but also in the coin of legitimacy and potency crucial for defining Englishness. Piracy on stage is by no means an uncomplicated mirror of the political phenomenon, yet precisely because pirate plays thematize the representation of national allegiance, they serve to chart social anxieties about the fidelity of piratical subjects, and their potential for destabilizing the consolidation of an English nation. Although my discussion so far has centered on the dyad of privateer and pirate, I would now like to introduce a third term – the *renegado* – in order fully to explore the trajectory of illegitimacy and betrayal that the pirate potentially embodies.

Renegadoes

Although English piracy might seem like a romantic, individualistic response to the age of empire-formation, it existed in a complicated web of geopolitical and religious exchanges. Piracy in the sixteenth century was hardly an isolated phenomenon. Fernand Braudel refers to it as "that secondary form of war" – another way of fighting the battle between Christianity and Islam.[18] But the religious motivations for piracy were largely cosmetic; the true stakes were economic. Every nation that attempted to trade in the Mediterranean faced the scourge of the Barbary pirates, who became increasingly well organized and powerful as the century progressed. The economic motive was in turn connected to the territorial struggles in the area, for once the Barbary states came under the control of the Ottoman emperor, an increase in piracy essentially equaled an advance by the Turk.

Although piracy was by no means an exclusively Islamic pursuit – some of the most able Mediterranean pirates were the Knights of Malta[19] – the Barbary corsairs were the most infamous of the pirates. Thus the English turn to piracy in the Mediterranean established a connection between England and Islam, the satanic other of Christian Europe. This connection was strengthened in the early years of the seventeenth century when more English pirates actually made the Barbary Coast their base of operations and when the English state considered the North African Moors as a probable ally against Catholic Spain.[20] Spain, meanwhile, used this alliance as further proof that its Protestant enemy was truly demonic.

By 1604, when the peace was signed between England and Spain, the Barbary states were often considered "renegade states," commanding a navy of corsairs.²¹ This again brings up the question of the imprecise boundary between the categories of privateer and pirate – it is Europe that classifies the North Africans as renegade states, thus suggesting that they cannot authorize any licit privateering, but only pirating. Such a European perspective seems somewhat self-serving. At the same time, however, the Barbary states offered a powerful attraction to European pirates, for they afforded safe markets for disposing of stolen goods and ports at which to replenish stores and repair ships. Once piracy had become more widely condemned by the European countries, the Barbary states also offered renegades respectability within a disreputable polity. These states thus proved a strong magnet for English pirates who were no longer protected by the government's espousal of privateering. As the soldier and colonist John Smith explained in his *Generall Historie of Virginia*:

After the death of our most gracious Queen Elizabeth, of blessed memory, our royal King James, who from his infancy had reigned in peace with all nations, had no employment for those men of war, so that those who were rich rested with what they had; those that were poor, and had nothing but from hand to mouth, turned pirates; some because they became slighted of those who had gotten much wealth; some for that they could not get their due; some that had lived bravely, would not abase themselves to poverty; some vainly, only to get a name; others for revenge, covetousness, or as ill; and as they found themselves more and more oppressed, their passions increasing with discontent, made them turn pirates. Now because they grew hateful to all Christian princes, they retired to Barbary.²²

Spurned pirates often renounced all allegiances to Europe by converting to Islam, and becoming "renegadoes."²³ The English renegadoes built up a reputation for incredible perfidy. Samuel Purchas locates the scandalous confusion of Moors and English renegadoes in Algiers, "the Whirlepoole of these Seas, the Throne of Pyracie, the Sinke of Trade and the Stinke of Slavery; the Cage of uncleane Birds of Prey, the Habitation of Sea-Devils, the Receptacle of Renegadoes of God, and Traytors to their Country."²⁴ According to one's perspective, then, the renegadoes were thieves, traitors, or apostates. Yet the figure of the English renegado seemed threatening, I conjecture, mainly in shattering the carefully constructed fantasy of privateering as a way of controlling piracy. If England could imagine its own patriotic privateers mirroring the pirates of the Barbary Coast, they could also imagine a role for themselves in controlling the Mediterranean. Once the English pirates effectively became outlaws and went over to the other side, England was at a disadvantage, having no official expansionist presence in such contested territory.

Perhaps the most infamous of the English renegadoes' achievements was the transfer of nautical technology to the Barbary pirates. In the early seventeenth century, these began to use the larger northern ships, which allowed them to sail beyond the straits of Gibraltar and into the open sea. Although this technological transfer may have occurred in other ways – through trade with Northern Europe before the European pirates arrived, or through the expelled Moors from Spain – the renegade pirates are a likely source. John Smith explicitly accuses the renegadoes: "those were the first that taught the Moores to be men of warre."[25] From the perspective of cultural history, what matters is the widespread perception that it *was* European pirates who enabled their Barbary counterparts to go beyond the Mediterranean and mount increasingly daring attacks in the Atlantic and the North Sea. Such attribution is at once a subtle colonialist rewriting (they can only hurt us because we taught them how) and a more chagrined recognition that, despite the Elizabethan adventures, harnessing piracy to a particular state's goals was impossible, unless that state were itself to become piratical.

The movement from the paradox of privateering, in which supposed private quarrels were harnessed to the service of the state, to the murky lawlessness of piracy, to, finally, the absolute break of the renegadoes, may thus be read as a trajectory of increasing independence of the subject vis-à-vis the English state. That is, if for the privateer even a personal quarrel had to be authorized by the state, the renegado abandons that state so completely as to be branded a traitor. Moreover, this unstable continuum of privateer, pirate, and renegado disrupts the legitimacy of a view of the English nation based in commerce. While the privateer's heroics call into question the duller ethics of the merchant, and the pirate's depredations threaten the very possibility of licit commerce, the alliance of the renegade subject to the Barbary States produces a highly unstable identity, one often represented as extremely fragile. Robert Daborne's play *A Christian Turn'd Turk* (1612), for example, recounts a highly embroidered story of the historical pirate Ward's conversion to Islam. When the Algerians turn against him after his conversion, Ward attacks them for being ungrateful after all the service he has done them. He describes himself as, "He that hath brought more treasure to your shore, than all Arabia yields, he that hath showne you/ the way to conquer Europe."[26] Unlike Ward, who proved too generous with what he knew, the text withholds its knowledge of the pirate's economic betrayal of Europe. Instead, it focuses on Ward's descent to what the prologue calls "the heart itself of villainy" – religious apostasy.[27] The disclosure of Ward's betrayal of sensitive knowledge at the end of the play reveals the text's real stakes: minimizing the role of the European pirates as "double agents" vis-à-vis the supreme perfidy of their final conversion. This postponement displaces the narrative's moral and ideological thrust from the troubling technological exchanges that the renegado effects to the religious exchange that ultimately damns him. The emphasis on placing Ward so firmly beyond the bounds of a Christian community as a renegado, however, suggests a kind of textual retribution for the pirate's cultural duplicity. Ward's pitiful death exemplifies precisely that representation of the renegade subject's fragility that I discussed above: although he might betray England, the text suggests, he cannot be allowed to survive his betrayal.

Double the pirates

Heywood and Rowley's *Fortune by Land and Sea* (1607–09?) stages a more complex account of the interactions between piracy and respectable English commerce. Like *A Christian Turn'd Turk*, the play presents historical pirates – Purser and Clinton – amid imaginary characters. The pirates are crucial to the plot and yet remain strangely marginal, with their lines directed mainly at each other and their scenes generally set very much apart. Thus the play thematizes its ultimate goal, of containing piracy in a frame of respectable activity. Yet once again the distinction between categories of licit and illicit commerce appears less than clear.

The land plot of *Fortune by Land and Sea* is typical of city comedy: a rich father disapproves of his son's marriage to a poor woman. The plot swirls around this couple, Philip and Susan, but they remain strangely apathetic, debasing themselves as servants to the rich father, who has disowned his disobedient son upon his marriage. Meanwhile, the plot by sea pits the young hero, Susan's brother Forest, against Purser and Clinton, the notorious pirates. Forest is forced into hiding after killing his brother's murderer in a righteous duel and is saved by a merchant who provides him with passage on one of his ships, bound for France. Subsequently, the merchant himself is attacked by the pirates, but Forest saves the day, restores the merchant's wealth, and is granted both a pardon and a knighthood for his services in capturing the famous corsairs. He returns with a fortune and tries to save his sister and her husband from their fate, only to find that Philip's father has conveniently died without managing to change his will, so that Philip inherits after all. Forest then marries Anne, Philip's father's young widow, and all live happily ever after, except for the pirates, whose farewell execution scene is one of the play's set pieces.

The interesting twist, however, is Forest's own use of piracy to make his fortune. Before he encounters Purser and Clinton, he has already been named captain of the ship that bears him to France, and has led the crew in taking "many a rich prize for Spain." The reasons given for Forest's embrace of piracy are similar to those attributed to Drake: to right a wrong and seek just revenge. But the justification wears thin when the mariners praise Forest for their many successes:

> FIRST MARINER: Our captain being lately slain in fight,
> We by your valour scap'd our enemies,
> And made their ship our prize, since we first knew you
> All our attempts succeeded prosperously,
> And heaven hath better blest us for your sake.
> SECOND MARINER: When first we took you to our fellowship,
> We had a poor bark of some fifteen tun,
> And that was all our riches, but since then
> We have took many a rich prize for Spain,
> And got a gallant vessel stoutly man'd,
> And well provided of Ordnance and small shot,
> Men and ammunition, that we now dare coap
> With any Carract that do's trade for Spain.[28]

To reinforce the morality of such an apparently immoral situation, Forest responds: "We dare do any thing that stands with justice,/ Our country's honour, and the reputation/ Of our own names" (4.2, 1690–92). When the captain announces that their next goal will be to capture "the valiant Pirats" Purser and Clinton (4.2, 1693), the First Mariner stresses the honor of such a goal by underscoring the difference between the pirates chased and the ones doing the chasing:

> FIRST MARINER: The ocean scarce can bear their outrages,
> They are so violent, confounding all,
> And sparing none, not their own countrimen,
> We could not do our country greater service
> Than in their pursuit to engage our lives. (4.2, 1700–1704)

The concept of loyalty to England, and the possibility of defining that Englishness by a subject's behavior at sea, runs through these lines. What makes the mariners loyal English subjects is their stipulation that the "real" pirates are un-English, precisely because they will not recognize English ships and consequently spare them. In fact, the pirate Purser wants nothing of English nationality, if he must be an outlaw to be English: "Nay since our country have proclaim'd us pyrats,/And cut us off from any claim in England,/We'l be no longer now called English men" (4.1, 1618–20).[29]

Yet it is not so simple to draw the line between English friend and foreign foe: one of the pirates' favorite tricks, which Heywood reproduces in the text, was to fly a false flag, thus pirating the very symbols of national allegiance and trumping the careful distinctions that "good" pirates like Forest might establish between legitimate and illegitimate targets. Purser and Clinton's ship in fact approaches flying "the Cross of England and St. George" (4.2, 1759). The counterfeit symbols of state fool Forest, thus increasingly complicating the distinction between lawful and unlawful piratical attacks. For if state symbols can themselves be plundered on the open main, there are no guarantees that one is ever in fact attacking subjects of one state rather than another. This appropriation of nationality by mimicking the symbols of the state highlights the subversive possibilities of mimesis. As Taussig suggests, following James Frazer, the threat consists of a copy, "*in magical practice, affecting the original to such a degree that the representation shares in or acquires the properties of the represented.*"[30] In the case of the pirate-pretenders, the very act of mimetic representation renders the state fundamentally vulnerable. Representation here equals reproduction, and a state reproduced finds itself hopelessly open to the possibility of counterfeit.

When the pirates, once captured by the valiant Forest, reminisce about their golden years, it becomes obvious just how profoundly they have colonized the symbolic realm of the English state, for they imagine their own dominion as a kind of shadow realm, one which reproduces the trappings of English power while in no way subservient to it. In the pirates' farewell scene, Purser reminds Clinton:

> Oh the naval triumphs thou and I have seen,
> Nay our selves made, when on the seas at once
> Have been as many bonefires as in Towns,
> Kindled upon a night of Jubilee,
> As many Ordnance thundring in the Clouds
> As at Kings Coronations, and dead bodies
> Heav'd from the hatches, and cast over-board,
> As fast and thick as in some common Pest
> When the Plague sweeps Cities. (5.1, 2182–90)

The pirates read their own triumphs at sea as a mirroring of a monarch's coronation on land; even death at sea is couched in terms of a polity, albeit one suffering the ravages of the plague. This vision of the piratical realm as a parallel state is again recalled when Purser speaks of captains "that commanded Ilands, some to whom/the Indian mines pay'd Tribute, Turk vayl'd" (5.1, 2205–2206). As the pirate-state of this account achieves what remain for England wishful imperial aspirations, the double comes perilously close to superseding the original. The analogy between the innumerable deaths of warfare and the plague, furthermore, makes empire seem like a dubious goal.

Thus, although the pirates' shadow realm is only recollected once it has disappeared, it presents a retrospective threat to English power: in this cultural fantasy, at least, piracy was the simplest way to acquire an empire. In Taussig's terms, the problem resides in the double, and in this case contradictory, meaning of fidelity.[31] The pirates cannot be *loyal* to England precisely because their reproduction of the English state is dangerously *faithful* to the original. The situation is further complicated by the temporal dimension: Heywood's play nostalgically rewrites the Elizabethan era from a Jacobean standpoint; in such rewriting, recollection itself complicates fidelity – to the queen or to historical facts.[32] That is, in order to stress the continuity of English sovereignty the narrative might faithfully emphasize the ultimate power of Elizabeth's state over the pirates. A regretful longing for the empire never achieved under Elizabeth, on the other hand, might account for the more rueful mirage of empire in the pirates' own nostalgic speech. One might thus read here a veiled critique of Elizabethan expansionism both when the pirates are most like England – i.e. when they behave like a shadow state – and when, in surpassing it, they resemble it the least.

How does this frantic activity at sea correspond to the plot on land? Fortune seems to have a much stronger hold on those who stay home – although the good triumph in the end, they by no means take Fortune into their own hands as does Forest, the young upwardly mobile pirate. This contrast seems significant considering Hakluyt's ambivalent account of English sluggishness in his prologue to the *Principal Navigations*, where he encourages those demobbed in the recent peace to head for the New World. The doubleness of the plot of *Fortune by Land and Sea* deeply complicates the play's ideological stakes. On the one hand, making one's fortune at sea is clearly a positive achievement that may even lead to a knighthood. On the other hand, such activities at sea place one dangerously close to the reviled pirates, who come to a bad end. And, to make things worse, staying home does not necessarily mean one does *not* make one's fortune, especially if patient and trusting enough to leave it *up* to Fortune. If fortune by sea is achieved by narrowly skirting criminal activity and being a pirate unto foreigners, on land the unpredictable goddess Fortune takes care of the slackers who stay home. The rabid self-fashioning of the young Forest does not really achieve more for him than passivity does for the subdued Philip. Thus Heywood's play offers seafaring trade as a valuable source of accumulation and national recognition and simultaneously withholds that offering by contrasting it to a plot of rewarded passivity.

The land plot further undermines young Forest's career at sea by presenting royal authority as highly compromised. The crucial proclamation on which his well-being depends, a proclamation that ostensibly promises a reward for capturing the pirates and a pardon for the capturer, should he need it, is barely delivered. The representative of royal authority in the play, the "Pursevant" is already one degree removed from the office of herald: he "comes after." To make matters worse, this particular pursuivant is hoarse, and must employ a mouthpiece for himself, who is already but a mouthpiece.[33] Such a diluted performative of a promise bears but faint traces of the authorizing monarch's voice. To make the denigration of the royal command even more apparent, the chosen mouthpiece is the play's Clown, who mangles the speech. The repetition with a difference here produces a debased version, again sounding a cautionary note about Forest's near-repetition of the pirates' activities. The same-but-different is not necessarily an improvement. Although Heywood is not nearly as adroit as Shakespeare with malapropisms – and therefore not particularly humorous – the Clown's version manages to undo precisely the most important part of the proclamation: the rewards for capturing the pirates. Where the Pursevant, speaking for the queen, promises "A thousand pound sterling," the Clown offers "A thousand Stares and Starlings" (3.4, 1562–63). More importantly, he reverses the terms of the pardons:

PUR.: If a banisht man his country.
CLOWN: If a man he shall be banisht his country.
PUR.: If a condemned man liberty.
CLOWN: If a man at liberty condemned. (3.4, 1564–67)

This disruption of royal authority, while less threatening than the actual pirates, constitutes a similar instance of state power disabled through doubling. At the same time, it undoes the hypothetical heroic Englishman's motivation for chasing pirates, and suggests that the Crown may be quite capricious in distributing rewards and punishments where piracy is concerned. State power is thus ventriloquized and undermined even as it attempts to control the threat of piracy.[34]

Thus piracy casts a shadow over a simple plot of bourgeois enrichment and happy unions by proving the dark double of peaceable trade. If James' England essentially renounces piracy, and most certainly condemns piracy against English trade, the world of the text presents the practice in a more ambiguous light, as a method of self-fashioning into rank and riches, and of benefiting England, but also as a dangerous double to state authority and legitimate trading.

"A girl worth gold"

The feminization of the pirate ship in *Fortune by Land and Sea* – as in "She bears the cross of England and St. George" – brings to mind the identification between such symbols of state power and Elizabeth herself.[35] Although the queen is largely absent or misrepresented in that play, a closely related text by Heywood, *The Fair Maid of the West*, gives the sovereign a different kind of presence. Jean E. Howard has suggestively analyzed the complicated identification of Bess Bridges, the "fair maid" of the title, with Elizabeth. Although Howard argues that Bess Bridges is primarily a simple West Country maid and only secondarily a stand-in for the "fair maid" of England, she nonetheless identifies the character as "a device for uniting men of different classes into a homosocial community of brothers, into a nation."[36] Howard's analysis of the workings of gender and race in the constitution of an English identity is highly illuminating; I propose here to expand upon her discussion in terms of class.

The Fair Maid of the West bears a distinct resemblance to Fortune by Land and Sea: both texts feature tavern fights, self-imposed exiles, and sea-combats.[37] It is, however, far more straightforward in its definition of an English identity against the Spaniards and the Moors. Probably written in the last years of Elizabeth's reign, the play opens with an enthusiastic port scene where two captains and a gentleman speculate with great expectation about the gallant earl of Essex's upcoming voyage of plunder to the Spanish Azores:

> FIRST CAPTAIN: Most men think
> The fleet's bound for the Islands.
> CARROL: Nay, 'tis like.
> The great successe at Cales [Cádiz] under the conduct
> Of such a noble general hath put heart
> Into the English; they are all on fire
> To purchase from the Spaniard. If their carracks
> Come deeply laden, wee shall tug with them
> For golden spoil.
> SECOND CAPT.: O, were it come to that!
> FIRST CAPT.: How Plymouth swells with Gallants! How the streets
> Glister with gold! You cannot meet a man
> But trick'd in scarf and feather, that it seemes
> As if the pride of England's Gallantry
> Were harbor'd here. It doth appear, methinks,
> A very court of soldiers.[38]

Written before the disgrace and execution of Essex, The Fair Maid of the West rides the crest of Elizabethan privateering. The nation imagined in the passage above is highly combative, gallant, and, more importantly, successful. The expeditions against Spain serve to gild the average man in Plymouth and raise him beyond his station, until the whole town seems both courtly and martial, marvelously restored to an epic time.

Despite the optimistic rhetoric of nationalism surrounding the expedition to the Azores, Bess's gentlemanly suitor, Spencer, joins for rather less exalted reasons. Early in the play, he carefully differentiates his motives from those of his less wealthy friend, Goodlack:

GOODLACK: Pray resolve me,
        Why, being a gentleman of fortunes, means,
        And well revenu'd, will you adventure thus
        A doubtful voyage, when only such as I,
        Born to no other fortunes than my sword,
        Should seek abroad for pillage?
SPENCER: Pillage, Captain?
        No, 'tis for honor; and the brave society
        Of all these shining gallants that attend
        The great lord general drew me hither first,
        No hope of gain or spoil. (1.2, 3–11)

No matter how noble his intentions, however, Spencer ends up joining the expedition for rather more interested reasons. Enraged by a gentleman who insults Bess at the tavern, Spencer kills him in a fight. Like Forest, then, he must take to the seas to save himself from justice. But whereas Forest was both fugitive and hero, the heroics here are left to Bess.

When news comes of Spencer's death, she is the one who outfits a ship and, dressed as a man, sails off to rescue Spencer's body from the Spanish, her black ship of mourning significantly named the *Negro*. But the news of Spencer's fate involves a double set of misrepresentations: first, a man named Spencer has actually died at Fayal, but he was not Bess's Spencer. Second, the strong expectations set up in the text by the early flag-waving about the Islands Voyage and the subsequent scenes against the Spaniards confuse the facts of the actual Spencer's actual wound. Instead of dying in combat against the Spaniards, he has merely been hurt in a quarrel between Englishmen over the division of booty (2.2, 18–50).[39] Although the two English captains, who are shown fighting over the spoils, had in fact engaged successfully with the Spaniards, any claims of national unity are undone by their lust for gold. The central plot device of the play is thus an injury inflicted by Englishmen on one of their own.

The motive for revenge against the Spanish is supplemented much later, when the story is told of the *other* Spencer's exhumation by fanatical Catholics (4.4, 39–44). And by the time Bess finally confronts the Spaniards, the scene has been set: 4.1 shows the injured Spencer and the surgeon who cured him captured by a Spanish ship, itself seeking revenge for the attack on Fayal. But Bess begins attacking Spanish ships long before she knows any of this, and relishes a combat the audience does not even see: "Oh, this last sea fight/ Was gallantly perform'd! It did me good/To see the Spanish carvel vail her top/Unto my maiden flag" (4.4, 1–4). As in *Fortune by Land and Sea*, there is a sense of multiple encounters beyond those staged.

Bess's expedition reflects some of the ambiguities between piracy and privateering. She sets out on her private mission to recover Spencer's body but is easily distracted into fighting Spaniards. The conflation of motives is conveyed nicely when she exclaims before battle: "Then, for your country's honor, my revenge,/For your own fame and hope of golden spoil,/Stand bravely to't" (4.4, 84–86). Her greatest success as a symbol of England lies in bringing these disparate motivations together. The play's setting during the war with Spain and its frank recognition that Essex's expedition is one of looting complicate the distinctions between licit and illicit activities at sea to the point where it is difficult to separate the motives of English and Spanish, although Heywood is careful to show the English as more charitable and honorable. Howard argues that this equation between the European powers is reinforced by the introduction of a clearly differentiated third term, the Moors:

These Moors who dare to interfere with English merchants and to court an English woman are made to embody a dangerous but effeminate otherness that finally renders them safely inferior to their European visitors. A much vaster gulf of difference yawns between them and the English than between those sworn enemies, the English and the Spanish.[40]

Yet what Howard's reading fails to account for is the odd closeness between the English and the Moors, a proximity that corresponds not only to the historical contacts between England and Morocco in the period but, more significantly, to the text's othering of the English themselves. Where Howard reads Bess's sailing on the *Negro* as "a desire for command and mastery" over Africans,[41] I would argue that it signals a conflation between the English and the Moors, one that Spain and Portugal, for example, would certainly have identified. Not only does Bess herself sail on a ship that establishes her relation to the Barbary corsairs, the English merchant she rescues was himself headed to Mamorah, an important corsair base in Morocco, before being intercepted by the Spaniards. A symbolic closeness belies the play's apparent distinction between English and Moors, and although the text stresses the difference between Bess and a pirate ("The French and Dutch she spares, only makes spoil/ Of the rich Spaniard and the barbarous Turk," 4.5, 7–8), it succeeds only in presenting her and her crew as surprisingly close to the Moors themselves.

When Bess and her crew journey to the Moorish court of Fez, being "forc'd for want of water/To put into Mamorah in Barbary" (4.5, 10–11), the fair maid's English beauty quickly wins over the ruler Mullisheg. Her servant Clem uses Bess's favor with Mullisheg to bribe foreign merchants, who pay him considerable amounts to influence the ruler in their favor. Clem fancies himself a courtier, but his quotation from Kyd's *The Spanish Tragedy* introduces a note of foreboding:

"It is not now as when Andrea liv'd," – or rather Andrew,
our elder journeyman. What, drawers become courtiers?
Now may I speak with the old ghost in Jeronimo:
    When this eternal substance of my soul
    Did live imprisoned in this wanton flesh,
    I was a courtier in the court of Fez. (5.1, 110–15)

Why does Clem so pessimistically imagine himself a ghost? And why does
he invoke Andrea, whose rise in the world and love affair with the noble
Bel-Imperia is cut short by his suspicious death? Perhaps one answer can
be found in the punishment the play subsequently deals to this drawer-
turned-courtier. When Bess requests preferment for her lover, Spencer,
Mullisheg kindly offers to make him his eunuch. Bess protests, and Clem
steps in to receive the honor meant for Spencer (5.2, 89–100). When the
Moorish ruler promises to have the Englishman *gelded*, Clem hears *gilded*
and rushes to volunteer.[42] He is, after all, merely aping his mistress,
the "girl worth gold." But whereas her chastity affords her a symbolic
status that locates her beyond class struggle, her servant does not fare as
well. Perhaps the difference lies in the fact that Bess's rise in the world
stems from Spencer's charitable bequests to her; no matter how virtuous,
she would never have gotten rich without him. When Clem attempts to
supplant Spencer, however, it is a different matter. Howard partially
accounts for the castration by focusing on Clem's entrance dressed "as a
fantastic Moor" (5.1, 109), reading the episode as "a grotesquely hideous
warning of the dangers of 'going native.'"[43] Although I agree that the play
seems very much exercised by Englishmen (and a woman) who are too
much like the Moors, when Clem suffers castration it is not primarily for
being like the natives but for trying to stand in for his betters. The warning
seems to be more clearly directed at an apprentice trying to appear a
gentleman than at an Englishman playing Turk. Clem is identified as an
interloper by his class, while the Moors as a whole are represented as
inferior to the English. Those marked by race or class, then, are excluded
from the nation that coalesces around Bess. Yet the lines of demarcation
can never be clearly drawn: Bess herself is raised from the lower classes,
and her own gender transgressions suggest a "good lack" of English
masculinity that recalls the supposed effeminacy of the Moors. As Howard
herself points out, there is a dangerous effeminacy within England herself:
it is not every nation that can boast of a female sovereign and cross-dressed
privateers.

    Rather than warn the English about the emasculation they risk if they
become too much like the Moors, Heywood's text presents that emasculation as already characteristic of England's relation to other empires.
This less than potent account of the English nation is reinforced by the

continuously postponed nuptials between Bess and Spencer. Although the marriage is always imminent, it is never presented during the course of the play.[44] Instead of domesticating Bess, the text focuses on the actual emasculation of the upstart, who threatens the socioeconomic hierarchy of England more than its gender hierarchy.

"I am made! an eunuch!"

The punishment for social mobility based on commerce recurs in Philip Massinger's *The Renegado* (1623), where it seems more closely connected to the relationship between trade, English potency, and social class. *The Renegado* reformulates the questions of masculinity and trade even more directly. The text owes much to source stories in Cervantes, but Massinger places the emphasis squarely on commerce. The protagonist, Vitelli, is a Venetian gentleman who comes to Tunis disguised as a merchant to save his sister, Paulina, who has been captured by the pirate Grimaldi and sold to the Turk. Vitelli's servant, Gazet, takes advantage of his master's success with the Turkish princess Donusa to take over both his wares and his social position. When Donusa's liaison with Vitelli is discovered, they are both thrown in prison. She attempts to save them by entreating him to convert and marry her, but he refuses, strengthened by the ministrations of the Jesuit Francisco. Instead, Vitelli manages to convince Donusa to convert and face a Christian death with him. Meanwhile, the renegade pirate Grimaldi falls into disgrace with the Turks for failing to defeat the Maltese corsairs and returns to Christianity. Finally, with Paulina and the repentant Grimaldi's help, all the Christians escape, leaving their Turkish captors discomfited. It is striking that the Spanish completely disappear from the play (although one could argue that the Jesuit Francisco sounds like a Spanish character) while the English are introduced through their habitual stand-ins, the Italians. The moments of direct reference to England satirize that nation's supposed capitulation to female power and subsequent loss of masculinity, as when Donusa asks her eunuch Carazie to describe the liberties that women enjoy in England, which he as a native of that country knows full well.[45]

Although the play's title ostensibly refers to the Grimaldi subplot, I would argue that it also alludes to what fails to happen in the main plot, as Vitelli resists Donusa and escapes conversion. While Vitelli never becomes a renegado, Grimaldi reneges on his renegado state. Perhaps the best way to interpret Massinger's title, then, is as a commentary on the constant diegetic betrayals that characterize the play, for the characters who surround Vitelli almost constantly represent the possibility of crossovers between Christians and Turks, chastity and venery, merchants and

courtiers, loyalty and treachery. This kind of oscillation complicates the
boundaries between Turks and Christians – there is a numerous class of
"in-betweens" – while mapping onto the religious/national difference a
gendered difference that often confounds the former. Furthermore, as in
Marlowe's *The Jew of Malta*, the constant problems of keeping faith
versus keeping *the* Faith amid multiple religions locate *The Renegado* in a
world of epistemic uncertainty. As Gazet states at the very outset:

> And if it be lawfull
> In a Christian shopkeeper to cheat his father,
> I cannot find but to abuse a Turke
> In the sale of our commodities, must bee thought
> A meritorious worke. (1.1, 19–23)

But of course it is not at all clear whether it is lawful for a Christian
shopkeeper to do such a thing in the first place.

Although Vitelli, the hero of *The Renegado*, is a disguised gentleman
from Venice, this is barely alluded to in the play. Instead, he appears as a
merchant, selling in his tent the stuff of European culture: Greek myths,
reproductions of Michelangelo, and so forth. The play opens with a scene
of trade as traffic in women, as Gazet offers the various painted ladies on
his master's wares to any possible takers. The merchant functions as
panderer not only of women in general but more specifically of European
ladies: the women Gazet touts include the "Mistris to the Great Duke of
Florence/ That Neece to old King Pippin, and a third/ an Austrian
Princess by her Roman lippe" (1.1, 9–11). The merchant's role as purveyor
of sexuality becomes doubly loaded when "wares" are connected to male
potency. At the bazaar, Donusa's servant Manto disdainfully taunts the
eunuch Carazie with his lack of the proper "wares;" he cannot "serve the
turne" (2.3, 3–8). The metaphoric relation between "wares" and testicles
depends on the several meanings of "stones" as precious commodities (a
polysemy that Gazet later ignores at his peril). Yet by entering the realm of
metaphor male potency also becomes oddly unstable: stones can be lost,
stolen, or foolishly bartered away. The resulting relation of castration to
commerce, and the description of the castrated eunuch Carazie as the sole
English character in the play suggest a troubling connection between
England's trade and its vulnerable masculinity.

This relation is maintained throughout as Vitelli, busy with Donusa,
abandons his merchant guise and leaves all the merchandise to his servant.
Gazet rises in the world and develops an ambition to join the court, but as
he goes from small change (a "gazet" was a Venetian coin of small value)
to greater stakes, he risks emasculation. Although Gazet is determined not
to be a "Sanzacke" (an administrator in the Ottoman empire), for it

sounds to him perilously close to "Sans-iacke" (3.4, 40–41), he is captivated by the possibility of becoming a eunuch. He can buy that post, Carazie tells him, "but parting with a precious stone or two" (52–53). Only a grammatical hiatus stands between Gazet and castration as he unwittingly exclaims, "I am made! an Eunuch!" (56). Being "made" in economic terms (becoming a self-made man) here implies being *unmade* as a man. From this perspective, of the paradoxical unmaking of self-fashioning, the optimistic predictions for commerce as a national means to empire in *Fortune by Land and Sea* seem all too sanguine.

Like Clem in Heywood's *Fair Maid of the West*, Gazet risks being punished for his excessive climb in the social world with a diminution of potency. Gazet rises perilously, as does his master, but while Vitelli is condemned for taking the Turkish princess' virginity, Gazet barely hangs on to his masculinity. If, then, *The Renegado* replaces the model of Grimaldi, the renegade pirate, with that of the successful merchant, it does so with certain caveats. Although the merchant can presumably come and go without changing allegiances and enjoy a greater fluidity than the reviled renegado, he also risks losing his masculinity through his excessive aspirations. The path from the ambiguity of piracy to the legality of commerce is hardly a smooth one. Of course, Gazet only encounters the threat of castration when he attempts to join the court – perhaps castration is not the fate of every merchant but only of those who get above themselves. Yet the text suggests that social mobility is unstoppable; once Gazet finds himself in his master's clothes, he wants nothing more than to follow him into the court. Significantly, his master is really a gentleman, merely roughing it as a merchant because it provides a convenient disguise. Merchants and gentlemen are emphatically not the same in the world of *The Renegado*, a world which tolerates conversions far better than it does change in social status.

If the class distinctions of this play are mapped onto the mercantile world of Jacobean England, a number of interesting anxieties come to the fore: perhaps it is unreasonable, the play suggests, to expect gentlemen to concern themselves with trade for long; trade for them is but a means to an end. Perhaps, too, it is unduly optimistic to expect merchants to remain merchants; once subjects are offered the possibility of social mobility, they will take it as far as possible, even if their imperfect knowledge of upper-class mores threatens to emasculate them. In this model, being a merchant is but an illusory, temporary condition, somewhere between the lower and upper classes. The expanded world of commerce offers no safe havens, and the Christians' retreat to Europe at the end of the play contrasts vividly with the tantalizing sales of European culture to the infidels earlier in the text.

Although *The Renegado* expresses considerable anxieties about the development of a merchant class, it by no means romanticizes piracy as do Heywood's plays. The play's further remove from Elizabeth's reign may account for the absence of such nostalgia. But who, then, carries out the most successful transactions in *The Renegado*? Without a doubt, it is the shadowy Jesuit Francisco. As a redeemer, however, his transactions are ideally final and absolute. What he buys back goes out of circulation. Redeemed Christians remain redeemed, and distance themselves from the play's transactions and hard bargaining. (In fact, they leave the world of the Barbary Coast altogether.) Yet if this type of dead-end negotiation by a Catholic is ultimately the most successful Christian position vis-à-vis the Turks, the prognosis is not good for English commerce in the region.

More importantly, what the texts I have analyzed seem to challenge is the possibility of basing an empire upon the expansion of the merchant class in the wake of England's experience of piracy. Although an upwardly mobile figure like John Smith might argue that colonial adventures can profitably replace piracy, the threat of such a solution lies in its obfuscation of class lines. Thus, either because commerce bears too close a resemblance to piracy, or because the status of merchant seems but a convenient stepping-stone on the way to ever more exalted states, these plays seem deeply suspicious of a mercantile solution. At the same time, of course, they are comedies, offering largely positive resolutions to the conflicts they present. The development of the merchant class was hardly a tragedy for England; in historical terms it did establish the basis for empire. But in the first part of the seventeenth century, the scourge of piracy and its models of accumulation seriously complicated the adoption of trade as a part of national identity. The gradual involvement of the upper classes in commercial ventures also incurs a social cost that these plays reflect: if the aristocracy stoops to trade for the sake of riches, while the lower classes trade to improve their station, the hierarchies of the social echelon risk becoming meaningless in the pursuit of commerce. The clustering of castration anxieties around the upstart figures of Clem and Gazet suggests that a nation where class differences are minimized is a nation emasculated. In the texts analyzed, the virile nation seems to rely far more heavily on the romanticized figure of the epic pirate than on the more prosaic merchants, despite Richard Hakluyt's efforts to make of commerce an epic pursuit.

Postscript: survival in Utopia

How did the English reliance on outmoded aristocratic models of virile conquest and plunder complicate England's actual colonial ventures, as it attempted to imitate Spain in the Americas? The creation of the Virginia Company in 1606, after the repeated failure of the Roanoke settlements, was, as Ivor Noël Hume has put it, a move "to transform the practice of private adventuring with royal blessing, characteristic of the previous reign, into a more businesslike and unified arrangement operating as a controlled element of the nation's foreign policy."[46] Yet its members do not seem to have taken the shift to an ethic of hard-working, mercantile expansion to heart, and the change from an earlier aristocratic model of plunder and piracy to the "gentlemanly" excursions of the Company was hardly substantive. As Karen Kupperman points out, "The company expected to set up military outposts run by gentlemen and aristocrats who would be given ample scope for swashbuckling exploits suitable to their station."[47] That is, they expected to behave like Cortés in Mexico, or Pizarro in Peru.

How these aristocrats expected to feed themselves while engaged in such exploits is not quite clear: the Company's first crew included mainly gentlemen and their personal servants, and notably lacked farmers and husbandmen. The ensuing stories of starvation and misery in the colony soon became a source of acute embarrassment to the Company, and threatened the colony's survival. Yet even when starving, these gentlemen colonists do not seem seriously to have considered fishing.[48]

The main problem, as Smith himself repeatedly pointed out, was that the gentlemen colonizers never intended to engage in heavy labor. Yet there was no prodigal abundance in Virginia, or even enough for subsistence. Even in richer areas, the Spaniards had often depended upon the natives for their sustenance. Here, tense relations with the tribes made even trade for food sporadic, and the colony was always short of the labor to procure itself necessities. The vanishing banquet that tantalizes the starving Europeans in *The Tempest* serves well as a metaphor for the expected abundance that evaporated when the English arrived in the New World.

By the time the Company started shipping larger numbers of laborers to Virginia, around 1620, relations with the Indians had deteriorated to such a point that the colony faced threats other than starvation. Yet the early history of Virginia seems dogged above all by a sense of displaced and anachronistic expectations: although the Crown might have replaced the model of plunder with one of sober plantation and commerce, its subjects persisted in regarding themselves as dashing adventurers of an epic, rather than a mercantile, hue.

An empire besieged

Arriving first can be a mixed blessing. As the most advanced and established European empire in the Americas throughout the sixteenth century, Spain suffered repeated attacks from its imperial rivals. England, for example, gleefully disseminated the Black Legend of unprecedented Spanish cruelty in the New World, while simultaneously attempting to acquire through privateering the possessions that Spain had originally conquered.[1] Spanish territories in the New World experienced constant attacks by semi-official pirates such as Drake. These required defensive measures that taxed even the copious resources the Crown extracted from the Indies. After the defeat of the Armada, the Iberian Peninsula itself became more vulnerable, as England attacked with increasing boldness while Spain's scant naval resources were spread ever more thinly over the multiple conflicts in which the state engaged at the same time. It was not feasible for a single navy, no matter how powerful, effectively to protect the Spanish coasts, escort the treasure-laden galleons from the Indies, guard New World settlements and Spanish coasts from piratical attacks, and contain the rebellion in the Netherlands, as Philip's forces attempted to do during these years.[2]

Spain was beleaguered not only by rival European powers but by the forces of Islam in the Western Mediterranean. After the defeat of the Ottoman navy at Lepanto in 1571, corsairs from Tunis and Algiers, client states to the Turks, posed the primary threat to Spanish coastal settlements. The corsairs included a large population of renegadoes of European origin, whom Friar Diego de Haedo, in his *Topografía e historia de Argel*, calls "turcos de profesión."[3] When they chose to align themselves with Islam, the renegadoes brought with them a wealth of geographical as well as technical knowledge: Haedo notes that they were all "very well-versed in the beaches and coasts of all Christianity."[4] Because all of Christianity furnished the renegadoes who became corsairs, they could pilot their way to any European coast. Yet Spain found itself especially vulnerable to corsair attacks, first, because of its proximity to North Africa, and, second, because of the constant migration of Moriscos to the Barbary Coast.[5] With their detailed knowledge of Spanish and of the vulnerable coasts, the Moriscos could become the most effective of corsairs, passing for Spaniards.[6] Like the renegadoes, they muddle the distinction between self and other – or European and African – in this struggle: while recognizable as European, they are nonetheless just as clearly Europe's enemies.

This chapter analyzes the complex representation of Spanish identity in literary accounts of piracy and captivity. Whereas English accounts of piracy emphasize the commercial gains and class mobility of potentially wayward subjects, in Spain such representations are often concerned more with the nation's providential mission and the challenges to it from compromised religious identities and unheroic commercial transactions. Pirate attacks against the Spanish empire are incorporated into the grand narrative of its imperial mission, yoking together religious and colonial goals.[7] In this narrative, bellicose English attempts to emulate and supplant the Spanish are simply a heavenly scourge visited upon Spain, to be endured as were the attacks of Islam. Indeed, in that endurance lies the true essence of the nation. Such is the ideological thrust of Lope de Vega's *La Dragontea* (1598), an epic poem that aims, paradoxically, to diminish the epic stature of its hero, Sir Francis Drake. Lope struggles to fit his antipathy to his subject into an epic frame traditionally reserved for praising heroes, while allegorizing Spanish struggles against the infidel, whether Lutheran pirate or Moorish corsair.

Yet if pirate stories enable the discursive consolidation of a Spanish identity eternally committed to the defense of the Faith, they also challenge the integrity of that identity. The second part of this chapter analyzes the vulnerability of a Spanish identity based on religious difference, by focusing on such liminal characters as renegadoes and converts to Christianity. As ambiguous figures of change and mimetization, these marginal characters pose a serious threat to a Spanish identity based on an irreducible and *irreproducible* Christianity. Since renegadoes mimic Spanishness in their exercise of piracy, their double nature begs the question of how Spain can maintain its self-identity. How does the mimetic reproduction of not merely the state and its symbols (as in the case of Heywood's pirates, in Chapter 5), but of individual Spanish identities, undermine what it means to be Spanish?

As I have suggested earlier, the key image that links Spain's Mediterranean struggles to consolidate an "unadulterated" Christian identity with its imperial expansion in the New World is the purported equation between the *Reconquista* (of Peninsular territory from the Moors) and the

Conquista (of the New World). But the analogy provides only an unstable grounding for Spain's exploits. The necessary temporality of the comparison – in which the completed Reconquista guarantees the success of the ongoing Conquista – collapses in the face of Spain's continuing struggles against an encroaching Islam. Although the threat of Islam takes new forms in the late sixteenth century – as the continuing scourge of piracy on the coasts or the perceived danger of the Moriscos to Spain's "purity" – it is hardly contained in the past. The licit rhetorical reproduction of Spanish victories in the Reconquista/Conquista analogy – twice the conquests, twice the triumphs – collapses in the face of *illicit* reproductions of Spanish identity. The mimetic reproduction of Spanish identity by marginal actors – especially those targeted by the state – constitutes a sort of reverse conquest in its own right. The rhetorical performance of Spanishness by those Spain marginalizes subtly undermines the notion of an essential, unadulterated national self, and suggests instead that identity itself is merely a series of endlessly iterable performances.

A Dragon in paradise

Famous pirates such as Francis Drake appeared frequently in Spanish writing of the 1580s and 90s, both in high literary forms like epic and in popular ballads.[8] In 1598, ten years after England's defeat of the Armada Invencible and soon after the death of Philip II, the young Lope de Vega published *La Dragontea*, on Drake's last voyage to the Canaries and the Indies. Lope would become the preeminent Spanish playwright of his age, yet he chose to tell this story not as a *comedia*, but rather in the style of a Renaissance epic, more befitting a serious subject such as the defense of Spanish empire from the menace of piracy.

Although this was a departure for Lope, the prologue to the 1598 edition expresses far more anxiety over his choice of topic than of genre. Like Ercilla praising the Araucanians, Lope must explain his emphasis on Spain's enemy. The prologuist Francisco de Borja attempts to justify Lope's focus on Drake, even though *La Dragontea* actually presents an aging "Dragon" in his last and perhaps most disappointing venture. Borja's excuses seem oddly anachronistic – he is apologizing for Lope's writing about a past menace:

Esto hay en lo que toca al libro; más del sugeto dirá alguno, que si los ingleses han tenido felices sucesos en nuestras Indias y flotas ¿por qué se hace historia en España deste vencimiento? A esto se responde, que nunca los ingleses si no es por inclemencia del mar, o por grandes desigualdades en la gente, han tenido buen suceso, o por haber venido estando las costas seguras, o viniendo las flotas desarmadas.[9]

[So much for the book; but concerning the subject matter, one might ask why, if the

English have been successful in our Indies and against our fleets, these defeats are chronicled in Spain. To which I answer that the English have never succeeded except due to the inclemency of the sea or the great disparity in the forces, or because they came when they saw that the coasts were considered safe, or when our fleets were unarmed.]

In his rather thin excuse, Borja suggests that Lope portrays only the English reliance on luck, weather, or surprise in their victories over the Spaniards. Yet this does not fully address the question of why the poet should recount Spanish defeats in the first place. In another attempt to salvage *La Dragontea*, the prologuist points out that the ten cantos end with the destruction of Drake's fleet; thus an ideologically sound ending must justify the rather embarrassing initial focus on the English.[10]

Despite narrating the last, unsuccessful voyage of a diminished Drake, Lope banks on the English pirate's dangerous reputation to increase the poem's appeal. It is impossible to argue that Lope is sympathetic to Drake; nonetheless, the pirate towers over any other figure in the text, as its title indeed suggests. Lope faces the constraints of his chosen genre: Drake's exploits are simply greater and more heroic than those of the Spaniards, and epic requires that they be given their due. And although Lope purports to sing the defeat of Drake by "the famous lion" of Spain, Don Diego Suárez de Amaya, this Spanish captain never equals the "Dragon's" epic stature. In fact, Lope's focus on Suárez de Amaya seems to have been rather arbitrary, and much criticized by contemporary readers, who expected a more accurate account of recent events. An attempted first printing, in Madrid in 1598, was forbidden for the poem's "untruths" – namely the substitution of Suárez de Amaya, who does not appear in the historical documents on Drake's attacks, for the real leader against the English, Alonso de Sotomayor.[11] Unlike the irreplaceable, unmistakable Dragon of the epic's title, the Spanish hero turns out to be a rather shadowy and immaterial presence, whose place can be taken by another man. Despite Lope's concerted effort to portray Drake's actions as the work of Satan, the poem's focus on him suggested, at least to some readers, an unhallowed sympathy for the enemy.

Lope's critics seized on *La Dragontea* as a deliberate libel praising Drake to the detriment of the king and the shame of Spain.[12] Moreover, they specifically attacked Lope for his representation of the Spanish side, arguing that the rightful leader had been denied his place in the poem. This double attack was quite powerful: Lope could not shield himself from accusations of sympathy to Drake with a claim for the objective truth of his poem, since he had in fact altered the historical account. Never has an epic invocation sounded less convincing – if the poet is not singing the glory of Suárez de Amaya, what exactly is he singing? Ironically, Lope's logical choice of epic as the appropriate genre for glorifying the Spanish empire is fundamentally compromised by the absence of any notable Spanish leader to represent that empire. The dashing pirate, as a challenger to Spain's dominion, cuts a far more compelling figure than its staid defenders.

The generic conventions of epic complicate Lope's project from all sides: an authentic "Drakead" would have required a fuller account of the privateer's glorious exploits, but for a chronicle of his defeat and death the triumphalist codes of epic are woefully inadequate. How can the author diminish the epic stature of Drake while preserving the conflict's appeal? Lope's solution to this problem – a decisive turn to allegory in the service of empire – makes *La Dragontea* a fascinating text despite its generic limitations and negative reception. Bounded by the constraints of the epic form, Lope produces a religiously inflected poem without a real hero, more heavy-handedly allegorical than Tasso's *Gerusalemme liberata*, and ultimately less successful in rendering its ideological content in poetic form.[13] Yet with its awkward fluctuations between epic and biblical imagery, its hyperbolic figuration of an epic villain, and its blatant teleological framework, the poem proves an ideal case-study for the representation of piracy in the context of Spain's larger imperial ideology.

In this modified epic, Drake becomes the Dragon, transposing the imperial struggle into a biblical frame of reference. Under this guise, he embodies biblical evil from alpha to omega, from the Snake in Eden to the Dragon of the Apocalypse, and the struggle against him becomes a cosmological battle of good against evil. Given that Lope's poem focuses on Drake's late, less spectacular exploits in order to diminish the stature of the pirate, his allegorization into absolute Evil might seem somewhat disproportionate. Yet it enables the superimposition of a theological code on the political events of recent history, magnifying the importance of Spain's own religious mission. Lope's use of apocalyptic motifs, moreover, appears quite timely at the end of the century, when the imminence of the Kingdom of God was widely proclaimed.[14]

The repeated recourse to biblical typology in the poem allows Lope to glorify Spain through more exalted imagery than mere epic motifs. By 1598, claiming an imperial inheritance from Rome through epic was hardly a unique gesture – similar claims are implicit not only in Ariosto and Tasso but in Spenser's *Faerie Queene* and Camões' *Lusiadas* (1572). In Spain such claims were reinforced by an imperial rhetoric that equated the furtherance of Spanish temporal power with that of the Christian faith. Spain's Hapsburgs were not only the true inheritors of Rome's universal empire, but, more importantly, uniquely responsible for the extension of Christian empire into the New World.[15] In attempting to describe Spain as an empire that valiantly fends off imperial imitators, therefore, Lope generally eschews clichéd classical motifs and focuses instead on religious imagery, presenting Spain as the only and unalienable representative of Christian empire.[16] By resorting to the teleology to end all teleologies – the biblical Apocalypse – as the primary motif for his poem, and reserving explicit references to epic for hellish messengers such as Greed or Allecto, Lope emphasizes Spain's central role in the preservation of Christianity against heretics and infidels.

Summarily ignoring the political and commercial dimensions of the conflict between Spain and England, Lope frames the Spanish struggle against Drake's depredations as a religious battle. Spain he casts not as a rich empire busily extracting riches from American mines but rather as the beleaguered citadel of the true Faith. After an initial dedication to the newly crowned Philip III, Lope introduces a heavenly allegory in which a religious figure stands in for Spanish political authority. Spain is represented by "La Religion Cristiana perseguida,/ A España, a Italia, a América turbadas,/ De propias y de bárbaras espadas" (14) – the persecuted Christian Religion, with her three handmaids, Spain, Italy, and America, all threatened by "barbaric swords."

Christian Religion – larger than Spain, yet notably coterminous with its empire – begs God to spare her the scourge of the English Dragon, when she suffers already from Islamic corsairs:

> ¿Ha de arrojar este Dragón el río
> Como el que desde el cielo vino al suelo
> Contra mujer que tiene el nombre mío,
> Inmenso Padre de la luz del cielo?
> ¿No basta de Mahoma el señorío
> Que causa a Italia, a España tal desvelo,
> También quieres que crezca y se derrame
> La vil simiente de Lutero infame?
>
> Mira las almas que perdidas lloran
> Italia triste, España miserable,
> Cautivas de los Bárbaros que adoran
> La rapiña de cuerpos lamentable.
> Los cuatro que en Argel corsarios moran
> Con daño mío y perdición notable,
> Chafer, Fuchel, Mamifali y Morato,
> De Tripol, Túnez y Bizerta el trato.
>
> Eliz, Caratali, Mami, Arnauto,
> De aquestas dos destruyen las riberas,
> Tomando como mísero tributo
> Barcas, tartanas, zabras y galeras.   (22–24)

[Must the river bring this Dragon, like the one that came from Heaven to earth, against a woman of my name, oh Immense Father of the Heavenly Light? Is not Mohammed's domination enough, which causes Italy and Spain so much anxiety? Do you want also the vile seed of infamous Luther to grow and spread?

Look at the lost souls who cry for sad Italy and miserable Spain, captives of the Barbarians who adore the deplorable theft of bodies; look at the four who live in Algiers as corsairs, to my harm and considerable loss: Chafer, Fuchel, Mamifali, and Morato; look at the trade of Tripoli, Tunis and Bizerta.

Eliz, Caratali, Mami, Arnauto destroy the coasts of these two, taking as their miserable tribute barks, *tartanas*, *zabras*, and galleys.]

Religion describes in careful detail the scourge of Islamic attacks on shipping and the coastal areas of Spain and Italy; her catalogue of corsairs reads like a Mediterranean "Most Wanted" for the period.[17] The real threat of piracy, she suggests, lies not in commercial or fiscal losses but in captives' temptation to renege by converting to Islam in their cells, where, as she complains, "my divine name is forgotten" (25). The infamous names of the corsairs thus efface the proper name of Christian Religion in the contested territory of the Mediterranean world.[18]

The three territories that concern Religion – Spain, Italy, and the Americas – were the bulwarks of the Spanish empire. Muslim attacks against Italy were largely Spain's responsibility, for it controlled Sicily, Naples, Sardinia, and Milan. Thus Lope's allegory conveniently identifies God's protection for the true Christian religion – whether in the Mediterranean or in the Atlantic – with his favor for Spain's empire. More significantly, it equates the New World and the Old as threatened citadels of the true Faith, rhetorically solidifying Spain's position in the Americas, as though its control over those territories were as absolute as its authority over mainland Spain.[19]

Once Islam and England have been equated as threats, the old analogy between the Reconquista of Spanish territory from the Moors and the Conquista of the New World plays itself out in reverse: because both Spain and America are newly threatened by infidels and heretics, they now merit equal protection as strongholds of the Faith. Religious discourse cloaks imperial competition in the borrowed dignity of a crusade, much as the talk of conversions had dignified Spain's original New World conquests. Even as the allegory serviceably conceals the important differences between Spanish control in the New World and the Old, it highlights the connection between Mediterranean and Atlantic as stages for the "shadow navies" of corsairs, pirates, and privateers that challenged Spanish dominion.

The relation between Reconquista and Conquista takes a fascinating turn in one of the most poignant episodes of the epic, when Drake's men attack the Spanish settlement of Nombre de Dios, in Panama. Unable to escape due to the illness of both her husband and her father, one Spanish woman gathers her children to her and awaits the attackers. She pleads with the raiders to let her children live, for they will pay tribute if allowed to reach maturity: "Que permitáis que crien estos pechos/ a quien os pague cuando grandes, pechos" (369) [Allow these breasts to nurture those who will pay you, when grown, tribute]. The pleading mother elides the distance between the two senses of *pecho* – the breast and a synecdochic personal tax – as though to dispel the distance between her children's threatened present and their adult future. When she develops the image of the tribute, however, the acutely personal, New World conflict is located squarely in Spain's experience of Islamic domination:

> Que si es preciso hado que esta tierra
> Y la demás que a su comarca alinda,
> Pague tributo injusto a Ingalaterra,
> Bien es que crezca quien le pague y rinda.
> Dio el cielo a España de Africa la guerra
> Por el pecado o fuerza de Florinda,
> Si muzárabes fueron sus cristianos,
> Dracárabes seremos los indianos.   (370)

[For if fate decrees that this land and that around it pay an unjust tribute to England, it is fitting that those who will pay and render it should increase. Heaven visited war from Africa on Spain because of Florinda's sin or rape; if its Christians were *mozárabes*,[20] we in the Indies will be *Drakarabs*.]

The plea for mercy becomes a rather defiant statement of cultural resistance, as the stanza equates the colonists beleaguered by Drake with the *mozárabes*, Christian minorities who subsisted in Islamic Spain as tributaries under the Moors. But the odd neologism *dracárabes*, while reducing England to the figure of Drake, oddly preserves the "Arabic" portion of *mozárabe*, making the Spanish colonists into an odd chimera of English piracy and Moorish culture.[21] The very system imagined as a solution by this threatened Spaniard suggests how close Reconquista and Conquista remained in the Spanish imaginary, while emphasizing the dangers inherent in constantly rehearsing the scene of conquest.[22]

When, in Canto VIII, the Spanish leader Don Diego Suárez de Amaya encourages his scant troops to resist the English, his exhortation moves from biblical struggles to the Reconquista to the present situation of his men. In a highly condensed passage, he encourages their resistance to Drake by appealing to their national character and invoking the possibility of a new Islamic threat to Spain:

> Y fuera de que el cielo nos ampara,
> Sólo el ser españoles nos obliga
> A no volver al fiero inglés la cara,
> Cuando con más poder nos busque y siga.

Que por ventura volverá la jara
Al arco y mano alarbe y enemiga,
Y cuando no, para morir nacemos,
Y después de la muerte viviremos.   (523)

[And beyond the fact that Heaven protects us, simply our being Spanish compels us
not to turn the other cheek from the fierce Englishman, when with greatest might
he seeks and follows us. For perchance the arrow will return to the Arabic bow and
hand of the enemy, and, should it not, we are born to die, and will live after death.]

In his enthusiasm, Don Diego makes the Muslim threat to Spain a near
and constant one. Yet there, precisely, lies the problem with the Reconquista as a model for the struggle against the English pirates: the conflict
with Islam cannot be fixed safely in the past, for it presents a continued
threat to Spain. The same rhetorical equation between the struggles
against Muslims and Lutherans that Lope uses to frame his narrative here
makes the defenders of Panama into virtual martyrs, fighting an ever-
recurring enemy and looking forward only to death and heavenly peace.
Although this characterization may underscore the profound, even heroic,
devotion of the Spanish, it by no means guarantees that they will be able to
preserve their conquests.

This instability of imperial conquest is alluded to again and again in *La
Dragontea*, through repeated laments for the heroic sufferings of the first
Spanish conquistadors: "¡Ay de los tristes que tocaron antes/De las re-
motas playas las arenas/Y por los nunca vistos horizontes/Abrieron las
entrañas a los montes!"(113) [Woe to the sad ones who once touched the
sands of these remote beaches, and, through horizons never before seen,
opened the entrails of the mountains!]. In his exhortation, Don Diego
invokes the sacrifices of the earliest conquistadors as justification for
Spanish dominion: the English, he argues, never suffered with Columbus
or Cortés as they tamed the New World and became its "first inhabitants"
(525). Native peoples are not "first" in these accounts; in fact, they are
singularly absent from the entire narrative – one gets the sense that the
only thing originally conquered was a conveniently empty landscape. Very
much the locals, the entrenched Spaniards now refer to themselves as
indianos (see stanza 370 above), to stress their long-term connection to the
endangered empire.[23] If Columbus originally thought he had discovered
the Earthly Paradise in the Indies, Drake now appears as the Snake in the
grass. And, despite Spanish claims for their own primacy, secular conquests appear fundamentally unstable, as evinced by the English attacks.
At the end of his speech, Don Diego returns to biblical teleology, recalling
the promise in Apocalypse that the Dragon will be killed. Thus the
constant appeal to religious imagery deliberately replaces unstable epic
conflicts with a more reliable plot.

Meanwhile, classical versions of imperial ideology are reserved for Drake's hellish instigators. The pirate is first presented at rest (29), a reluctant hero in need of encouragement. The traditional messenger from heaven is here replaced by Greed, who comes to Drake in a dream, in the guise of a beautiful woman. Unlike Aeneas, urged on to a licit empire by Mercury, Drake is spurred to his illicit conquests by a deceptive imago. Beneath her radiant exterior lies a shriveled and monstrous body, which more accurately reflects her moral valence, and recalls the enchantress Alcina in *Orlando Furioso* 7, or the stripping of Duessa, in *Faerie Queene* I.8. Greed's words are preceded by a catalogue of false prophecies and a long *occupatio*: she will not tell Drake of Spanish successes against Islam, Spanish weapons, or Spanish might.[24] Instead, she dwells on his past exploits, encouraging him with her careful rhetoric:

> Con fábulas, con sombras, con engaños
> Le refirió sus hurtos y blasones,
> Sus provechos también, y nuestros daños,
> Buscados por tan ásperas regiones.
> Encubriéndole al fin los desengaños,
> La capa de retóricas razones
> Dio con alborotar su pensamiento,
> Esta imagen al sueño, y voz al viento.   (41)

[With fables, with shadows, with deceit, she told of his thefts and glories, his profit, too, and the damage to us that he had sought in such inhospitable regions. Finally, concealing disenchantments under the cloak of rhetorical reasons, she excited his thought, bringing this image to his slumber, and this voice to the wind.]

Note the dissimulation of disenchantments – *desengaños* – in Greed's speech to Drake. The word choice is surely significant: *desengaño* was the term for a generalized disillusion and disappointment in Spain in the period, a kind of widespread cultural malaise. The first symptoms of this disillusion were very much in place by Philip II's death, for his reign had included not only the defeat of the Armada and the revolt in the Netherlands but repeated bankruptcy. Thus it is not only Greed who tells a partial truth in this passage; the reference to *desengaño* invokes a grimmer picture of Spain than Lope intends to paint.

In the long exhortation that follows, Greed sings the praises of Drake and imperial England. Like Satan in Milton's *Paradise Lost*, Greed uses rhetoric so well that the reader forgets all preambles and warnings against the suspect message. First she narrates Drake's past successes, so spectacular that they threaten to replace mere recounting with the literal (ac)counting of riches: "¿Quién hay que vuelto a Inglaterra crea/ Tu viaje, tu grande empresa y celo?/ Más poco entonces de contarla trata,/Ocupada en contar tanto oro y plata" (62) [Who would believe your trip, your great enterprise and zeal, once you returned to England? But she hardly tried to recount it, busy with counting so much gold and silver]. The powerful image of material wealth so immense that it upstages rhetoric counters the prefatory warnings against Greed's false speech – it is hard to argue with the numbers.

Greed's enticements range from the practical and sensible – Philip's power cannot reach the distant Indies undiluted (67) – to the mythical-world historical – she wants to make of England a "Julian Roman Olympian Macedonia" (75). Her rhetorical flights arrogate to England every imperial predecessor; Spain's rival is equated with all the great empires of antiquity, rolled together into a hyperbolic epic monstrosity. Drake's *impresa* of a dragon, both powerful and ominous, is traced through their imperial battalions. Greed's speech obliquely raises, in the unauthorized voice of a messenger from Hell, some of Spain's greatest concerns: how can it project its strength across the seas? How can it prove its own unalienable right to the imperial mantle of Rome? Letting the enemy speak, even by putting words in her mouth, can be dangerous: Greed's rhetoric of empire betrays Spain's anxieties about its own fragile dominion, even as it inflates English prospects.

While almost all the classical allusions fall on the side of the devilish Englishmen, there are some notable exceptions. One is the narrator's comparison of a pious Spanish son who bears his mother on his shoulders to Aeneas (506); another is the ironic embrace of classical exemplars by the *cimarrones*, escaped slaves who remain improbably faithful to Spain.[25] As they refuse to betray the Spaniards and join Drake, the leader of the *cimarrones* protests that, "no somos por negros hombres viles,/Sino las sombras de Héctor y de Aquiles" (437) [we are not, though black, vile/ but rather the shades of Hector and Achilles]. The classical imagery is stretched thin, as New World slaves claim to imitate Greek and Trojan warriors.[26] In general, the classical references on the Spanish side seem scattered and flimsy, while the repeated claims of a providential mission for Spain's empire brace the poem like a backbone, from the initial allegory of Religion as holy supplicant, to the desperate plea to Mary that she should stomp out the piratical Snake (339–43), to Don Diego's martyr speech cited above.

Religion also serves to help Lope resolve cruxes in the plot, where sympathy for a particular character threatens to undo the careful ideological distinctions of the poem. To mitigate his excessive focus on Drake, Lope attempts a strategy of "divide and conquer." No sooner is the Dragon's fleet armed and launched than the poem digresses to the story of Ricardo Achines (Hawkins), who undertakes his own expedition to the New World as an act of filial devotion, to avenge the offenses suffered by his father at the hands of the Spaniards. But this strategy brings new problems, for Ricardo's story makes him highly sympathetic. With a detailed description of the young captain's separation from his wife – a Dido figure – the episode introduces romance motifs into the text. Pleading with him to stay by her side, Hawkins' wife points out the strengths of Spain, and the foolish daring of his enterprise, invoking the Bible to argue for her husband's greater duty to her than to his father. Ricardo nonetheless sails to Peru, where he is swiftly captured by the Spaniards. He immediately regrets his expedition, conceding that his wife had been right all along. Finally, the text yields an explanation for the surfeit of sympathy that has characterized the description of the young adventurer: in defeat, Ricardo at last sees the light, and longs to become a Catholic (189). This is resolution by teleology: what might have appeared as a suspiciously sympathetic account of a marauding Englishman turns out to be prescient appreciation of good Catholic material.

The somewhat suspect conversion after defeat – reminiscent of Tasso's Armida and her late transformation into Rinaldo's "handmaiden" – finds a more convincing echo as the story is doubled within Drake's own ranks. When his men, too, encounter defeat, a certain Guillermo, "who seemed Catholic in his works and in his looks" (616) deserts to join the Spaniards. This latter episode provides an elaborate context for conversion: Guillermo's family had always been Catholic; his brother was martyred by Henry VIII. The defining moment for the Englishman's transformation comes when he finds the crucifix that an escaping priest has hidden in a tree trunk (636–39). Whereas the hasty conversion of Ricardo functions as a narrative about-face to justify post facto his intensely sympathetic portrayal, this more elaborate account, towards the end of the epic, lingers on the final conversion of a man who has clearly always been a crypto-Catholic. The tale retold is less blatantly opportunistic – both character and author seem more deliberate in choosing conversion. Yet it takes the retelling and doubling of the conversion episode before the powerful crucifix – an "idol" to Protestants – is finally given its due.

Even Drake's death from fever at the end of the poem is rendered through the unsubtle dichotomy of epic vs. Christian imagery. The final betrayal of Drake by his men is provoked by the fury Allecto, who incites them to violence against their leader. Thus for his diabolical ending Lope once more resorts to the Hell of the epic tradition – all that epic can provide for this poem, it seems, are the figures of classical evil that compound Drake's satanic nature. Allecto persuades the sailors to poison Drake, and the much-reduced fleet makes its return to England covered in ignominy. To close the allegorical frame, and return to the privileged Christian imagery, Religion thanks God for Drake's defeat.

Yet certain loose ends mar the neat embroidery of Lope's allegory. After Drake's death, Christian Religion must remind Him that there is still the small question of Islam to be solved:

> ¡Oh! gran Señor, que humillas al gigante,
> Al humilde David vuelve tus ojos,
> Al moro agora pirata arrogante
> Cargado de católicos despojos.
> Revuelve, eterno Júpiter tonante
> Los rayos de tus ímpetus y enojos
> Sobre mis enemigos y de España,
> Que su daño, Señor, me aflige y daña.   (729)

[Oh! Great Lord, who humiliates the giant, turn your eyes now to the humble David, to the Moor, arrogant pirate, now laden with Catholic spoils. Cast, oh eternal thundering Jupiter, the bolts of your violence and anger on my enemies and those of Spain, for its distress, Lord, saddens and afflicts me.]

This new religious allusion, after the shots have died down, complicates the hitherto clear terms of the biblical metaphorics. For where is Spain in the vertiginous perspective of this analogy? The Moors – figured as David in this plea – were hardly the ones fighting the "giant" Dragon in the New World. Islam is equated with David, clearly the virtuous hero of his own story, and threatens to take over the role that Spain previously played in defeating an outsized Drake. The Spaniards, meanwhile, go from playing David against an English Goliath to becoming the giant themselves, needled by Islamic corsairs. The bewildering instability of this image, with its transitive movement from one referent to the next in a game of metaphorical musical chairs, threatens to undo the careful differences between Spaniard and Englishman, Catholic and heretic that the text has so deliberately constructed. If they can change (rhetorical) places so easily, how distinct can they actually be? Moreover, this last-minute appeal to God – "oh, and by the way, there *is* one more thing . . ." – introduces an awkward rem(a)inder into the tidy teleology of the text. After the death of the Dragon, the unresolved question of the relation between Spain and its Islamic others looms large. The tidy allegorical end is not quite the last word, despite the invocation of the Bible's own finale, and the sequel promises to be considerably more confusing than Good versus Evil.

"Moros en la costa"

There is strong historical evidence for the connections Lope establishes in *La Dragontea* between Moorish corsairs and English pirates. A Spanish ballad of 1611 tells of Englishmen, Turks, and Moors sailing together as pirates, an indiscriminate threat to Spain and its empire,[27] while contemporary English accounts of notorious pirates often chronicle their association with Barbary corsairs.[28] As Chapter 5 argues, the English state experienced a considerable anxiety over the possible transformation of state-authorized privateers to pirates of dubious legality to, finally, renegadoes with no allegiance to European political or religious institutions. In Spain, the fears were more pressing, more concrete. No coastal town was safe as marauding pirates captured fishing boats, travelers passing near the shore, and anyone else unfortunate enough not to have reached safety behind town walls. Under Philip II, the redemption of Spanish captives from North Africa became such a common affair, and involved such large sums of money, that the Spanish state began overseeing the work of the religious orders who had generally performed such transactions.[29]

But the most troubling development for Spain in the period was the alliance – sometimes real, sometimes imagined – between the Morisco population in Spain and the Moors of North Africa. As Pérez de Hita's *Guerras civiles de Granada* makes clear, the long-standing cultural conflict between Moriscos and Christians in the south of Spain led to claims that the former acted as a fifth column, rendering Spain vulnerable to attack by Turks or North African Moors at any moment.[30] Haedo describes the Moriscos within Spain as willing allies of the corsairs who, "entering the land in Christian dress, and speaking very good Spanish, and being very well received in certain places by other Moriscos," are able to take many Christian captives.[31] These claims, combined with an increased intolerance for the Moriscos' ethnic difference, left this population increasingly vulnerable to those who argued for their complete expulsion from Spain. In 1609, Philip III finally decided to banish all Moriscos, converted or otherwise.[32]

The Spanish authorities seem not to have considered how these virtual Spaniards – fluent in Spanish, largely converted to Christianity, and often phenotypically indistinguishable from "real" Spaniards – would relate to Spain once expelled from the Peninsula. If the Moriscos had indeed sympathized with the Islamic corsairs who targeted both Mediterranean coasts and shipping, would they not logically join such attackers en masse once expelled?[33] One fascinating voice in this debate was the duke of Medina Sidonia, councilor to the king and sometime commander of the Armada. The duke did worry that the Moriscos would become enemies of Spain in Barbary if ill treated when expelled; his more humane solution involved sending them, as a hard-working labor-force, to New World lands such as Florida, Cuba, or Santo Domingo, which had suffered depopulation.[34] This incredible proposal, which displays so compactly the connections between Spain's control over the Peninsula and its imperial struggles overseas, was not heeded, and the Moriscos found their way to North Africa. As Medina Sidonia had feared, they there contributed to the expansion of corsair attacks against Spanish coasts in the Mediterranean and, increasingly, in the Atlantic as well.[35]

Although they were widely represented as violent aggressors who would aid the Barbary corsairs in capturing Spaniards, the Moriscos underwent their own experience of captivity within Spain. Despite claims for their essential Spanishness by advocates such as Núñez Muley, during the revolt of the Alpujarras the Moriscos were routinely taken captive as spoils of war and sold as slaves. In the 1570s, transactions for redeeming captives were as complicated between the different towns of Andalucía as between Spain and the Barbary States.[36] The notary documents from the period offer a poignant glimpse of the Moriscos' precarious standing and their tenuous hold on liberty: while some communities (and primarily their women and children) were summarily enslaved, others remained in a position to ransom their fellows, from the relative security of their perceived loyalty to Spain.[37]

The documents also provide a fascinating insight into the vexed question of the Moriscos' color, which apparently varied from one individual to the next, so that the records of slave sales and redemptions must specify the color of the person described: "de color moreno," "de color negra," "de color blanco que tira un poco a membrillo cocho," and even, frequently, "de color blanca" ["tawny," "black," "white tending to cooked quince," and "white"].[38] The fact that all these different shades are detailed makes it impossible to establish any standard physical appearance for Moriscos, and explains how at least some of them could have easily passed for Old Christians. So indistinguishable were certain Moriscos from "real" Spaniards that they could even pass for such in a Muslim context, seriously complicating the negotiations for redeeming captives from North Africa. The state felt the need to instruct the redemptionist religious orders to "watch with great vigilance that the captives you redeem are not Moriscos expelled from this kingdom."[39] These instructions seem to get at the very heart of the Morisco problem: how could they be persecuted and eventually targeted for expulsion from Spain as a threat to the homogeneous nation, and yet also be identified incorrectly as "real" Spaniards in desperate need of repatriation?

More than forty years after the revolt of the Alpujarras, the expulsion decrees provided another opportunity for Christians to acquire Morisco slaves. While adults were summarily expelled, the authorities often forced young Morisco children to remain in Spain, in order to "save" them for Christianity. They then sold them as slaves to Old Christians who would guard their spiritual well-being.[40] The captivity and forced conversion of these Moriscos, too young to resist Christianity, is the dark double of the Spanish fear that young Christian captives in North Africa would convert to Islam, and replicates at a much larger scale the abuses decried by the literature on captivity.

Captives' tales

Literary representations of Mediterranean piracy often focus on the problem of captivity and the threat it presents to a Christian identity. Spanish renegadoes, new or false converts to Christianity, fake captives – the frequent presence of such characters in Spanish depictions of piracy troubles the notion of a homogenous national identity based on an ancestral Christianity. The re-presentability of that identity in these accounts renders it both vulnerable and adulterate, and the image of Spaniards as defenders of the Faith, which Lope goes to such pains to construct in his *Dragontea*, is threatened by those actors who best mimic its attributes. In the murky world of captivity and redemption, religious and national identities become so many tradable commodities.

Although the topos of captivity harks back to Greek romances such as Heliodorus' *Æthiopica*, it acquires a new veneer of realism in the works of Cervantes, who was himself held captive in Algiers for five years.[41] Cervantes stresses that his own experience guarantees the authenticity of his Algerian play, *Los baños de Argel*: "No de la imaginación/ este trato se sacó/ que la verdad lo fraguó/ bien lejos de la ficción"[42] [This business was not taken from imagination but rather forged by truth, very far from fiction], although literary elements nonetheless abound in the plot. The historical context for Cervantes' writing career – a Mediterranean world full of dubious transactions of commerce and identity – accounts in part for his complex use of such models, and makes his work a remarkably rich trove for assessing Spanish attitudes towards Islam. While Islam plays a significant role in a large portion of Cervantes' writings, from the plays and novellas to the longer prose works, I will focus here on those texts that anatomize the relationship between the experience of captivity and Spanish identity.[43]

The more orthodox version of this relationship echoes the certainties of Lope: it features a heroic, resistant Christian subjectivity unmoved by the advisability of converting, even strategically or temporarily, to Islam. This is the vision of captivity portrayed in the fourth part of Haedo's *Topografía*, an account of the "martyrs" of Algiers. Here Haedo, who elsewhere presents a more compassionate (and realistic) account of the doubts to which captivity can lead the faithful, stresses the unwavering faith of Spaniards who die stoically, with the name of Jesus on their lips.[44] In Cervantes' earliest surviving play, *El trato de Argel* (ca. 1582), the heroic Christian role is played by a captive named Saavedra – a name choice that hints, perhaps, at the author Cervantes Saavedra's identification with the character. In order to convey its propagandistic anti-Islamic message, the play proceeds so haltingly that the plot barely advances. The main story of lovestruck Moorish masters falling for their Spanish captives (upon which Massinger was to base his *Renegado*) limps along, as Cervantes stages scene after static scene of stalwart Christians proclaiming that they will remain so against all obstacles. The most bombastic rhetoric surrounds the (offstage) torture and killing of an innocent priest, in retribution for the burning in Spain of a renegade Morisco who had become a dangerous corsair. This shadowy figure represents the Spanish fear of an internal threat: "de Cristo había renegado/ y en Africa se pasó,/ y que por su industria y manos,/ traidores tratos esquivos,/habían sido cautivos/ más de seiscientos cristianos" (509–514) [he was a renegade from Christ and had gone to Africa, and by his industry and hands, his treacherous dealings, more than six hundred Christians had been taken captive]. Although loosely based on a true story,[45] the scene of Algerian Moors united to take revenge on a Christian for the death of a Morisco in Spain suggests a tighter connection between the two scenarios – and a more religiously inflected singularity of purpose to the corsair adventures – than was in fact the case. As in *La Dragontea*, the text underscores the religious dimension of the struggle against pirates, while ignoring its geopolitical and economic dimensions. Moreover, the scene glosses over the usual freedom of conscience that the Christians enjoyed in Muslim Africa: Friedman points out that captives were allowed to hold Mass and perform all religious observances; they were also rarely forced to apostatize, since their economic worth to their captors evaporated with their conversion.[46]

Cervantes depicts Spanish captives less exemplary than Saavedra at constant risk of becoming renegadoes (as Christian Religion had warned in *La Dragontea*), either because they are too young to understand the consequences of their actions or because they understand only too well the advantages to be gained from conversion to Islam. The play's most interesting discussion of apostasy centers around the figure of Pedro, a picaresque captive who is truly making the best of things by spying for the king of Algiers and selling to credulous Christians places on his nonexistent escape boat. He claims to be getting richer in Algiers than he ever was in Spain, despite having fought in the uprising in the Alpujarras for nine months (2075–77). In North Africa, he can fleece Christians and Moors alike.

The logical next step would seem for Pedro to convert to Islam, which would afford him even greater liberty of action. The *pícaro* confesses his intentions to the good Christian Saavedra:

Ni niego a Cristo ni en Mahoma creo;
con la voz y el vestido seré moro,
por alcanzar el fin que no poseo.
Si voy en corso, séme yo de coro
que, en tocando en la tierra de cristianos,
me huiré, y aun no vacío de tesoro.   (2150–55)

[I neither deny Christ nor believe in Mohammed; with my language and dress I shall be a Moor, to achieve my ends. If I go out as a corsair, I know full well that when I land on Christian soil I shall be able to escape, and not without treasure, either.]

But Saavedra – the exemplary Christian – refuses to accept the expediency of conversion for the sake of liberty.[47] He insists that the very miming of Islam will damn Pedro, and that his resolve to remain "here, in my heart, always a Christian" is not enough. Here, Christianity seems to require its own performance: its essence resides in its accidental manifestations – the same argument Deza used to counter Núñez Muley's pleas for tolerance, as discussed in Chapter 4. Saavedra thus eschews the opportunities of picaresque performance in favor of Christian resignation; bereft of trans-formative strategies, the play ends with a clunky deus ex machina in the form of an expedition of friar-redemptors from Spain. Self-transform-ation, the play suggests, is an unreliable way out, one that presents too many risks for Christian identity. Here, true Christianity seems to require a timeless uniformity, a consistent commitment, and, to some extent, the relinquishing of personal agency.

"¡Cuán cara eres de haber, oh dulce España!"

Cervantes reworks the basic plot of *El trato de Argel* in his later comedia *Los baños de Argel* (published 1615), which includes a good deal more lively action. The play opens with corsairs attacking a coastal town in Spain, enabled by the renegade Yzuf, who knows the territory like the palm of his hand: "Nací y crecí, cual dije, en esta tierra,/ y sé bien sus entradas y salidas/ y la parte mejor de hacerle guerra" (10–12) [As I said, I was born and raised in this land, and know well the ways in and out, and the best places to make war on it]. Yzuf's detailed knowledge of the coast renders his home town supremely vulnerable to the corsair's attack, and dozens of captives are taken, including his uncle and nephews.

The play contrasts Yzuf's perfidy to the goodness of Hazén, a renegade who intends to renege again – i.e. return to Christianity – and make his way to Spain:

                                  soy
buen cristiano en lo escondido

y quizá hallaré ocasión
para quedarme en la tierra
para mí de promisión.   (395–99)

[I am a good Christian undercover, and perhaps I will find an opportunity to stay in
what is for me the promised land.]

Yet, although Hazén shares the firm commitment to Christianity in the
face of danger that is the mark of a strong Spanish identity, that commitment must be certified by others, because he appears to be an infidel.[48]
Indeed, the Christian captives in Algiers meet him with mumbled insults
("*perro* . . .") until he reveals his secret purpose of becoming a counter-
renegade. He begs them for their signatures to guarantee that he has been
good to them, and had been forced to convert as a child (again, as
Christian Religion had lamented in *La Dragontea*).[49] The captives praise
Hazén's secret Christianity (400–09); because his dissimulation tends towards a final conversion from Islam, it proves far less problematic than
Pedro's proposed "temporary" conversion to Islam in *El trato de Argel*.
Yet it remains questionable whether such an opaque figure, adept at
dissimulation and marked by his experience of Islam, can find a place
within Spain.

The climactic encounter between good and bad renegadoes comes when
Hazén reproaches Yzuf for his recent attack against what was once his
homeland. Hazén becomes more and more incensed as he recounts Yzuf's
offenses against Spain: "¿Contra tu patria levantas la espada? . . . ¿No te
espanta haber vendido a tu tío y tus sobrinos y a tu patría, descreído?"
(797–804) [Do you raise your sword against your native land? Are you not
horrified at having sold your uncle and your nephews and your land,
unbeliever?]. Finally, carried away by the force of his own accusations, he
stabs Yzuf to death. Particularly intriguing in this scene is Hazén's rhetorical transformation of Yzuf into a Spaniard, whose fatherland is unques-
tionably Spain. The lapsed Christian Yzuf must be compelled to return to
the fold, although the play gives little evidence that Yzuf was an Old
Christian. If Yzuf had in fact been instead a Morisco or New Christian
forced to leave Spain, then the Spanishness that Hazén holds out as a
reproach would have been beyond him, for he would have been targeted
precisely as a *non*-Spaniard within Spain.

One explanation for Hazén's generous inclusion of the dubious renegado Yzuf in the Spanish polity clearly lies in his own indeterminate
status: here is an *avowed* Christian who must nonetheless be certified by
true Christians before he can make his way to Spain as a counter-renegade.
The text carefully avoids the problem of Hazén's reinsertion into Spanish
society by having him die a martyr, condemned for the death of Yzuf,

while still in Algiers. The scene grants him the exalted status of a Christian martyr while preempting all questions of his eventual inclusion within Spain. Thus the strongest case for the essential Spanishness of those who have crossed over to Islam is presented by a liminal character who is never able to return to the fold, even though he devoutly wishes it. The scourge of vengeful renegadoes is not enough to make Spain open its borders to all those who would be Spanish. The refrain the captives sing in their longing: "¡Cuán cara eres de haber, oh dulce España!" (1407, 1420) [how dear you are to have, oh sweet Spain!], ironically voices the situation of the repentant renegadoes – or exiled Moriscos – who can never attain their "promised land."

A welcome romance

The central plot of *Los baños de Argel* suggests that perhaps Spain is only accessible to such marginal figures when the devices of romance erase the boundaries and obstacles that bar their way. This story tells of a captive, Don Lope, redeemed by the gold of Zara, a Moor eager to convert to Christianity – a variation of the famous "Captive's Tale" from *Don Quijote*, Part I (1605).[50] Introduced to Christianity by an old female captive, Zara is determined to get to Spain and become a Christian, and enlists Don Lope to arrange the escape using her considerable wealth. This romanticized narrative suggests that a man of strong Christian faith may well survive the experience of captivity to emerge magically equipped with a beautiful and rich wife. But perhaps what it romanticizes most fully is the possibility of a welcome for Zara: although it never follows her there, it suggests a Spain that welcomes converts with open arms, regardless of their origins. The romance of the tale, however, masks the reality of Spain at the turn of the seventeenth century, where being a New Christian was a suspect and vulnerable state, and mere conversion could not confer the benefits of Spanishness upon even the most devout Moor. Could an actual Moorish woman, no matter how rich, beautiful, or devout, have been welcomed in Spain? It seems highly unlikely – her language, dress, eating habits, and even the "taint" of her blood would probably have made her *essentially* unwelcome. As Hazén's unsatisfied longing in the same play suggests, the lived experience of Islam could make Spain unattainable for ambiguous figures like the would-be counter-renegades; only the conventions of romance hold out any promise of inclusion for Zara.

The far more complex version of the tale in *Don Quijote* actually follows the captive, here named Ruy Pérez de Viedma, and the beautiful Moor Zoraida to Spain.[51] When they arrive at the inn where Don Quijote is staying, Zoraida's beauty and her exotic garb excite everyone's curiosity, and the captive is asked to tell their story. It seems clear from the tale that Zoraida has always been intent on leaving her father's house for Spain and Christianity – what is less clear is that she understands what Christianity is all about. For while on the one hand Zoraida functions as a virtual captive, as desperate to escape Algiers as any Christian slave, on the other hand she is a counter-renegade like Hazén, whose allegiance to Christianity requires certification.

In this version of the story, Zoraida finances the escape with money stolen from her father's house, and a friendly renegado orchestrates it. Ruy Pérez's own role pales by comparison – Zoraida does not even care if he marries her, as long as he gets her to Spain, and her abundant funds stand in for any heroism that might have been necessary on his part.[52] Agi Morato, her rich father, is presented as a most sympathetic character, whose heart breaks when his ungrateful daughter robs and abandons him. Her disloyalty to her father undoes the tidy correspondences between ethical behavior and Christian faith. As if to underscore this, the tale tells how the fugitives abandon Agi Morato, whom they have been forced to take with them, on the cape named after the "Cava Rumía" – the Florinda of legend who betrayed Spain to the Moors:

es llamado el de la *Cava Rumía*, que en nuestra lengua quiere decir la *mala mujer cristiana*; y es tradición entre los moros que en aquel lugar está enterrada la Cava, por quien se perdió España, porque *cava* en su lengua quiere decir *mujer mala* y *rumía*, *cristiana*; y aun tienen por mal agüero llegar allí a dar fondo cuando la necesidad les fuerza a ello, porque nunca le dan sin ella; puesto que para nosotros no fue abrigo de mala mujer, sino puerto seguro de nuestro remedio, según andaba alterada la mar.[53]

[called by the Moors that of the *Cava Rumía*, which in our language means the *wicked Christian woman*, and it is a tradition among the Moors that La Cava, through whom Spain was lost, is buried there – *cava* in their language means *wicked woman*, and *rumía*, *Christian*. They consider it unlucky to anchor there even when forced to by necessity, and they never do so otherwise. Yet for us it was not the shelter of the wicked woman, but a haven of safety from the angry sea.]

The repeated emphasis on female treachery in this passage, with a double translation to underscore female duplicity, points an accusing finger at this daughter who must betray her earthly father for the sake of religion.[54] If the Cava Rumía of legend gave Spain away to the Moors, this new evil Christian woman betrays her Moorish father to the Spanish captives.

When the escaped captives finally arrive on a desolate coast in Spain, the Moorish dress of Zoraida and the renegado so alarms a local shepherd that he runs for help, shouting, "¡Moros, moros! ¡Arma, arma!" (I. 509) [Moors, Moors! To arms! To arms!]. Clearly, the Christian conviction of these characters cannot be perceived at first glance. After sorting out that confusion, Zoraida is taken to church for the first time, where she learns to recognize religious images as versions of Lela Marién. Although she has claimed to be a Christian all along, she has in fact very little knowledge of theology and Christian ritual. When questioned at the inn, Ruy Pérez confesses that she has not yet been baptized:

– No ha habido lugar para ello – respondió el captivo – después que salió de Argel, su patria y tierra, y hasta agora no se ha visto en peligro de muerte tan cercana, que obligase a baptizalla sin que supiese primero todas las ceremonias que nuestra Madre la Santa Iglesia manda, pero Dios será servido que presto se bautice con la decencia que la calidad de su persona merece, que es más de lo que muestra su hábito y el mío. (I. 467)

["There has been no time to do so," he replied, "since we left Algiers, her country and her homeland, and until now she has not been so close to death as to oblige us to baptize her without her first knowing all the ceremonies that Our Holy Mother the Church requires. But please God that she soon be baptized in a manner befitting a person of her rank, which is greater than her dress or mine suggest."]

Ruy Pérez's version of events is surely questionable – his own subsequent narrative relates in great detail situations (such as being attacked by French corsairs and set adrift in a small boat) that would seem to call for immediate baptism in order to safeguard Zoraida's soul from the instant peril of death. The Spaniard's concern here for the authenticity of Zoraida's baptism, when it finally occurs, and his insistence that she must first master the complexities of Christian ritual, suggests that Cervantes is obliquely addressing the forced conversions of Moriscos in Spain. Soon after the fall of Granada, mass conversions became the Church's favored method for Christianizing Moors; unlike them, Zoraida is to be instructed before being baptized.[55] And unlike the Moriscos targeted by the Inquisition at the end of the century, she neither becomes an object of suspicion nor forfeits her place in Spain when her initial claims to be a (New) Christian are proved hollow by her ignorance of Christian forms. The exotic, and highly romanticized, foreigner seems to find a place in Spain far more easily than those suspect domestic others, the Moriscos.[56]

Despite the complex portrayal of Zoraida's filial impiety as a blot on her religious devotion, and her ignorance of Christianity, she is welcomed into Spain with open arms. Although when she arrives at the inn she still speaks no Spanish, wears Moorish clothes, and has not been baptized, there is no question that she will be transformed into a proper Spaniard, even if we barely hear her own opinion on the matter. (Notice that the whole story has been related by the captive; Zoraida's single intervention, in basic Spanish, is to insist that she be called María and not Zoraida.) The appeal of the story is such that authenticity hardly seems an issue. But the magic of romance is sorely taxed: in this case, in order to achieve the Moor's conversion and her religious "repatriation," the Spaniards must both overlook her ethical lapses – which the text underscores – and be willing to accept a flawed, incomplete Christian subject. The barriers for non-fictional converts were, as I have suggested, significantly higher.

Performing captivity

Porque no hay negro en España
ni esclavo en Argel se vende
que no tenga mejor vida
que un farsante, si se advierte . . .

Agustín de Rojas, *Viaje entretenido* [57]

Dramas of captivity may challenge the ideological certainties of Spanish identity even when they occur safely within Spain. Such is the case in the episode of the false captives in Cervantes' last novel, the Byzantine *Los trabajos de Persiles y Sigismunda* (published posthumously in 1617). In their travels, the protagonists come to a small town where two young captives, newly rescued, relate their sad story in the town square to wring alms out of passersby. These glib survivors put on an elaborate show for money, displaying on a canvas the central elements of their story: Algiers, the galley where they were forced to row, the corsair captains. They read the canvas as though it were a book, and pepper their tale with words in Arabic and the infamous names of corsairs and renegadoes. Suspicious of their story, the mayor of the town, a former captive himself, decides to quiz them on the particulars of captivity, to which one of the would-be captives responds with a flood of words, in a vain attempt to hide his ignorance.

When caught in his lies and threatened with punishment, the young man, apparently an enterprising student from Salamanca, begs the authorities not to punish them for a trifle. In doing so, he claims, the mayor would deprive the king of two valiant soldiers, "for we were going to Italy and Flanders to break, smash, maim, and kill all the enemies of the holy Catholic faith we might run into."[58] With such authentic champions, one might observe, the Church hardly needs any enemies. The pursuit of Catholic empire seems doubly compromised in this satire: not only is the fealty of these young would-be soldiers somewhat suspect, but their enlistment actually depends on the collapse of a previous performance, in which they play Catholic victims rather than conquerors. The performance of captivity is presented as a common trade that spreads through the land: these fake captives bought their Algerian props and learned their tale from another troupe, "though they, too, like us now, were probably counterfeit" (249). Despite Rojas' claim, in the epigraph to this section, that no life was harder than the actor's, the trade in misfortunes appears more profitable, and certainly safer, than the soldier's life. We are a long way from *El trato de Argel,* where the authenticity of the captive's experience served to cement a Christian Spanish identity. In the Spain depicted in the *Persiles,* the performance of captivity is far more common than the real thing; the currency of suffering has become disconnected from any real referent, and serves mostly to yield profits.

Most surprisingly, the only real captive in this episode, the astute mayor who discovers the ruse, comes around and forgives the students their trespass against his own authentic sufferings. His authority on matters Algerian strangely cancels out his political and civic authority, as he not only condones but encourages the mimicry of captivity. After threatening for a while to punish the students, he relents and invites them to his house in order to teach them the real story, bequeathing upon them his own authenticity: "les quiero dar una lición de las cosas de Argel, tal que de aquí en adelante ninguno les coja en mal latín, en cuanto a su fingida historia"[59] [I'll teach them a lesson on things about Algiers, so that from now on no one will catch them [with bad Latin, where their faked story is concerned]]. The pedagogy is somewhat perverse: the mayor teaches the truth so that the students can better pass off their simulacrum. The problem is again one of verisimilitude: the performance of the false captives – presumably improved by the mayor's teachings – undoes the authenticity of a resistant Spanish identity by suggesting that it can be successfully pirated.[60] Even those characters in the story with the greatest authority – political, personal, and moral – seem to have accepted the fact that captivity no longer serves as a test for true Spanish virtue; as a reproducible, representable phenomenon, it has become the stuff of spectacle. Yet even when exposed as frauds, the captives' tales retain their appeal, an appeal that has somehow become separated from the ideological reaffirmation they ostensibly provided.

Whether they depend on discreet dissimulation, romance convention, or overt performance, the stagings of opaque selves in Cervantes' texts suggest the difficulty of distinguishing the true Spaniard from the pirated, or piratical, copy. Identity remains surprisingly fluid in these representations, despite, or perhaps because of, the Counter-Reformation context in which they were written. Whether they exist within Spain or menace it from North Africa, renegadoes, Christian Moors, and false captives complicate the consolidation of Spanish identity around notions of timeless Christianity and pure blood. In many of these tales, it is not clear what constitutes an authentic commitment to Christianity, or where a Spanish identity begins or ends – the individual cases challenge the usefulness of any blanket definitions.

Whereas the representation of piracy as a clash of religions in Lope's *La Dragontea* and Cervantes' early play *El trato de Argel* presents Spain as a nation of devoted Christians on a holy imperial mission, the transactions of religious identity in later Cervantine tales of captivity profoundly question the parameters of that mission, and its exclusionary force. These accounts of captivity do not in fact serve to distinguish true Christians from false ones – they only complicate matters further by suggesting that religious identity can be lost and found, strategically hidden, or vociferously adopted. Moreover, these tales of ambiguity in the *baños* of North Africa and the Mediterranean in-between powerfully engage also the domestic space of Spain, where the Moriscos, as unconvincing Christians, were denied a full Spanish identity. They suggest a more permeable Spain, where the Moors have not only landed at the coast, as the old warning would have it, but are intimately ensconced – albeit unwelcome – within the porous territory of Spain's national imaginary.

Conclusion: *Contra* originality

Scratch a Russian and you find a Tartar. Scratch a Spaniard and you find a Saracen.

Gertrude Stein, Everybody's Autobiography

¡Si parecen españoles!

Fernando Trueba, La niña de tus ojos.[1]

In our post-romantic era, we still assign disproportionate value to originals – this, we feel, makes us discriminating critics and connoisseurs. The legacy of romanticism also encourages us to think of resistance – especially cultural resistance – as an original gesture that upends established hierarchies. My larger aim in this project has been to question the privileging of originality by suggesting how closely it is tied to exclusion and political discrimination. I have argued instead for a revaluation of imitation as a cultural and political practice that challenges established national narratives. The early modern confrontations that I have traced throughout suggest that the most interesting mode of resistance to orthodox ideologies of exclusion may often be imitation with a difference. In the face of repressive attempts at homogenization, a calculated deployment of similarity often proves more effective, and more strategically feasible, than the defense of difference.

Mimesis poses a particular challenge to early modern national and imperial identities predicated on exceptionalism and ethnoreligious homogeneity. In the first place, similarity bridges the divide between self and Other. Where ideologies of difference seek to solidify distinctions, mimesis recalls underlying likenesses. Moreover, it undermines the original by showing how easily it can be reproduced, despite claims to singular entitlement. The exceptionalism of Spain's Catholic destiny; England's belated imperial mission, itself imitative; Europe's putative cultural superiority vis-à-vis both Islam and New World cultures – all are surprisingly vulnerable to imitation.

Expanding the notion of mimesis from literary to cultural, religious, and political exchanges enables the relocation of what is fundamentally a deconstructive insight – the power of the imitator to destabilize the original – squarely within a historical context. As I have shown, the dynamics of pointed imitation are comparable whether the problem is one of literary verisimilitude in a transatlantic context, of religious facsimiles in Granada, or of cultural impersonation on any number of imperial stages. As a theoretical concept, cultural mimesis is particularly suited for comparing disparate but related sites, such as the transatlantic and the Mediterranean. The comparison reveals both how imperial competition dilutes imperial ideologies and how resistance itself may translate from one contact-zone to another. The deliberate enactment of imitation as a strategy for inclusion links New World subjects such as Inca Garcilaso de la Vega and Pablo Nazareo de Xalcotán with Morisco advocates such as Francisco Núñez Muley and Miguel de Luna. Tasso, Ercilla, and Lope de Vega's late sixteenth-century epics all reflect a similar anxiety about the limits of literary imitation as a device of imperial ideology. The threat of unauthorized or ambiguous agents who usurp *imperium* pervades English pirate plays and the Spanish literature on Islam, as authors from Pérez de Hita to Cervantes to Heywood chart the counterfeiting of national identity.

But these are only my own privileged cases. There are clearly other early modern encounters that might benefit from a similar reading: the relation between colonizer and colonized in the Elizabethan conquest of Ireland, fundamentally complicated by a whole class of earlier mimetic conquerors; the position of Spanish *conversos*, who were sometimes grouped with the Moriscos but often performed national identity from positions of much greater political power; the competition among European powers and their efforts to construct their own racial and national difference in the Spice Islands. My purpose is not to forge mimesis into the all-purpose key that unlocks every imperial conundrum – that would in itself constitute an exclusionary gesture. Instead, I hope to have shown that while the operations of mimesis vary across different imperial stages, the manipulation of sameness and difference appears as a constant preoccupation.

The years since I began this project have seen a new wave of work on the early modern period that crosses traditional geographic and disciplinary boundaries in order to examine a wide range of imperial relations. These studies on the connections between England and Islam, on the transatlantic aspects of "Golden Age" fictions, and on the cultural dimension of Anglo-Spanish relations, inter alia, suggest the rich possibilities of theoretical approaches across disciplinary fractures that connect problems previously divided by an unreflective acceptance of difference. Moreover, as the study of empire expands to consider *imperium*, in its internal as well as external incarnation, the concept of cultural mimesis serves to challenge our received notions of the inevitability of early modern national consolidation. Instead of originality and singularity, this focus reveals a panorama of vivid imitations, contested origins, and transparent contaminations.

As such, the study of mimesis recovers the fragility and tentativeness of the originary exclusions that continue to color our world today. Without ignoring the specificity of early modern conflicts, it is useful to remember the long pre-history of modern structures of discrimination. My twentieth-century epigraphs suggest the connections between the early modern dynamics of internal and external colonialism and their more recent avatars. Stein playfully rehearses Western prejudices against Russia and Spain as less-than-European, while underscoring these European nations' own self-fashioning through homogenizing repression. Trueba's 1998 film portrays a company of Spanish actors engaged in a co-production with Nazi Germany. When Jewish prisoners are brought in to play Andalusian extras, the Spanish producer speaks the unspeakable: the Jews make perfectly good Spaniards. The scene collapses the distance between the Nazis' racialized persecution of Jews and Spain's own efforts to excise all traces of its Semitic culture in the early modern period, all while humorously suggesting the futility of such efforts: the Spaniards still look Semitic; the Jews Spanish.

The problems with basing national identity on racial, ethnic, or religious homogeneity have never really left us. The recent failure of anything remotely approaching *convivencia* in the Balkans or Northern Ireland; violent Russian efforts to incorporate the Caucasus on Russian terms; attacks on North African and Turkish immigrants across Europe; the uneasy reformulation of ethnic identities as Great Britain undergoes devolution into its constituent parts; the continued struggles over the constitution of truly multi-ethnic nations in so many parts of Central and South America – these are all problems intimately connected to the early modern history of *imperium* that I have charted here. They reveal the pressing stakes in identifying similarity when difference is much touted, in reading dominant cultures *contra* originality, and in revealing the often transformative power of mimesis. By exposing the constructedness of homogeneity, challenging and ironizing narratives of difference, and effectively enabling subjects to cross boundaries, mimesis introduces or preserves cultural variance under the guise of similarity.

Notes

INTRODUCTION

1 The account of the viceroy's entrance into Cuzco is based on text in Stephen Clissold, *Conquistador* (London: Derek Verschoyle, 1954), 64. The second account is quoted in Samuel Chew, *The Crescent and the Rose: Islam and England during the Renaissance* (New York: Oxford University Press, 1937), 462.

2 I purposely use the term Islam here to recall the European confusion between the very different groups – Moors, Turks, Saracens, and so forth – which were perceived as a cultural and military boundary to Europe in the sixteenth and early seventeenth centuries.

3 Some of the main proponents of such theories of imitation were the Spanish Arabist Julián Ribera y Tarragó and the French philosopher and sociologist Gabriel Tarde. An overview of these theories can be found in R. P. Pinard de la Boullaye, "Le mouvement historique en ethnologie," *Semaine Internationale d'Ethnologie Religieuse* (1925): 33–46.

4 Hayden White, *Tropics of Discourse: Essays in Cultural Criticism* (Baltimore: Johns Hopkins University Press, 1978), 70 and passim.

5 Ibid., 4.

6 While Stephen Greenblatt, for one, has alerted us to the powers of representation, conceptualizing mimesis in Marxist terms as a social relation of production, so that "representations are not only products but producers, capable of decisively altering the very forces that brought them into being," his formulation concerns representation in general rather than pointed imitation or mimicry. Joseph Roach's fascinating study of performance and memory focuses on the dynamics of *surrogation* to suggest how the reproduction of cultures transforms them even while rehearsing them. See Greenblatt, *Marvelous Possessions: The Wonder of the New World* (Chicago: University of Chicago Press, 1991), 6, and Roach, *Cities of the Dead: Circum-Atlantic Performance* (New York: Columbia University Press, 1996).

7 René Girard, *"To double business bound": Essays on Literature, Mimesis, and Anthropology* (Baltimore: Johns Hopkins University Press, 1978), vii.

8 Michael Taussig, *Mimesis and Alterity: A Particular History of the Senses* (London: Routledge, 1993), 21.

9 Ibid., 237.

10 Homi Bhabha, "Of Mimicry and Man: The Ambivalence of Colonial

Discourse," in his *The Location of Culture* (London: Routledge, 1994), 85. The essay originally appeared in *October: Anthology*, 1987.

11 Ibid., 88.

12 Roach, *Cities*, 6.

13 Francisco López de Gómara, *Historia general de las Indias* (1552), 2 vols. (Madrid: Espasa Calpe, 1932), I.8.

14 In "Reconquista and Conquista" (*Homage to Irving A. Leonard*, ed. Raquel Chang-Rodríguez and Donald A. Yates [New York: Mensaje, 1977]), Charles Gibson points out that the very term *reconquista* is an eighteenth-century neologism, so that the linguistic analogy – Reconquista/Conquista – can only be made from our retrospective point of view (21).

15 María Rosa Menocal, *Shards of Love: Exile and the Origins of the Lyric* (Durham: Duke University Press, 1994), 45, 211–12.

16 The small corpus of Morisco texts written in Hispanicized Arabic during this period provides a version of the Morisco's experience in Spain in their own words. See Luce López-Baralt, *Islam in Spanish Literature, from the Middle Ages to the Present*, trans. Andrew Hurley (New York: Brill, 1992). For Islam's relation to England, see the recent work of Nabil Matar, *Islam in Britain, 1558–1685* (Cambridge, England: Cambridge University Press, 1998), and *Turks, Moors, and Englishmen in the Age of Discovery* (New York: Columbia University Press, 1999).

I   TRUTH, FICTIONS, AND THE NEW WORLD

1 For a good summary of the moralists' opposition to romances of chivalry, see Ida Rodríguez Prampolini, *Amadises de América: La hazaña de Indias como empresa caballeresca*, second edition (Caracas: Centro de Estudios Latinoamericanos Rómulo Gallegos, 1977).

2 See Rolena Adorno, "La construcción cultural de la alteridad: el sujeto colonial y el discurso caballeresco," *Primer Simposio de Filología Iberoamericana, Facultad de Filología, Universidad de Sevilla* (Zaragoza: Pórtico, 1990).

3 Irving Leonard, *Books of the Brave*, second edition (Berkeley: University of California Press, 1992). See especially Chapter 7.

4 José Torre Revello reproduces the documents from the Archivo General de Indias related to the circulation of books in the New World in the appendix to his *El libro, la imprenta y el periodismo en América durante la dominación española* (Buenos Aires: Publicaciones del Instituto de Investigaciones Históricas, 1940). I have modernized the spelling of the decrees.

5 A note on the term "romance": in sixteenth-century Spanish, it did not connote the *novelas de caballerías* or the Italian *romanzo*. Covarrubias (*Tesoro de la lengua castellana o española*, ed. Martín de Riquer [Barcelona: Alta Fulla, 1998]) gives as its only meaning "el lenguage que oy se usa"; the term was also used for traditional ballads. It is nonetheless clear that the decrees refer to chivalric romances; the second one, which I cite below, even gives *Amadis* as an example of the dangerous books making their way to the New World. Thus when I use the term in English, I am in fact referring to that literary mode that exercised both censors and literary theorists of the period.

6 Torre Revello, *El libro*, v.

7 For an analysis of romance's erring waywardness, see Patricia Parker's seminal study, *Inescapable Romance* (Princeton: Princeton University Press, 1979).

8 Torre Revello provides an account of the exportation of Ariosto to the Spanish colonies in the New World (223). *Orlando Furioso* was translated as early as 1543 and exported under the title *Caballerías de Orlando en prosa*. Leonard cites the reports filed when the Inquisition inspected the books on incoming ships (including passengers' baggage) to note that the *Furioso*, in either the original Italian or the Spanish translation, is mentioned more often than any of the chivalric romances (163). It thus seems certain that such an exuberantly inventive text as the *Furioso* was included in the condemnations of romance in the New World.

9 Ludovico Ariosto, *Orlando Furioso* (Vicenza: Mondadori, 1976), 35. 26–29.

10 Ariosto, *Orlando Furioso*, trans. Guido Waldman (Oxford: Oxford University Press, 1974).

11 Not surprisingly, John's "revelations" suggest that the most important myth for male rulers to propagate is that of imperial might; for their consorts, as for female rulers, chastity is the central concern.

12 Parker, *Inescapable Romance*, 51. For a similar reading, see also David Quint, "Astolfo's Voyage to the Moon," *Yale Italian Studies*, o. s. 1 (1977): 398–408. Other critics read St. John's claim as less profoundly subversive. Robert Durling suggests that Ariosto's praise of his own patron earlier in the canto guarantees, as it were, the counter-irony of the Evangelist's claims (*The Figure of the Poet in the Renaissance Epic* [Cambridge, Mass.: Harvard University Press, 1965], 149), a reading that Quint disputes in *Origins and Originality in Renaissance Literature* (New Haven: Yale University Press, 1983), 88–90. Albert Ascoli, on the other hand, suggests that St. John's claims constitute an undecidable "double paradox," for the Evangelist expects the reader to believe in the truth of his claim that he, like other writers, has lied. For Ascoli, "the poem is suspended between inauthenticity and authenticity, blasphemy and belief" (*Ariosto's Bitter Harmony: Crisis and Evasion in the Italian Renaissance* [Princeton: Princeton University Press, 1987], 300–301).

13 Ascoli imagines two possible kinds of imitation: "Is John an 'imitator di Cristo' in the sense that his words are a poetic imitation which create and sustain the fiction of Christ's divinity? Or . . . in the sense that his words derive from, and point toward, the truth of the 'Verbo Incarnato'?" (301).

14 Leonard, *Books of the Brave*, 25 and passim. Although Leonard grants that the influence of the romances "does not lend itself to exact measurement," the hypothesis is highly persuasive. For other discussions of the influence of imaginative fiction on the Spanish explorers, see Rodríguez Prampolini, *Amadises de América*, Luis Weckmann, *La herencia medieval de México* (México: Colegio de México, 1984); Juan Gil, *Mitos y utopías del descubrimiento* (Madrid: Alianza, 1989); and Adorno, "La construcción cultural de la alteridad."

15 Clearly, the model is not a straightforward one, combining, as it does, the wanderings of romance with more teleological imperial and erotic pursuits. Petrarchan models of desire and female perversity – such as the elusive

Amazons – are central to what one might call "conquest by tantalization."
16 Leonard, *Books of the Brave*, 36.
17 Adorno, "La construcción cultural," 157.
18 Juan Gil, "El latín en América: lengua general y lengua de elite," *Primer Simposio de Filología Iberoamericana, Facultad de Filología, Universidad de Sevilla* (Zaragoza: Pórtico, 1990), 116–17.
19 Pilar Gonzalbo Aizpuru, *Historia de la educación en la época colonial: El mundo indígena* (México: Colegio de México, 1990), 36.
20 For the way indigenous writers used this argument in Peru, see Chapter 3.
21 Gil, "El latín en América," 119.
22 For a detailed discussion of Nazareo's suit and his sources, see Gil, "El latín en América." Ignacio Osorio Romero reproduces the letters with a Spanish translation in *La enseñanza del latín a los indios* (México: Universidad Nacional Autónoma de México, 1990).
23 Gil, "El latín en América," 125–26.
24 Ibid., 127.
25 Taussig, *Mimesis and Alterity*, 49.
26 Gonzalbo Aizpuru, *Historia de la educación en la época colonial*, 37.
27 For an account of such practices as resistance among the Mayas, see Inga Clendinnen, "Landscape and World View: The Survival of Yucatec Maya Culture under Spanish Rule," *Comparative Studies in Society and History* 22 (1980): 374–93. Her focus on specific elements that have traditionally been considered a disadvantage for the Indians (fatalism, circular conception of time) as sources of cultural strength is especially powerful.
28 Gonzalbo Aizpuru, *Historia de la educación*, 121.
29 Cited in Osorio Romero, *La enseñanza del latín*, 61.
30 See Timothy Hampton, *Writing from History: The Rhetoric of Exemplarity in Renaissance Literature* (Ithaca: Cornell University Press, 1991), 82–83.
31 As Margaret Ferguson has so ably demonstrated in *Trials of Desire: Renaissance Defenses of Poetry* (New Haven: Yale University Press, 1983), the younger Tasso's need to justify his father's meandering romance seriously complicates his own rejection of Ariostan modes of romance.
32 For the role of America in Tasso's epic, see Sergio Zatti, *L'ombra del Tasso: Epica e romanzo nel Cinquecento* (Milano: Bruno Mondadori, 1996), especially the chapter entitled "Nouve terre, nuova scienza, nuova poesia: la profezia epica delle scoperte"; Theodore Cachey, "Tasso's *Navigazione del Mondo Nuovo* and the Origins of the Columbus Encomium," *Italica* 69.3 (1992): 326–43; and Jane Tylus, "Reasoning Away Colonialism: Tasso and the Production of the *Gerusalemme liberata*," *South Central Review* 10.2 (1993): 100–14.
33 Quint points out that, because of quarrels between the Duke of Ferrara and the Pope, "Tasso, the poet of the First Crusade, wrote under the patronage of one of the few major Italian courts that did not participate at Lepanto" (*Epic and Empire: Politics and Generic Form from Virgil to Milton* [Princeton: Princeton University Press, 1993], 223).
34 See the chapter entitled "Political Allegory in the *Liberata*" in ibid.
35 Ferguson, *Trials of Desire*, 54. See also Sergio Zatti's highly perceptive reading, *L'uniforme cristiano e il multiforme pagano: Saggio sulla* Gerusalemme liberata

(Milan: Il Saggiatore, 1983).

36 For a thorough account of the literary quarrels over Tasso's poem, see Bernard Weinberg, *A History of Literary Criticism in the Italian Renaissance*, 2 vols. (Chicago: University of Chicago Press, 1961).

37 Tasso, *Apologia della Gerusalemme liberata*, in *Scritti sull'arte poetica*, I, ed. Ettore Mazzali (Torino: Einaudi, 1977), 72.

38 Tasso, *Jerusalem Delivered*, trans. and ed. Ralph Nash (Detroit: Wayne State University Press, 1987), 468. The characterization of the poetry as monstrous also raises interesting connections to the European apprehension of the American marvelous through bestiaries.

39 Discourse I of *Discourses on the Art of Poetry*, from Lawrence Rhu, *The Genesis of Tasso's Narrative Theory: English Translations of the Early Poetics and a Comparative Study of Their Significance* (Detroit: Wayne State University Press, 1993), 103–104.

40 On Tasso's transformation of the epic motif, see Thomas Greene, *The Descent from Heaven: A Study in Epic Continuity* (New Haven: Yale University Press, 1963).

41 Discourse I, 105.

42 Tasso, *Discourses of the Heroic Poem*, trans. Mariella Cavalchini and Irene Samuel (London: Oxford University Press, 1973), 40.

43 Ibid., 50.

44 Ibid., 57.

45 Zatti, *L'ombra del Tasso*, 172.

46 Tasso, *Gerusalemme liberata*, ed. Lanfranco Caretti (Milano: Mondadori, 1979), 15.31–32. The translation is Nash's, with my corrections in brackets.

47 As Jane Tylus has noted, publishers and artists occasionally magnified this passage for their own purposes. The 1590 edition of the poem, printed in Genoa – birthplace of Columbus – features as its frontispiece "a portrait of the harbor of Genoa and just above it, a picture of Tasso himself . . . The poet is looking out from the harbor into the great West beyond." The engraving by Castello suggests the centrality of westward exploration in the poem's metaphorics, even if represented in the text primarily by the stanzas in Canto 15 (Tylus, "Reasoning Away Colonialism," 100).

48 Cachey provides a detailed reading of this earlier appearance of the New World in the poem, arguing that the Columbus encomium, which remains in the poem as a sign of Tasso's knowledge of and interest in New World matters, constitutes "the record of a polemical stance vis-à-vis the detractors of the Genoese among contemporary Spanish historiographers" (340).

49 Lanfranco Caretti's edition (Milano: Mondadori, 1979), for example, includes these stanzas in an appendix of "ottave estravaganti."

50 Cachey, "Tasso's *Navigazione*," 335.

51 The classic work on this topos is Bartlett Giamatti's *The Earthly Paradise and the Renaissance Epic* (Princeton: Princeton University Press, 1966), 179–210.

52 The fifteenth canto of the *Orlando Furioso* includes a similar prophecy to Astolfo by Andronica, the personification of Fortitude, as they sail *from* the witch Alcina's enchanted isle. Andronica's prophecy, unlike Fortuna's, describes both eastern and western voyages, and focuses on the political – i.e.

imperial – rather than the religious consequences of the discoveries for Charles V.

53 Zatti, *L'ombra del Tasso*, 171.

54 Ibid., 175; the translation is my own.

55 See also Tylus' brief account of this problem, "Reasoning Away Colonialism," 108.

56 Albert Ascoli describes Armida in these terms in "Liberating the Tomb: Difference and Death in *Gerusalemme liberata*," *Annali d'italianistica* 12 (1994): 159–80.

57 Clorinda, the beautiful pagan who was always meant to be a Christian, converts when the Christian warrior Tancredi deals her a fatal blow in combat [emphasis mine]:

> Ella, mentre cadea, la voce afflitta
> movendo, disse le parole estreme;
> parole ch'a lei novo un spirto ditta,
> spirto di fé, di carità, di speme:
> virtù ch'or Dio le infonde, e se rubella
> in vita fu, la vuole in morte *ancella*.   (12.65)

[She, while she was falling, with weakened voice was uttering her last words: words that a new spirit is teaching her, a spirit of faith, of charity, of hope: a grace that God now sheds upon her, and if she has been a rebel in her life, He wants her now in death His *handmaiden*].

58 Giamatti, *Earthly Paradise*, 210–11.

59 Tylus, "Reasoning Away Colonialism," 107–108. Tylus argues that the *Liberata* holds out the possibility of conversion as an "intensely emotional and individual" process, which operates by "holding others' identity in ambivalence and affirming in them a central sameness" (109). She thus contrasts conversion with Geoffrey's straightforward violence against religious others. Yet I cannot help but feel that the vision of conversion that Tylus presents is unrealistic and somewhat romanticized; throughout the sixteenth century, in the Americas as in Spain, conversions were more often than not violent and highly repressive. Conversion itself functioned as an unabashed tool of empire.

60 This central problem applied of course not only to the conversion of New World natives, but to the forced baptisms of Jews and Moors in Spain, and the often repeated conversions and recantations of subjects caught between Protestantism and Roman Catholicism, virtually across Europe.

61 Quint, *Origins and Originality*, 118.

2   LITERARY LOYALTIES, IMPERIAL BETRAYALS

1 Leonard, *Books of the Brave*, second edition (Berkeley: University of California Press, 1992), 118–19.

2 Recent readings of the *Aeneid* have identified a darker vision of empire in the poem and argued that it does not wholeheartedly support imperial ideology. Nevertheless, and regardless of the text's ambiguities, it is possible to consider the *Aeneid*, and especially its long and fruitful afterlife as a model for other

epic texts, as a primary example of the connections between epic and empire. In his powerful study of that title, Quint makes a distinction between epics of the winners and epics of the losers, placing the *Aeneid* squarely within the winners' camp. See especially chapters 1–2 of *Epic and Empire: Politics and Generic Form from Virgil to Milton* (Princeton: Princeton University Press, 1993).

3 The classic account of these debates is Lewis Hanke's *The Spanish Struggle for Justice in the Conquest of America* (Philadelphia: University of Pennsylvania Press, 1949). See also Anthony Pagden, *The Fall of Natural Man: The American Indian and the Origins of Comparative Ethnology* (Cambridge, England: Cambridge University Press, 1986).

4 Pagden, *Lords of All the World: Ideologies of Empire in Spain, Britain and France c.1500–c.1800* (New Haven: Yale University Press, 1995), 92.

5 This anxiety about loyalty to Philip accounts in part for Ercilla's repeated address to the king in his poem. For their textual relationship, see Carlos Albarracín Sarmiento "El poeta y su rey en *La Araucana*," *Filología* 21 (1986): 99–116. See also Quint, *Epic and Empire*, 172–74.

6 The term *araucano* was first used by Ercilla as a generic name for all indigenous peoples in the region of Arauco, in Southern Chile. The indigenous people's name for themselves, generally used to refer to them today, is *mapuche*. There are 900,000 mapuches living in Chile today.

7 Alonso de Ercilla, *La Araucana*, ed. Isaías Lerner (Madrid: Cátedra, 1993), "Declaración de algunas dudas que se pueden ofrecer en esta obra," pp. 975–77 (subsequent references to the poem are in the text by canto and octave number only).

8 In "L'umanesimo etnografico e l'*Araucana* di Alonso de Ercilla" (*Tre studi sulla cultura spagnola* [Milan: Varese, 1967], 7–72) Ariella dal Seno points out that Ercilla carefully distinguishes the martial excellence of the Araucanians from the kind of innocence and docility on which Bartolomé de Las Casas' conceptions of the "good savage" were largely predicated.

9 For the term's etymology and its use in later texts on the natives of Chile, see Isaías Lerner, "América y la poesía épica áurea: La versión de Ercilla," *Edad de Oro* 10 (1991): 125–40.

10 For the dynamics of interlacing and authorial control, see Daniel Javitch, "Cantus Interruptus in the *Orlando Furioso*," *Modern Language Notes* 95 (1980): 66–80.

11 Ramona Lagos, "El incumplimiento de la programación épica en *La Araucana*," *Cuadernos Americanos* 40 (Sept.–Oct. 1981): 157–91.

12 Quint, *Epic and Empire*, 164.

13 Michael Murrin, *History and Warfare in Renaissance Epic* (Chicago: University of Chicago Press, 1994), 214.

14 Note that the explicitly ethnographic section of the poem actually occurs before the narrator announces that he witnesses the action, but is narrated in the "eternal present" of ethnography.

15 The term is from Jaime Concha's "El otro nuevo mundo," *Homenaje a Ercilla* (Concepción, Chile: Universidad de Concepción, 1969), 31–82.

16 Perhaps the classic example of this topos is Anchises' prediction of Roman

greatness to Aeneas, in Book VI of the *Aeneid*. Although the epic tradition includes many forms of prophecy, such as the ekphrastic prophecy on armor, I am focusing on the vision afforded to the hero and which describes events leading to the readers' (and especially the imperial patron's) present. For an account of the different kinds of prophecy in the *Aeneid*, see James J. O'Hara, *Death and the Optimistic Prophecy in Virgil's* Aeneid (Princeton: Princeton University Press, 1990), which argues that the disjunction between Roman reality and the optimistic prophecies of the text undermines traditional readings of Virgil as an ideological mouthpiece for Augustus. See Quint, *Epic and Empire*, 45.

In Spain, the tradition of prophecy was not merely literary; political discourse included "fulfillment prophecies," which, as Richard L. Kagan suggests, "were intended to convince the populace that a king or some other important individual had received divine approval and would achieve momentous or long-awaited results" (Kagan, *Lucrecia's Dreams: Politics and Prophecy in Sixteenth-Century Spain* [Berkeley: University of California Press, 1990], 86).

17 William Mejías-López provides a summary of anthropological accounts of these figures in "El Fitón de Alonso de Ercilla: ¿Shamán araucano?" *Atenea* 462 (1990): 97–117.

18 Although gender does not play a significant role in Ercilla's representation of Philip, such representation nonetheless subjects the king to his own subject's imagination in terms akin to those discussed for Elizabeth I and Spenser in Louis A. Montrose's "The Elizabethan Subject and the Spenserian Text," *Literary Theory/Renaissance Texts*, ed. Patricia Parker and David Quint (Baltimore: Johns Hopkins University Press, 1985).

19 See also the connection of the moon to epic fame in 10.4:

> ¡Quién vio los españoles colocados
> sobre el más alto cuerno de la luna
> de sus famosos hechos rodeados
> sin punto y muestra de mudanza alguna!

[Who had seen the Spaniards placed on the highest horn of the moon, surrounded by their famous feats, with no hint or sign of any change!]

20 Lucan's *Civil War*, trans. P.F.Widdows (Bloomington: Indiana University Press, 1988), VI. 728. I have given the translator's line numbers.

21 In his "Fitón's Aleph, Ercilla's World" (*Revista de estudios hispánicos* 15.3 [October 1981]: 349–63), Aden W. Hayes argues that, from the reader's extratextual position, "the accuracy of Ercilla's report of the vision in Fitón's aleph . . . gives greater credence to Ercilla's other reports" (354), and reads Fitón's display of Lepanto as the magician's recognition of "the need for variety in the epic poem." I would argue instead for a more suspicious reading of Fitón's refusal to provide Ercilla with information on Chile: the inclusion of the immediate Chilean scenario in the panorama of epic success is problematic, to say the least, given the embarrassingly incomplete campaign against the Araucanians.

22 Hayes, "Fitón's Aleph," 354–55.

23 See, most famously, the extensive writings of Las Casas based on the abuses he witnessed, or Alvar Núñez Cabeza de Vaca's *Naufragios* (Madrid: Alianza, 1998), on his shipwreck in Florida and subsequent encounters with native peoples across the North American continent.

24 Quint, *Epic and Empire*, 157–59. In his "Ercilla, lector de Lucano" (*Homenaje a Ercilla* [Concepción, Chile: University of Concepción Press, 1969], 83–109), Dieter Janik points out that the Araucanians are identified with the republican side through their emphasis on liberty, especially in the rhetoric of Colocolo and Galbarín.

25 Quint, *Epic and Empire*, 17.

26 It is interesting to note that Tasso does not consider the problems posed by the description of a different, but contemporary culture; he imagines a "modern story" as being necessarily one which is culturally transparent to the poet: "Modern stories offer a great advantage and convenience in the matter of custom and usage, but almost entirely remove the freedom to invent and imitate, which is essential to poets, particularly epic poets," (*Discourses of the Heroic Poem*, trans. Cavalchini and Samuel [London: Oxford University Press, 1973], 40).

27 Lucan's *Civil War*, I. 1–5.

28 For an account of the Moriscos' experience in the period, see Julio Caro Baroja, *Los moriscos del reino de Granada* (Madrid: Istmo, 1976).

29 Deborah Root, "Speaking Christian: Orthodoxy and Difference in Sixteenth-Century Spain," *Representations* 23 (Summer 1988): 118–34.

30 Ginés Pérez de Hita, *Guerras civiles de Granada*, Part II, ed. Paula Blanchard-Demouge (Madrid: Bailly-Baillière, 1913), 3. All subsequent references are to this edition.

31 Caro Baroja, *Los moriscos*, 158–59.

32 The 1604 edition, by Juan Gracián in Alcalá de Henares, is referred to in an "Aprobación," itself dated 1610 and included in the Cuenca 1619 edition, which Blanchard-Demouge reproduces. The editor points out that there are no extant copies of either of the earlier editions.

33 The title pages of the 1595 and 1619 editions, respectively, are reproduced in Blanchard-Demouge's edition.

The censor's approval for the Barcelona 1619 edition, which Blanchard-Demouge cites in her "Bibliografía" (xxxv), tellingly conflates Pérez de Hita's narrative with much later events. The censor states that in the second part of the *Guerras civiles*, "se tocan variedad de sucesos históricos de nuestros tiempos con apacible estilo y se acaba de dar cuenta de la total expulsión de los moriscos: no sólo de aquel Reyno sino de toda Castilla" [a variety of historical events of our time are described in a gentle style, and the total expulsion of the Moriscos, not only from that kingdom but from all of Castile, is recounted]. The censor misreads the "destierro de los Moros por toda Castilla," in the title, which actually refers to the forced relocation of Moriscos throughout Castile after the rebellion, taking it as a reference to the far more drastic decrees of 1609. Although Pérez de Hita wrote long before the expulsions, the text is only conceivable for the censor if he imagines it as tending to that extreme resolution. As I will show, the author is actually far more sympathetic to the Moriscos than the censor's description would suggest.

34 Francisco Márquez Villanueva, "El problema historiográfico de los moriscos," *Bull. Hisp.* 86 (1984): 61–135.

35 This formulation gets at the root contradiction of Spanish religious proselytism in a climate of quasi-racial intolerance: "New" or converted Christians remain ostracized by Old Christians, who are untainted by a Moorish or Jewish past.

36 For the influence of the *Austríada* on the *Guerras civiles*, see Blanchard-Demouge's introduction, xv–xxiii.

37 Ibid., xiii.

38 Pérez de Hita's Tuzani inspired Calderón's 1633 play on the uprising, *Amar después de la muerte, o el Tuzani de la Alpujarra*. In Calderón's version, penned long after the Moriscos had been expelled, the rebels are highly romanticized, although the hero, Tuzani, is never recuperated through conversion. Interestingly, in the play the ability to pass is determined by class: the Morisco *gracioso*, Alcuzcuz, protests to Tuzani that while the hero may be able to speak Spanish flawlessly, wear Christian clothes comfortably, and so forth, his servant cannot.

39 For an account of this tradition, see Márquez Villanueva, "El problema historiográfico," 94–100.

40 Blanchard-Demouge, *Guerras civiles*, xxx.

41 The echo was first recognized by Marcelino Menéndez Pelayo in his *Orígenes de la novela* (Madrid: Bailly-Baillère, 1925), 365.

42 Although Blanchard-Demouge attempts to establish the historical existence of this Moor in her introduction (*Guerras civiles*, I, xxviii–li), the evidence is less than compelling. See Enrique Moreno Báez, "El manierismo de Pérez de Hita," *Homenaje a Emilio Alarcos*, II (Valladolid: Universidad, 1965–7), 353–67, and María Soledad Carrasco-Urgoiti, *The Moorish Novel: "El Abencerraje" and Pérez de Hita* (Boston: Twayne, 1976), 93–4.

43 In her unpublished dissertation, "Beyond the Limits of Genre: The Rhetoric of History in the *Guerras Civiles de Granada*" (Princeton University, 1993), Diane S. Williams suggests that Pérez de Hita attempts to enhance his authority by inventing "a plausible eyewitness" for the events he narrates (112). What seems to me particularly interesting in this borrowing of authority, as in Cervantes' similar move, is the location of authority within the camp of the religious other.

44 In his reading of the two episodes, L. P. Harvey suggests that Cervantes is mocking the pretensions of "pseudo-history," placing within this camp both Hita's text and Miguel de Luna's *La verdadera historia del Rey Don Rodrigo* ("The Moriscos and *Don Quijote*," Inaugural Lecture in the Chair of Spanish delivered at University of London, King's College, November 11, 1974.) I would argue, first, that these are two very different texts, and, second, that in light of the sympathetic representation of the Morisco Ricote and his family in *Don Quijote*, Cervantes' gesture is actually more sympathetic than mocking. For my reading of Miguel de Luna, see Chapter 4.

45 Carrasco-Urgoiti, *The Moorish Novel*, 77.

46 Ibid., 111–12. Márquez Villanueva discusses the feudal aristocracy's defense of the Moriscos in "El problema historiográfico," 81–83.

47 Carrasco-Urgoiti provides an introduction to the history of these genres in *The Moorish Novel*, 43–52.

48 In her "The Frontier Ballad and Spanish Golden Age Historiography" (*Hispanic Review* 65.3 [Summer 1997]: 291–306) Diane E. Sieber argues that the romances were in fact acceptable documentary evidence by the standards of late sixteenth-century historiography. While this may be the case, Pérez de Hita himself seems quite aware of a generic and epistemological distinction between his narrated text and the ballads he appends. Moreover, Sieber's argument minimizes the differences between the two parts of the *Guerras civiles*, which seem to me crucial.

49 Carrasco-Urgoiti, *The Moorish Novel*, 113.

3 LETTERED SUBJECTS

1 Michel Foucault, "On the Genealogy of Ethics: An Overview of Work in Progress," in *Michel Foucault: Beyond Structuralism and Hermeneutics*, second edition, ed. Hubert L. Dreyfus and Paul Rabinow (Chicago: University of Chicago Press, 1983), 250.

2 For information about Garcilaso's life, I rely primarily on John Grier Varner's extensive biography, *El Inca: The Life and Times of Garcilaso de la Vega* (Austin: University of Texas Press, 1968). See also Aurelio Miró Quesada, *El Inca Garcilaso y otros estudios garcilasistas* (Madrid: Ediciones Cultura Hispánica, 1971).

3 See Foucault's "On the Genealogy of Ethics," and Louis Althusser's classic essay, "Ideology and Ideological State Apparatuses," in *Lenin and Philosophy*, trans. Ben Brewster (London: NLB, 1971). For a recent account of how the subject may "misrecognize" an injurious interpellation, and the productive consequences of that misrecognition, see Judith Butler, "Subjection, Resistance, Resignification: Between Freud and Foucault," in her *The Psychic Life of Power* (Stanford: Stanford University Press, 1997).

4 Francisco López de Gómara, *Historia general de las Indias* (1552), 2 vols. (Madrid: Espasa Calpe, 1932), II. 188.

5 Sebastián de Covarrubias, *Tesoro de la lengua castellana o española* (1611), ed. Martín de Riquer (Barcelona: Alta Fulla, 1998), 866–67.

6 *Comentarios reales de los Incas* in *Obras completas del Inca Garcilaso de la Vega*, ed. Carmelo Sáenz de Santa María (Madrid: Atlas, 1960), Bk. 1, Ch. 2. All subsequent references to the second part of the *Comentarios reales* are to this edition by book and chapter number only. Translations are from *Royal Commentaries of the Incas and General History of Peru*, trans. with an introduction by Harold V. Livermore (Austin: University of Texas Press, 1966), unless otherwise stated.

7 "Carta que Lope de Aguirre escribió al Rey Nuestro Señor Don Felipe Segundo," from Diego de Aguilar y Córdova, *El Marañón* (1578), reprinted in *Cronistas de las Guerras Civiles*, ed. Francisco Carrillo (Lima: Horizonte, 1989).

8 For a detailed account of these justifications, see Anthony Pagden, *Lords of All the World* (New Haven: Yale University Press, 1995), 94–102.

9 On the *encomienda* see Kenneth J. Andrien, "Spaniards, Andeans, and the Early Colonial State," in *Transatlantic Encounters: Europeans and Andeans in the Sixteenth Century*, ed. Rolena Adorno and Kenneth J. Andrien (Berkeley: University of California Press, 1991), and James Lockhart, "Encomienda and Hacienda: The Evolution of the Great Estate in the Spanish Indies," *Hispanic American Historical Review* 49 (August 1969): 411–29.

10 On the New Laws, see Hanke, *The Spanish Struggle for Justice in the Conquest of America* (Philadelphia: University of Pennsylvania Press, 1949).

11 Varner, *El Inca*, 283.

12 Despite general admiration for the translation, it was censored by the Inquisition. Garcilaso tactfully approves of the censorship, writing that the *Diálogos* were not for the *vulgo* (common readers) but only fit for a learned audience (*Comentarios reales*, "Prólogo a los indios mestizos y criollos de los reinos y provincias del grande y riquísimo imperio del Perú," 13–14).

13 The translation is my own. Livermore inexplicably omits the "Preface to Mestizos and Creoles" from his translation of Part II.

14 One of his most important sources for Part I was actually the work of a mestizo, the Jesuit Blas Valera. Unfortunately, Garcilaso complains, he has access only to a few fragments, because most of the writing was destroyed in Essex's sack of Cádiz in 1596. Garcilaso's lament recalls how closely the rivalry between England and Spain was intertwined with the Spanish imperial conquests.

15 Margarita Zamora, *Language, Authority and Indigenous History in the* Comentarios reales de los Incas (Cambridge: Cambridge University Press, 1988), 47.

16 Garcilaso's work was certainly successful in conferring upon him (posthumous) fame and glory. He is generally regarded as the first Peruvian/"truly American"/mestizo writer, the father of Peruvian letters, and so forth. But perhaps the greatest testimony to how his writing afforded him a Spanish identity is the publication of Garcilaso's works in the Biblioteca de Autores Españoles series, the edition that I myself use for Part II of the *Comentarios reales*. B. Sánchez Alonso, in his *Historia de la historiografía española*, II (Madrid: Consejo Superior de Investigaciones Científicas, 1944), grudgingly grants Garcilaso a place among "our" writers, arguing that the second part of the *Comentarios reales* is not very different from "las demás historias peruanas que nuestros cronistas publicaron" (256) [the other Peruvian histories published by our chroniclers].

17 Roberto González Echevarría, *Myth and Archive: A Theory of Latin American Narrative* (Cambridge, England: Cambridge University Press, 1990), 71.

18 Ibid., 73, 77.

19 It is not only Garcilaso who finds this model appealing: Varner makes much of Sebastián Garcilaso's allegiance to a chivalric code of conduct in his biography of the Inca Garcilaso.

20 See, for example, the chapter "Nowhere is Somewhere" in Zamora, *Language, Authority*.

21 Garcilaso de la Vega (1501–1536) was himself a soldier and poet, most noted for his adaptation of Petrarchan forms to Spanish. He died in the disastrous imperial invasion of France, after participating in Charles V's campaign against the Moors in Tunis.

22 Quoted in Miró Quesada, *El Inca Garcilaso y otros estudios garcilasistas*, 13. The subsequent translation is my own.

23 Garcilaso purposely recalls the story of his famous ancestor in his text. He presents Part II of the *Comentarios* to the Virgin Mary herself, recalling not only the grace of her protection for the Spaniards in the New World, and his own mother's conversion, but the tale of the first Garcilaso de la Vega, who fought the profane Moor for the Virgin's sake.

24 Varner, *El Inca*, 247.

25 Ibid., 249.

26 By the early seventeenth century nostalgia for an older Spain had become widespread. Two very different literary manifestations of this are Cervantes' *Don Quijote*, which parodies it, and Quevedo's "Letrilla satírica," which voices it wholeheartedly.

27 F. de Jerez, *Conquista del Perú*, quoted in Sabine MacCormack, "The Fall of the Incas: A Historiographical Dilemma," *History of European Ideas* 6.4 (1985): 421–45. The translation is my own.

28 Pagden, *Lords of All the World*, 74.

29 Stephen Clissold, *Conquistador: The Life of Don Pedro Sarmiento de Gamboa* (London: Derek Verschoyle, 1954), 64.

30 For a fascinating description of these representations in the New World, see Robert Ricard, "Contribution à l'étude des fêtes de 'Moros y Cristianos' au Mexique," *Journal de la Société des Americanistes* 26 (1932): 51–84. Ricard's account suggests that Indians often played both Christians and Moors in these elaborate pageants.

31 Varner, *El Inca*, 282.

32 On the cult of Santiago "Matamoros" (Moor-Killer), see T. D. Kendrick, *St. James in Spain* (London: Methuen, 1960).

33 This term, which dates from the Reconquista, comes from the Arab for lookout.

34 See especially the chapter "Contexts and Intertexts: the discourse on the nature of the American Indian and the *Comentarios reales*," in *Language, Authority*.

35 Garcilaso de la Vega, *Comentarios reales de los Incas*, ed. Aurelio Miró Quesada (Sucre, Venezuela: Biblioteca Ayacucho, 1976), 3.1. All references to Part I are to this edition; subsequent references are by book and chapter number only. Translations are from Livermore.

36 For an account of the role of letters in the administration of the Indies, see Antonia M. Heredia Herrera, "La carta como tipo diplomático indiano," *Anuario de estudios americanos* 34 (1977): 65–95. For some of the literary implications of this form, see González Echevarría, *Myth and Archive*.

37 I am grateful to Richard Menke for pointing out the refraction of native culture in this episode.

38 Garcilaso explicitly recalls the Ariostan personification of Discord in 2.19:

"La discordia, habiendo hecho entre los indios una de sus hazañas, que fue la muerte de Quizquiz, se metió entre los españoles a hacer otras semejantes" [Discord having achieved one of its feats among the Indians – the death of Quizquiz – went among the Spaniards to achieve more of the same.]

39 González Echevarría recalls how in colonial politics even the authorities were used to acknowledging, but not following, orders, with the infamous "Acato, pero no cumplo" (a response along the lines of "I acknowledge, but do not carry out this order").

40 Zamora, *Language, Authority*, 4–5. In the prologue to his edition, Aurelio Miró Quesada states that it was translated into English, French, and Dutch, all within the seventeenth century (xl).

41 Rolena Adorno, *Guaman Poma: Writing and Resistance in Colonial Peru* (Austin: University of Texas Press, 1986).

42 For an account of the interrelations between text and image, see Mercedes López Baralt, *Guaman Poma, autor y artista* (Lima: Fondo Editorial de la Pontificia Universidad Católica del Perú, 1993), especially the chapter "La metáfora como traslatio: del código verbal al visual en el texto ilustrado del autor andino."

43 Pratt defines the *Nueva corónica* as autoethnography in her "Arts of the Contact Zone," *Profession* 1991: 33–40.

44 Felipe Guaman Poma de Ayala [Waman Puma], *El primer nueva corónica y buen gobierno*, critical ed. Rolena Adorno and John V. Murra, trans. and textual analysis of Quechua Jorge L. Urioste (Mexico: Siglo Veintiuno, 1980), 4. All references are to this edition and appear in the text by page number only.

45 Adorno, "Waman Puma de Ayala: 'Author and Prince,'" *Latin American Literature and Arts Review* 28 (1981): 15, and introduction to her edition of the text, xli.

46 I am thinking here, for example, of the adoption of the master's name by slave populations.

47 Poma's claim to an *encomienda* must be located within a historical context of Indians who were, on occasion, awarded the labor of other Indians. As Steve J. Stern emphasizes in his *Peru's Indian People and the Challenge of Spanish Conquest* (Madison, Wis.: University of Wisconsin Press, 1982), the imitation of Spanish strategies of accumulation and labor exploitation enabled these natives to achieve economic success even during the first century of the Conquista (165–66). Even as they adopted Spanish economic patterns, Stern points out, these Indian entrepreneurs "disturbed the racial hierarchy which legitimated colonial exploitation" (180).

48 For the parodic version of the convention of knightly naming in the romances of chivalry, consider Don Quijote, who would much rather be known as the Knight of the Lions than of the Sad Figure, but who bears his name as a constant reminder of his adventures (*Don Quijote*, II, 17).

49 Adorno, *Guaman Poma*, 15.

50 Raúl Porras Barrenechea, in his *El cronista indio Felipe Huaman Poma de Ayala* (Lima: Lumen, 1948), states that, "Los indios Lucanas, según el Palentino y otros documentos, tampoco se limitaron a atacar a Hernández Girón, de-

spués de la batalla de Chuquinga. Atacaron a los dos bandos . . . Huamán
Poma convierte este acto de represalia indígena en un servicio a la causa del
Rey" (17). [The Lucanas, according to Palentino and other documents, did
not merely attack Hernández Girón after the battle of Chuquinga. They attacked both sides . . . Guaman Poma transforms this instance of indigenous re-
prisals into a service to the King's cause.] Cited in Adorno and Murra (eds.),
El primer nueva corónica y buen gobierno, 1144.

51 Adorno, *Guaman Poma*, 30–31.

52 Adorno argues for the influence of Las Casas' *Tratado de las doce dudas* in
"Colonial Reform or Utopia? Guaman Poma's Empire of the Four Parts of
the World," *Amerindian Images and the Legacy of Columbus*, ed. René Jara
and Nicholas Spadaccini (Minneapolis: University of Minnesota Press, 1992).

53 For an account of the Hapsburg's reliance on myths of universal rule, see
Marie Tanner, *The Last Descendant of Aeneas: The Hapsburgs and the Mythic
Image of the Emperor* (New Haven: Yale University Press, 1993), and Anthony Pagden, "Instruments of Empire: Tommaso Campanella and the Universal Monarchy of Spain," in his *Spanish Imperialism and the Political Imagination* (New Haven: Yale University Press, 1990).

54 It is of course intriguing to consider where Poma would locate the Jews in his
World Monarchy, for although the Moors have a king and an assigned territory, there is no such territory assigned to the Jews in the model proposed.

55 Adorno, "Colonial Reform or Utopia?" 357–58; see also Stern, *Peru's Indian
People*, 48.

56 Bartolomé de Las Casas, "Carta al maestro fray Bartolomé Carranza de
Miranda," *Obras escogidas de Fray Bartolomé de Las Casas* V, ed. Juan Pérez
de Tudela Bueso (Madrid: Atlas, 1958), 445.

57 MacCormack, "The Fall of the Incas," 428.

58 Ibid., 427–28.

59 In her chapter "La estridencia silente: oralidad, escritura e iconografía," Mercedes López Baralt suggests that this personal advice manual within the larger
manual for reform makes the *Nueva corónica* an American version of the
genre of *de regimine principum*, or instruction for princes.

4   VIRTUAL SPANIARDS

1 Pedro Córdoba, "Las leyendas en la historiografía áurea," *Criticón* 30 (1985),
242.

2 Deborah Root, "Speaking Christian: Orthodoxy and Difference in Sixteenth-
Century Spain," *Representations* 23 (Summer 1988): 119.

3 Ibid., 130.

4 For an account of these often competing histories, see Richard L. Kagan,
"Clio and the Crown: Writing History in Habsburg Spain," in *Spain, Europe
and the Atlantic World: Essays in Honour of John H. Elliott*, ed. Richard L.
Kagan and Geoffrey Parker (Cambridge, England: Cambridge University
Press, 1995), 73–99. The completion of a normative general history was a long
and drawn-out process. Juan de Mariana's immensely successful *Historia general de España* (published in Latin in 1592 and in Castilian in 1601) super-

seded a century's worth of failed attempts by royal chroniclers to write such a comprehensive account.

5 Robert B. Tate describes the context for Annius' both highly complimentary and interested account of the Spanish monarchy in his "Mythology in Spanish Historiography of the Middle Ages and the Renaissance" (*Hispanic Review* 22 [Jan. 1954]: 1–18).

6 Kagan, "Clio and the Crown," 88.

7 For a sense of the complexity of national identity in this period, see I. A. A. Thompson, "Castile, Spain and the Monarchy," in Kagan and Parker (eds.), *Spain, Europe and the Atlantic World*, 125–59.

8 See K. Garrad, "The Original Memorial of Don Francisco Núñez Muley," *Atlante* 2 (1954): 199–226.

9 See Chapter 2 for Pérez de Hita's description of these decrees in his *Guerras civiles de Granada*.

10 Garrad, "The Original Memorial," 202–203.

11 See, for example, the characterizations of Moriscos who managed to avoid expulsion in the village interrogatories collected in Ignacio Bauer Landauer's *Relaciones y manuscritos (Moriscos)* (Madrid: Editorial Ibero-Africano-Americana, n.d.), 17–134.

12 Garrad, "The Original Memorial," 209. Subsequent citations are in the text, by page number only. For a comparison of Núñez Muley and Guaman Poma as voices of protest against Spanish colonialism, in its internal and New World manifestations, see Rolena Adorno, *Cronista y príncipe: La obra de don Felipe Guaman Poma de Ayala* (Lima: Pontificia Universidad Católica del Perú, 1989), 225–45.

13 The terminology was in flux. Thompson points out that even after references to "the crown of the kingdoms of Castile, and of León, and of Granada" had given way to the singular "Castile," the territories contained within the crown of Castile continued to be described as "estos reinos" ("Castile, Spain and the Monarchy," 136).

14 After the shortened version of Núñez Muley's petition, rendered as a speech, Mármol gives Deza's answer to the Morisco. Deza's response, which relays the intentions of the king, illuminates the larger stakes of Núñez Muley's argument: "lo que su majestad quería dellos era que fuesen buenos Christianos, *en todo semejantes* a los otros Christianos sus vasallos" [what His Majesty wanted from them was that they should be good Christians, *resembling in all things* his other Christian subjects] [italics mine], Mármol, *Historia del rebelión y castigo do los Moriscos del reyno de Granada* (Malaga: Juan René, 1600), (fol. 40v). Mármol's monarch longs for uniform subjects, unmarked by regional peculiarities.

15 In fact, Moorish dress was very common not only in Granada but throughout Spain. As Garrad points out, "the adoption of veils and 'almalafas' by Old Christian women living in Granada had become so common that it was forbidden by a Royal Provision dated Valladolid, July 23, 1513" – more than twenty years, that is, after the fall of Granada ("The Original Memorial," 219, note).

16 In Mármol's version of Núñez Muley's petition, the Morisco astutely pro-

vides a Spanish proverb to make his point about appearances vs. essences: "el ábito no haze al monge" [the cloak does not make the monk] (fol. 38v). The ironic thrust of this tag is clear: even religious garb cannot guarantee Christian piety.

17 Mármol has Deza counter this point by stressing the importance of appearances; the king, he says, cares about such things: "su intención era que fuessen buenos Christianos, y no sólo que lo fuessen, mas que también lo paresciesen" [his intention was that they be good Christians, and that they not only be so, but seem so] (fol. 41).

18 As Francisco Márquez Villanueva points out in "La voluntad de leyenda de Miguel de Luna," *Nueva revista de filología hispánica* 30.2 (1981): 359–97, moderates such as Pedro de Valencia argued for assimilating the converted Moriscos by allowing them to hold public offices and honors. Núñez Muley's complaint that compliance was never rewarded with greater acceptance suggests how little these moderates affected state policy.

19 The family links among the protagonists of the Comunero revolt, the Morisco uprising, and New World struggles that I trace throughout this book are striking. The chronicler of the Alpujarras Diego Hurtado de Mendoza, for example, had a sister who was married to the *comunero* leader Juan de Padilla, and two brothers who were prominent viceroys: Antonio de Mendoza (New Spain, 1535–49; Peru, 1550–52) and Andrés Hurtado de Mendoza (Peru, 1556–60). For a fascinating transatlantic account of the Mendozas, see Roland Greene, *Unrequited Conquests: Love and Empire in the Colonial Americas* (Chicago: University of Chicago Press, 1999).

20 Antonio Garrido Aranda, *Organización de la Iglesia en el Reino de Granada y su proyección en Indias* (Seville, Spain: Escuela de Estudios Hispano-Americanos, 1979), 107. See also Mercedes García Arenal, "Moriscos e indios: Para un estudio comparado de métodos de conquista y evangelización," *Chronica Nova* 20 (1992): 153–75.

21 See Walter Mignolo, *The Darker Side of the Renaissance: Literacy, Territoriality, and Colonization* (Ann Arbor, Mich.: University of Michigan Press, 1995) for an account of this polyglot evangelism and its implications in New Spain.

22 Garrido Aranda (*Organización de la Iglesia*, 114–18) describes early catechisms in Arabic, such as the one contained in Pedro de Alcalá's *Arte para ligeramente saber la lengua arábiga* (Granada, 1505). The title of this work suggests the Church's ambivalence about Arabic even at this early date: the student must learn Arabic lightly or quickly, the title suggests, so as to preach Christianity to the Moriscos, but without lingering unduly in the dangerous linguistic space of the infidel tongue. Later bilingual catechisms, such as the *Doctrina Christiana en lengua aráviga y castellana compuesta por Martín de Ayala para la instrucción de los nuevamente convertidos deste Reino* (Valencia, 1566), suggest a certain pragmatism on the part of the Church: even as the Crown was passing laws forbidding the use of Arabic (the very laws that Núñez Muley is protesting), Ayala, as archbishop of Valencia, recognized that true conversion would be impossible if the tenets of Christianity were not translated for the Moriscos.

23 I have translated Núñez Muley's *memorias* as either "remembrances" or "memories," in an effort to convey the polysemy of the term. Núñez Muley's own document is a *memorial*, or petition, but a *memoria* could also be a memorial in the English sense: "algunas vezes se toma memoria por lo que dejan instituído nuestros mayores, por lo cual tenemos memoria dellos, como hospitales y obras pías. Y estas son las buenas memorias. Otros las dexan en mayorazgos o en suntuosos edificios," (Sebastián de Covarrubias, *Tesoro de la lengua castellana o española* [1611], ed. Martín de Riquer [Barcelona: Alta Fulla, 1998], 798.)

24 In his suggestive but ultimately inconclusive article, "Las leyendas en la historiografía áurea," *Criticón* 30 (1985): 235–53, Pedro Córdoba points out how the very term *cronicón* takes on pejorative associations because its neutral Greek ending is associated with the derogatory Spanish ending *-on* (as in *criticón* – one who criticizes too easily or too much!), while in fact there is no value judgment implicit in the term itself.

25 Córdoba, "Las leyendas," 238. In discussing the problem of truth, this critic sketches out a fascinating project along Foucauldian lines: "hay que intentar reconstruir, con la mayor precisión posible, una historia de la mentira a lo largo de los siglos porque también la mentira tiene su historia, tan digna de atención como la historia de la verdad" (248) [we must try to reconstruct, as precisely as possible, a history of the lie through the centuries, because the lie, too, has its history, as worthy of attention as the history of the truth].

26 T. D. Kendrick, *St. James in Spain* (London: Methuen, 1960).

27 Ibid., 53–54.

28 José Godoy Alcántara, *Historia crítica de los falsos cronicones* (Madrid: Rivadeneyra, 1868), 15–16.

29 Ibid., 30–33.

30 The term Pérez uses, in a letter to Higuera cited by Godoy Alcántara, is itself worthy of note: the *cronicones* are not *falsos* (false), but *fingidos* (faked). Thus the critic zeroes in on the agency in this mimetic creation of a Spanish history: someone is trying to pass off the false as true.

31 Cited in Godoy Alcántara, *Historia crítica*, 42. Note the subjunctive tense in the crucial phrase "que San Tirso *sea* de Toledo."

32 Cited in ibid., 43.

33 Miguel de Luna, *La verdadera historia del Rey Don Rodrigo* (Zaragoza, 1602), II. Q2r.

34 The first part was originally published in Granada by René Rabut in 1592; the second, also in Granada, by Sebastián de Mena, in 1600. My references are to the Zaragoza edition of 1602. The *Verdadera historia* had a long afterlife abroad; it was translated into English in 1627 as *Almansor the learned and victorious king that conquered Spaine. His life and death*, and Walter Ralegh used it to compile his *The life and death of Mahomet, the conquest of Spaine together with the rysing and ruine of the Sarazen Empire* (pub. 1637).

35 On the *Crónica sarracina*, see Israel Burshatin, "The Moor in the Text: Metaphor, Emblem, and Silence," *Critical Inquiry* 12.1 (Autumn 1985): 98–118. The traditional account of the fall of Spain tells of King Rodrigo, "the last of the Goths," who, blinded by lust, seduced Florinda. To take revenge, her fa-

ther, Count Julián, conspired with the Moors against Rodrigo, enabling the invasion.

36 Luna, I.5. Márquez Villanueva suggests that Luna relishes the *frisson* of not only introducing the odd word of Arabic – a proscribed language by the time the *Verdadera historia* was published – but treating the language with the reverence usually reserved for Greek and Latin ("La voluntad de leyenda" 384).

37 Márquez Villanueva, "La voluntad de leyenda," 363.

38 There are precedents for this opinion in the colorful history of Spanish prophecy: in the seventh century, St. Isidore of Seville prophesied that the sins of the Gothic rulers would lead to their downfall at the hands of the Moors. For an account of the prophetic tradition in Christian Spain, see Kagan, *Lucrecia's Dreams* (Berkeley: University of California Press, 1990). The Moriscos had their own tradition of prophecy, the *aljofores,* which predicted their glorious future and liberation from persecution. See Luce López-Baralt, *Islam in Spanish Literature, from the Middle Ages to the Present,* trans. Andrew Hurley (New York: Brill, 1992), 198.

39 Luna, I. 11.

40 Ibid., II. 25.

41 For the glorified role of peasants as Old Christians in the *comedias* of Lope de Vega, for example, see *El villano en su rincón* or *Fuenteovejuna.*

42 Luna, I.39. As Godoy Alcántara first pointed out, one of these marriages – that of Rodrigo's daughter Egilona to the Moorish general Abdalazís – gives the Moors a legitimate right to the Spanish throne.

43 See especially Márquez Villanueva's note in "La voluntad de leyenda" on the verdicts of Menéndez Pidal and Menéndez Pelayo, two of the most influential Spanish critics of the early twentieth century.

44 Luis de Góngora, "Al Monte Santo de Granada," *Sonetos completos,* ed. Biruté Ciplijaus Kaité (Madrid: Castalia, 1985), 232.

45 See, for example, Miguel Hagerty's very useful introduction to his edition of *Los libros plúmbeos del Sacromonte,* translated from the Arabic by Adán Centurión, Marqués de Estepa (Madrid: Editora Nacional, 1980), a text which I will discuss at some length later in this chapter, and Godoy Alcántara, *Historia crítica,* 78–79.

46 This attempt to erase the architectural memory of another religion and replace it with a triumphant Christian monument recalls Cortés' destruction of the Aztec temple in Tenochtitlan, which provided the stones to build the new cathedral there. It is ironic that "Turpin's Tower," when torn down, yields such fabulous truths – Turpin, legendary archbishop of Rheims, is the putative author of the *Chronicle of Charlemagne,* and the "reliable" source whom the narrator comically invokes to justify his improbable veracity in Ariosto's *Orlando Furioso.*

47 On Alonso del Castillo and his role in the finds, see Darío Cabanelas, *El morisco granadino Alonso del Castillo* (Granada: Patronato de la Alhambra, 1965).

48 Godoy Alcántara, *Historia crítica,* 4–7; Kendrick, *St. James in Spain,* 69–72.

49 Darío Cabanelas, *El morisco granadino Alonso del Castillo* (Granada: Patronato de la Alhambra, 1965), 185–95; Godoy Alcántara, *Historia crítica,* 6n.

50 Hagerty (ed.), *Los libros plúmbeos,* 37, 39.

51 L. P. Harvey, "The Moriscos and *Don Quijote*," Inaugural Lecture, King's College, University of London, November 11, 1974, 13.
52 Godoy Alcántara, *Historia crítica*, 95.
53 Hagerty (ed.), *Los libros plúmbeos*, 123–25. The emphasis on the excellence of the Arabs – and Arabic – among all of God's creatures is repeated in the "Book of the Doings of St. James Apostle and of His Miracles," 207.
54 So fraught were the discussions between Granada, Madrid, and the Vatican over the value and subsequent fate of the leaden books, that one eighteenth-century critic, Pastor de los Cobos, dubbed the entire episode the "Guerras Católicas Granatensis' (Hagerty, *Libros plúmbeos*, 41).
55 Kendrick, *St. James in Spain*, 108
56 Hagerty, *Libros plúmbeos*, 58. The Church and College still stand today, their incontrovertible reality presented as a challenge to critics. A plaque for visitors discreetly dismisses the controversies over the leaden books, arguing instead for the essential significance of the site: "Cuando haya finalizado su visita – que esperamos sea de su agrado – queremos que haya valorado el significado histórico de esta institución en la vida de la Granada cristiana: prescindiendo de algunas cuestiones debatidas entre los estudiosos, lo que es históricamente seguro es que la fe cristiana llegó a Granada y a Andalucía en los primeros siglos de la fundación del cristianismo. *Esta casa es un símbolo de esta verdad histórica.* La noticia de la religión del Evangelio y de Jesús está en esta tierra desde hace dos mil años, aunque durante ocho siglos – desde el siglo VIII al XV – predominara en Granada la religión musulmana que, por cierto, también venera a Jesús como un gran profeta," [When your visit is over – and we hope it was a pleasant one – we want you to have valued the historical significance of this institution in the life of Christian Granada: setting aside certain questions debated among scholars, what is historically certain is that the Christian faith came to Granada and to Andalucía in the first centuries of Christianity. *This house is a symbol of that historical truth.* The news of the religion of the Gospels and of Jesus has been in this land for two thousand years, even if for eight centuries – from the eighth to the fifteenth – Islam, which, actually, also reveres Jesus as a great prophet, predominated in Granada] [italics mine].
57 Hagerty, *Libros plúmbeos*, 61.
58 Ibid., 32.

5   FAITHLESS EMPIRES: PIRATES, RENEGADOES, AND THE ENGLISH NATION

1 Thomas Dekker, *If This Be Not a Good Play, the Devil Is in It* [1612], *The Dramatic Works of Thomas Dekker*, III, ed. Fredson Bowers (Cambridge, England: Cambridge University Press, 1958), 4.2. 58–9.
2 As Anne Pérotin-Dumon points out in "The Pirate and the Emperor: Power and the Law on the Seas, 1450–1850" (in *The Political Economy of Merchant Empires*, ed. James D. Tracy [Cambridge, England: Cambridge University Press, 1991]), "the history of piracy in this period shows that it arises above all from change in the political realm – either the will of a state to establish

commercial hegemony over an area where it had previously been weak or non-existent, or from the conflict between two political entities, one an established trading power and the other a newcomer. The prize of piracy is economic, but as a historic phenomenon, the dynamic that creates it is political" (197–98).

3 John Dee, *General and Rare Memorials Pertaining to the Perfect Art of Navigation*, in *John Dee: Essential Readings*, ed. Gerald Suster (London: Crucible, 1986), 51.

4 Richard Helgerson, *Forms of Nationhood: The Elizabethan Writing of England* (Chicago: University of Chicago Press, 1992). See especially "The Voyages of a Nation." Helgerson's description of the cultural stakes of this transformation is central to my analysis.

5 For the development of the joint-stock venture and the increasing participation by the upper classes, see Theodore K. Rabb, *Enterprise and Empire* (Cambridge, Mass.: Harvard University Press, 1967).

6 The modern editor of the abridged Hakluyt collection, which I cite below, quotes J. M. Keynes on the immense significance of Drake's loot: "the booty brought back by Drake in the Golden Hind may fairly be considered the fountain and origin of British Foreign Investment. Elizabeth paid off out of the proceeds the whole of her foreign debt, and invested a large part of the balance (about £42,000) in the Levant Company. Largely out of the profits of the Levant Company, there was formed the East India Company, the profits of which, during the seventeenth and eighteenth centuries, were the main foundation of England's foreign connections" (23).

7 "Voyage of Sir Francis Drake about the whole globe" in Richard Hakluyt, *Voyages and Discoveries*, ed. abr. and intro. by Jack Beeching (London: Penguin, 1985), 179. Drake traveled as far north as the area he called Nova Albion – some degrees north of the San Francisco Bay. There he claimed the land for Elizabeth and left as a marker "Her Highness' picture and arms, in a piece of six pence of current English money under the plate" (182–83). Was Drake unwittingly symbolizing the English reliance on commerce as a means to empire?

8 C. M. Senior, *A Nation of Pirates* (New York: Crane, Russak, and Co., 1976), 78–9. It is interesting to speculate that Antonio's argosies in *The Merchant of Venice* were as likely to be intercepted by English pirates as destroyed by "merchant-marring rocks."

9 In his *Unspeakable Subjects: The Genealogy of the Event in Early Modern Europe* (Stanford: Stanford University Press, 1997), Jacques Lezra suggestively links the counterfeit legality of pirates with the counterfeiting of texts in the period: "This relation itself, between a 'model' and what plays 'after' it, is of course precisely what 'pirating' was and remains about, both as it affected the publication of early texts (the history of the pirating of the First Folio is notorious), and as it concerned the masking or feigning by means of which ships at sea were able to claim to be other than they were" (275).

10 Cited in Lois Potter, "Pirates and 'turning Turk' in Renaissance drama," in *Travel and Drama in Shakespeare's Time*, ed. Jean-Pierre Maquerlot and Michèle Willems, (Cambridge, England: Cambridge University Press, 1996), 124–40.

11 See J. F. Larkin and P. L. Hughes (eds.), *Stuart Royal Proclamations*, (Oxford: Oxford University Press, 1973), 53–56, 98–99, 145–47, 203–06. The adventurer and colonist John Smith specifically blamed James' peace with Spain for the proliferation of pirates: "our royal King James, who from his infancy had reigned in peace with all nations, had no employment for those men of war, so that those who were rich rested with what they had; those that were poor, and had nothing but from hand to mouth, turned pirates" (*Generall Historie of Virginia, New-England and the Summer Iles*, II [London, 1629], 280).

12 Senior, *Nation of Pirates*, 10–11.

13 Ibid., 46

14 Cited in ibid., 53.

15 James' proclamation against pirates of September 30, 1603, specifically orders the king's subjects to "forbeare from ayding or receiving of any Pirat or Sea-Rover, or any person not being a knowen Merchant, by contracting, buying, selling or exchanging with them, or by victualling of them or any of their company" (Larkin and Hughes, *Stuart Royal Proclamations*, 55). The clause about "known merchants" suggests how pirates could pass as legitimate traders or, conversely, how their suppliers could claim to have aided them only because they believed they were legal.

16 Senior, *Nation of Pirates*, 54–7.

17 Arthur Chichester, quoted in ibid., 58.

18 Braudel, *The Mediterranean and the Mediterranean World in the Age of Philip II*, II, trans. Siân Reynolds (London: Collins, 1973), 865.

19 See Peter Earle, *Corsairs of Malta and Barbary* (London: Sidgwick and Jackson, 1970).

20 For a detailed account of Anglo-Moroccan relations, see Matar, *Turks, Moors, and Englishmen in the Age of Discovery*, (New York: Columbia University Press, 1999), 44–55, 63–71, and passim; and Jack D'Amico, *The Moor in English Renaissance Drama* (Tampa: University of South Florida Press, 1991), 7–40.

21 David Delison Hebb, *Piracy and the English Government, 1616–1642* (Aldershot, England: Scolar Press, 1994), 12.

22 John Smith, *Generall Historie of Virginia*, II, 280.

23 I use the Early Modern term from the Spanish rather than the modern "renegade" to emphasize the linguistic reflection of England and Spain's related concerns on these matters.

24 Samuel Chew, *The Crescent and the Rose* (New York: Oxford University Press, 1937), 344. In his "Voyage to Tunis: New History and the Old World of *The Tempest*" (*ELH* 64 [1997]: 333–57), Richard Wilson observes, "So, though it was reckoned that some 466 English ships were seized and their crews enslaved in the Berber states between 1609 and 1616, the irony was that they fell victim to a system commanded not by barbarians, but by Christians such as Prospero" (335). Although I find Wilson's attempt to map the historical figure of the renegade Robert Dudley onto Shakespeare's Prospero much too literal, his reconstruction of the Mediterranean context for *The Tempest* is highly suggestive. I myself have insisted on the importance of recontextualizing the play in my essay "Conquering Islands: Contextualizing *The Tempest*" (*Shakespeare Quarterly* 48.1 [Spring 1997]: 45–62).

25 Smith, *Generall Historie of Virginia*, 281.
26 Robert Daborne, *A Christian Turn'd Turk* (London: William Barrenger, 1612), Scena Ultima.
27 Ibid., Prologue.
28 Thomas Heywood and William Rowley, *Fortune by Land and Sea*, ed. Herman Doh (New York: Garland, 1980), 4.2, lines 1677–89. (Note that the line numeration in this edition is continuous.) Subsequent references are in the text.
29 Whereas Purser disdains Englishness because he refuses to be placed outside the law, historical pirates such as Peter Easton ignored English appeals even when James proclaimed a General Pardon, in 1612. Easton replied, "I have no intention of obeying the orders of one king when I am, in a way, a king myself." Cited in Christopher Lloyd, *English Corsairs on the Barbary Coast* (London: Collins, 1981), 66.
30 Taussig, *Mimesis and Alterity,* 47–48, italics in the original.
31 Ibid., 213.
32 Potter points to the execution of the historical Purser and Clinton in 1583 as proof of the play's "nostalgia for an age of simpler values," and attributes a similar nostalgia to Heywood's *Fair Maid of the West* (127).
33 Lezra analyzes a 1639 chapbook, "A True Relation, of the Lives and Deaths of the two most famous English Pyrats, *Purser*, and *Clinton*; who lived in the Reigne of Queen Elizabeth," which includes a similar scene of a royal proclamation against the pirates and pardoning their capturer, which a hoarse Pursevant must retransmit, with disastrous results, through a "plaine and crafty country fellow" (*Unspeakable Subjects*, 276–80). Although the chapbook may, as Lezra suggests, have existed in an earlier form, from which Heywood took this scene, it is possible also that the later chapbook may have imported the humorous scene from *Fortune by Land and Sea*, where it plays a central role in the plot.
34 Ibid., 280.
35 Recall also the sixpence with Elizabeth's image left by Drake to represent her possession of Nova Albion.
36 Jean Howard, "An English Lass Amid the Moors: Gender, Race, Sexuality, and National Identity in Heywood's *The Fair Maid of the West*," in *Women, "Race", and Writing in the Early Modern Period*, ed. Margo Hendricks and Patricia Parker (London: Routledge, 1994), 102.
37 Herman Doh, introduction to Thomas Heywood and William Rowley, *Fortune by Land and Sea*.
38 Thomas Heywood, *The Fair Maid of the West*, ed. Robert K. Turner (Lincoln, Nebr.: University of Nebraska Press, 1967), 1.1, 3–16. Subsequent references are in the text.
39 In a play that will later cite Kyd's *Spanish Tragedy*, it is striking how reminiscent this quarrel is of the struggle for booty among Spaniards that initiates that play.
40 Howard, "An English Lass," 113.
41 Ibid., 110.
42 The term "geld," however, is itself connected with money (from *gelt*), and was the name of an early land tax paid to the Crown.
43 Howard, "An English Lass," 115.

44 It would take the second part of *The Fair Maid of the West*, which Heywood wrote much later, and a whole new set of exotic (and ever more bizarre) adventures, before the marriage was finally solemnized.

45 *The Renegado*, in *The Plays and Poems of Philip Massinger*, II, ed. Philip Edwards and Colin Gibson (Oxford: Oxford University Press, 1976), 1.2, 21–24. Subsequent references are in the text.

46 Ivor Noël Hume, *The Virginia Adventure* (New York: Knopf, 1994), 108.

47 John Smith, *A Select Edition of his Writings*, ed. Karen Ordahl Kupperman (Chapel Hill: University of North Carolina Press, 1988), 20.

48 Hume, *Virginia Adventure*, 160.

6 PIRATING SPAIN

1 For a detailed account of the repeated English attacks against the Spanish territories in the New World, see the three volumes of documents translated and edited by Irene A. Wright for the Hakluyt Society: *Spanish Documents concerning English Voyages to the Caribbean 1527–1568* (1928), *Documents concerning English Voyages to the Spanish Main 1569–1580* (1932), and *Further English Voyages to Spanish America 1583–94* (1951). Also, see the volume of historical documents published as a companion to Félix Lope de Vega's *La Dragontea* (Burgos: Museo Naval, 1935).

2 On the history of Philip II's navy, see Magdalena de Pazzis Pi Corrales, *Felipe II y la lucha por el dominio del mar* (Madrid: San Martín, 1989), and Peter Pierson, *Commander of the Armada: The Seventh Duke of Medina Sidonia* (New Haven: Yale University Press, 1989).

3 Diego de Haedo, *Topografía e historia de Argel*, 3 vols. (Madrid: Sociedad de Bibliófilos Españoles, 1927). Haedo claims that there are renegades from almost every conceivable European ethnic group, from Russians to Scots to Castilians. More surprisingly, he includes also "Indios de las Indias de Portugal, del Brasil y de Nueva España" (I. 52–53).

4 Haedo, *Topografía e historia*, 79.

5 Under Charles V, Spain established military bases in North Africa as a way to counter the danger, yet it proved impossible to conserve these footholds.

6 For the historical background on this population, see Ellen G. Friedman, *Spanish Captives in North Africa in the Early Modern Age* (Madison: University of Wisconsin Press, 1983).

7 For the Hapsburg's harnessing of imperial goals to the "history of salvation", see Marie Tanner, *The Last Descendant of Aeneas: The Hapsburgs and the Mythic Image of the Emperor* (New Haven: Yale University Press, 1993), especially chapters VI and VII.

8 For a summary of literary references to Drake, see John Cummins, *Francis Drake: The Lives of a Hero* (London: Weidenfeld and Nicolson, 1995), 258–73.

9 Lope de Vega, *La Dragontea*, p. 15. All subsequent references are in the text by stanza number only. As Cummins points out, it was not easy to write of Drake's earlier successes. Juan de Castellanos' *Elegías de varones ilustres de Indias*, which included a long account of Drake's circumnavigation and early exploits, was censored and published without the offending section (264).

10 Borja's prologue recalls another discomfited attempt to explain why the en-

emy's successes are being sung, this time by a royal Scot singing Spanish praises. In an epic poem entitled *Lepanto*, written while he was still king of Scotland, James I praises the Spanish leader Don Juan de Austria as he celebrates the great battle. In James' later preface to the reader, he provides an extensive set of justifications for a Protestant monarch's praise of the Catholic alliance: "And . . . I knowe, the special thing misliked in it, is, that I should seeme, far contrary to my degree and Religion, like a Mercenary Poët, to penne a worke, ex professo, in praise of a forraine Papist bastard." Although the extraordinary circumstances of the battle justify his praise of Don Juan of Austria "as of a particular man," James suggests, the reader should not extrapolate from that praise any sympathy for the Catholic League: "Next follows my invocation to the true God only, and not to all the He and She Saints, for whose vain honors, DON-IOAN fought in all his wars." James' ambivalent un-writing of the poem's epic praise reflects the unsustainable nature of the European unity that had led to the great naval triumph. See *Lepanto*, in *The Poems of James VI of Scotland*, I, ed. James Craigie (Edinburgh, 1955), 198.

11	For the poem's publication and reception, see Ismael García, "*La Dragontea*: Justificación y visicitudes," *Lope de Vega y los orígenes del teatro español, Actas del I Congreso Internacional sobre Lope de Vega*, ed. Manuel Criado de Val (Madrid: EDI-6, 1981), 591–603. On the disappearance of Sotomayor, see also A. K. Jameson, "Lope de Vega's *La Dragontea*: Historical and Literary Sources," *Hispanic Review* 6 (1938): 104–19. The documents on Drake's last voyage housed in the Museo Naval are published in vol. II of the museum's edition of Lope's poem.

12	Joaquín Entreambasaguas, *Estudios sobre Lope de Vega* (Madrid: Gráficas Sol, 1946), 310. Lope complains about the reception of his patriotic epic in the autobiographical second part of *La Filomena* (1621): "pasé a *La Dragontea* . . . /Mas como nunca paga lo que debe /la patria, dejé aparte/ las trompetas de Marte" [I turned to *La Dragontea*, but as the fatherland never pays what it owes, I set aside Mars' trumpets].

13	In its allegorical dimension, its combination of biblical and epic topoi, and its gilding of imperial ambitions with religious concerns, *La Dragontea* strangely anticipates Milton's far more successful *Paradise Lost* (1667) and presents some elements, too, of Spenser's *The Faerie Queene* (1591, 1596), although without as strong a center in the allegorized figure of the ruler. For a recent account of the colonialist dimensions of Milton's text, see J. Martin Evans, *Milton's Imperial Epic : Paradise Lost and the Discourse of Colonialism* (Ithaca: Cornell University Press, 1996). For the context of imperialism for Spenser's poem, see Stephen Greenblatt, "To Fashion a Gentleman: Spenser and the Destruction of the Bower of Bliss," in *Renaissance Self-Fashioning* (Chicago: Chicago University Press, 1980), and, more recently, Andrew Hadfield, *Edmund Spenser's Irish Experience: Wilde Fruit and Salvage Soyl* (Oxford: Oxford University Press, 1997).

14	Tanner describes the apocalyptic fervor of such influential figures as the Abbot Hortolá, Philip II's representative at the Council of Trent, and the sensationalist political theorist Tommaso Campanella (*The Last Descendant of Aeneas*, 179, 181).

15 Ibid., 141–43.
16 In his study of Lope's sources, A. K. Jameson finds echoes of two minor poems by Claudian (A.D. 370–404) against enemies of Rome in *La Dragontea*. Yet I would argue that the most interesting aspect of this relationship is how Lope Christianizes his classical models.
17 For an account of these infamous corsairs, see Peter Earle, *Corsairs of Malta and Barbary* (London: Sidgwick and Jackson, 1970) and Christopher Lloyd, *English Corsairs on the Barbary Coast* (London: Collins, 1981).
18 In Cervantes' *El trato de Argel* (ca. 1582), much is made of the special vulnerability of young captives to pressures to convert. See also Friedman, *Spanish Captives in North Africa*, 147.
19 As Ercilla's *La Araucana* and Guaman Poma's protests to the king make clear, in the late sixteenth century there was still strong resistance – whether military or cultural – to Spanish control in parts of the New World.
20 "Mozárabe (from the Arabic *musta 'rab*, arabized): A member of the Hispanic minorities who, tolerated by Islamic law as tributaries, lived in Muslim Spain until the end of the eleventh century, maintaining their Christian religion and even their religious and judicial hierarchies" (*Diccionario de la Real Academia Española* [Madrid: Espasa Calpe, 1992]).
21 The term *mozárabe* evinces some of the fascinating ambiguities in Spain's relation to its Muslim heritage. Although it primarily designates Christian minorities under Arabic rule in the Iberian Peninsula, it also refers to Christians who had formerly lived under such rule but who migrated to Northern, Christian Spain, bringing with them many elements of Muslim culture (*Diccionario de la Real Academia Española*).
22 The female colonist's account of the mythic origin of Spain's original conquest by Islam is very interesting in this passage: note that she is unwilling to specify whether Florinda was sinner or sinned against. For the legend of Florinda, also known as the Cava Rumía, see Chapter 4.
23 The term *indiano* – not to be confused with *indio* – was used both for Spaniards born in the Indies (what would later be known as *criollos*), and for those who returned to Spain (usually enriched) after a long stay in the New World.
24 In his somewhat hostile account of the poem Jean-Louis Flecniakoska describes Greed as "la mauvaise conseillère, retorse, qui sait cacher la vérité défavorable et exalter les bas instincts," ("Lope de Vega Propagandiste Nationaliste: *La Dragontea*" in *Hommage des Hispanistes Français à Noel Salomon* [Barcelona: LAIA, 1979], 322).
25 Cummins accounts for the fabulous loyalty of the escaped slaves in Lope's version: alarmed at the *cimarrones*' alliance with Drake on his earlier, more destructive voyages, the Spaniards waged a brutal campaign against them, almost completely eradicating them by the time of Drake's last voyage (*Francis Drake*, 232).
26 Aeneas' *pietas*, referred to in this episode, is clearly a Christianized virtue, while the comparison of the *cimarrones* to the classical heroes locates them ambiguously both inside and outside the Christian camp.
27 "Relación de la sangrienta y naval batalla que a vista de la ciudad de Málaga tuvieron once galeras de España, con dos galeones de Turcos, Ingleses, y

Moriscos" (Málaga, 1611), *Los turcos en el Mediterráneo: Relaciones*, coll. Ignacio Bauer Landauer (Madrid: Ed. Ibero-Africano-Americana, n.d.), V of *Papeles de mi archivo*, 6 vols.

28 See Chapter 5. Robert Daborne's dramatization of the pirate Ward's exploits in North Africa in *A Christian Turn'd Turk* (London: William Barrenger, 1612) is one striking example. See also Nabil Matar, *Turks, Moors, and Englishmen in the Age of Discovery* (New York: Columbia University Press, 1999).

29 Friedman, *Spanish Captives in North Africa*, 107–23. The New World, too, participated in these cross-cultural exchanges, providing a large portion of the funds for the redemptions (115).

30 See Francisco Márquez Villanueva, "El problema historiográfico de los moriscos," *Bull. Hisp.* 86 (1984): 94–100.

31 Haedo, *Topografía e historia*, I.92.

32 For a detailed account of the cruelty of the expulsion, see Roger Boase, "The Morisco Expulsion and Diaspora: an example of racial and religious intolerance," *Cultures in Contact in Medieval Spain*, ed. David Hook and Barry Taylor (London: King's College London Medieval Studies, 1990), and Márquez Villanueva, "El morisco Ricote o la hispana razón de estado" in his *Personajes y temas del Quijote* (Madrid: Taurus, 1975).

33 Friedman points out that in fact Spain never intended to send the expelled Moriscos to Muslim lands, but they made their way there regardless, whether by bribing ship captains, or undertaking a second journey from their original destination (*Spanish Captives*, 13).

34 Pierson, *Commander of the Armada*, 229.

35 Friedman, *Spanish Captives*, 13–15.

36 See *Documentos notariales referentes a los moriscos 1569–71*, coll. Nicolás Cabrillana from the Archivo Histórico Provincial de Almería (Granada: Universidad de Granada, 1978).

37 Document 487 in Cabrillana's collection is an acknowledgment by one man of how he received a slave and her daughter from their owner, "la qual le a entregado para llevar a la villa de Albox y otras partes para si la quisieren rescatar vecinos de los dichos lugares" [whom he gave to him to take to the town of Albox and other places to see if the residents of those places might wish to redeem her].

38 The reference to "membrillo cocho" ("cooked quince") is from Document 304, the others are repeated throughout the collection.

39 Friedman, *Spanish Captives*, 147.

40 Boase, "Morisco Expulsion and Diaspora," 13. The system is reminiscent of the *encomienda*, which had led to huge abuses of the native population in the New World under the guise of spiritual instruction.

41 George Camamis, *Estudios sobre el cautiverio en el Siglo de Oro* (Madrid: Gredos, 1977), 14, 53.

42 Miguel de Cervantes, *Teatro completo*, ed. Florencio Sevilla Arroyo and Antonio Rey Hazas (Barcelona: Planeta, 1987), lines 3082–85. All subsequent references to the plays are in the text by line number only and are from this edition.

43 For a more general treatment of the subject, see Albert Mas' encyclopedic *Les Turcs dans la littérature espagnole du siècle d'or*, 2 vols. (Paris: Centre des Re-

cherches Hispaniques, 1967) and Ottmar Hegyi, *Cervantes and the Turks* (Newark, Del.: Juan de la Cuesta, 1992).

44 Haedo, *Topografía e historia*, III. 31 and passim.

45 The story is mentioned in Haedo; the version in Cervantes fails to mention that the Moors who instigated the burning were the brothers of the corsair captured by the Inquisition, and that they had expected that they would be able to exchange their own captive for the Inquisition's prisoner (Friedman, *Spanish Captives*, 87–88). The priest, therefore, was not burned primarily because of his religious function or significance.

46 Friedman, *Spanish Captives*, 89–90.

47 Ellen M. Anderson, "Playing at Moslem and Christian: The Construction of Gender and the Representation of Faith in Cervantes' Captivity Plays," *Cervantes* 13 (1993): 45–46.

48 For a discussion of the ambiguity of renegades, see Paul Julian Smith, " 'The Captive's Tale': Race, Text, Gender," *Quixotic Desire: Psychoanalytic Perspectives on Cervantes*, ed. Ruth Anthony El Saffar and Diana de Armas Wilson (Ithaca: Cornell University Press, 1993).

49 In "The Captive's Tale," in *Don Quijote*, the protagonist expresses his own mistrust of these documents, which, he avers, are used as alibis by captured corsairs just as often as by renegades who truly seek reconciliation with the Church. The ambiguity surrounding such documents, although not explicitly mentioned in the play, adds another level of complexity to the renegade Hazén.

50 For the relationship between the two stories, and the historical background for the characters, see Jaime Oliver Asín, "La hija de Agi Morato en la obra de Cervantes," *Boletín de la Real Academia Española* 27 (1947–48): 245–339, and Márquez Villanueva, "Leandra, Zoraida y sus fuentes franco-italianas," in *Personajes y Temas del Quijote*.

51 There is a vast literature on "The Captive's Tale," which proved so popular that it acquired a life of its own, with a title and identity quite separate from the novel that contained it. See especially Asín and Márquez Villanueva; also Leo Spitzer, "Linguistic Perspectivism in *Don Quijote*," in *Linguistics and Literary History: Essays in Stylistics* (New York: Russell and Russell, 1962), E. Michael Gerli, *Refiguring Authority: Reading, Writing, and Rewriting in Cervantes* (Lexington, Ky: University Press of Kentucky, 1995), and David Quint, "Narrative Interlace and Narrative Genres in *Don Quijote* and the *Orlando Furioso*," *MLQ* 58.3 (September 1997): 241–68.

52 Ibid., 263.

53 Cervantes, *El ingenioso hidalgo Don Quijote de la Mancha*, ed. Martín de Riquer (Buenos Aires: Ed. Kapelusz, 1973), II. 492–93. Subsequent references are in the text, by page or chapter number only.

54 Spitzer, "Linguistic Perspectivism," 67–68.

55 See Chapter 4 for Núñez Muley's criticism of such methods, and his praise for the syncretic proselytism of Talavera.

56 By reading Zoraida as a figure for Mary, Gerli takes the argument much further, suggesting that Cervantes "redefines the legend [of La Cava Rumía] into one of deliverance – deliverance from the racial hatred and intolerance that

preside over the Spanish discourse of history and the foundational fiction of Reconquest, as he leaves La Cava entombed on an African promontory and, through Zoraida's public profession of faith, reminds his readers of humanity's salvation through the agency of a Semitic woman" (*Refiguring Authority*, 54).

57 Agustín de Rojas, *El viaje entretenido*, 2 vols., ed. Jacques Joset (Madrid: Espasa Calpe, 1977), I.305.

58 Cervantes, *The Trials of Persiles and Sigismunda, A Northern Story*, trans. Celia Richmond Weller and Clark A. Colahan (Berkeley: University of California Press, 1989), 249.

59 Cervantes, *Los trabajos de Persiles y Sigismunda*, ed. Juan Bautista Avalle-Arce (Madrid: Castalia, 1969), 349–50.

60 Alban Forcione, in his *Cervantes, Aristotle and the "Persiles"* (Princeton: Princeton University Press, 1970), discusses the episode in light of contemporary literary debates about verisimilitude in representation (171 and following).

CONCLUSION: *CONTRA* ORIGINALITY

1 Gertrude Stein, *Everybody's Autobiography* (New York: Vintage, 1973), 21; Fernando Trueba, *La niña de tus ojos* (Spain, 1998).

Bibliography

Adorno, Rolena. "Waman Puma de Ayala: 'Author and Prince.'" *Latin American Literature and Arts Review* 28 (1981): 12–15.

Guaman Poma: Writing and Resistance in Colonial Peru. Austin: University of Texas Press, 1986.

Cronista y príncipe: La obra de don Felipe Guaman Poma de Ayala. Lima: Pontificia Universidad Católica del Perú, 1989.

"La construcción cultural de la alteridad: el sujeto colonial y el discurso caballeresco." *Primer Simposio de Filología Iberoamericana, Facultad de Filología, Universidad de Sevilla*. Zaragoza: Pórtico, 1990. 153–70.

"Colonial Reform or Utopia? Guaman Poma's Empire of the Four Parts of the World." *Amerindian Images and the Legacy of Columbus*. Ed. René Jara and Nicholas Spadaccini. Minneapolis: University of Minnesota, Press, 1992. 346–74.

Aguilar y Córdova, Diego de. "Carta que Lope de Aguirre escribió al Rey Nuestro Señor Don Felipe Segundo." *El Marañón* (1578). Reprinted in *Cronistas de las Guerras Civiles*. Ed. Francisco Carrillo. Lima: Horizonte, 1989.

Albarracín Sarmiento, Carlos. "El poeta y su rey en *La Araucana*." *Filología* 21 (1986): 99–116.

Althusser, Louis. "Ideology and Ideological State Apparatuses." *Lenin and Philosophy*. Trans. Ben Brewster. London: NLB, 1971.

Anderson, Ellen M. "Playing at Moslem and Christian: The Construction of Gender and the Representation of Faith in Cervantes' Captivity Plays." *Cervantes* 13 (1993): 37–59.

Andrien, Kenneth J. "Spaniards, Andeans, and the Early Colonial State." *Transatlantic Encounters: Europeans and Andeans in the Sixteenth Century*. Ed. Rolena Adorno and Kenneth J. Andrien. Berkeley: University of California Press, 1991.

Ariosto, Ludovico. *Orlando Furioso*. Vicenza: Mondadori, 1976.

Orlando Furioso. Trans. Guido Waldman. Oxford: Oxford University Press, 1974.

Ascoli, Albert. *Ariosto's Bitter Harmony: Crisis and Evasion in the Italian Renaissance*. Princeton, N.J.: Princeton University Press, 1987.

"Liberating the Tomb: Difference and Death in *Gerusalemme liberata*." *Annali d'italianistica* 12 (1994): 159–80.

Asín, Jaime Oliver. "La hija de Agi Morato en la obra de Cervantes." *Boletín de la Real Academia Española* 27 (1947–48): 245–339.

Auerbach, Erich. *Mimesis: The Representation of Reality in Western Literature.* Trans. Willard R. Trask. Princeton, N.J.: Princeton University Press, 1953.

Bauer Landauer, Ignacio, ed. *Relaciones y manuscritos (Moriscos).* Madrid: Editorial Ibero-Africano-Americana, n.d.

Los turcos en el Mediterráneo: Relaciones. Madrid: Editorial Ibero-Africano-Americana, n.d.

Bhabha, Homi K. *The Location of Culture.* London: Routledge, 1994.

Boase, Roger. "The Morisco Expulsion and Diaspora: An Example of Racial and Religious Intolerance." *Cultures in Contact in Medieval Spain.* Ed. David Hook and Barry Taylor. London: King's College London Medieval Studies, 1990.

Braudel, Fernand. *The Mediterranean and the Mediterranean World in the Age of Philip II.* 2 vols. Trans. Siân Reynolds. London: Collins, 1973.

Brownlee, Kevin and Walter Stephens, eds. *Discourses of Authority in Medieval and Renaissance Literature.* Hanover, N.H.: University Press of New England, 1989.

and Marina Scordilis Brownlee, eds. *Romance: Generic Transformation from Chrétien de Troyes to Cervantes.* Hanover, N.H.: University Press of New England, 1985.

Burshatin, Israel. "The Moor in the Text: Metaphor, Emblem, and Silence." *Critical Inquiry* 12.1 (Autumn 1985): 98–118.

Butler, Judith. "Subjection, Resistance, Resignification: Between Freud and Foucault." *The Psychic Life of Power.* Stanford: Stanford University Press, 1997.

Cabanelas, Darío. *El morisco granadino Alonso del Castillo.* Granada: Patronato de la Alhambra, 1965.

Cabeza de Vaca, Alvar Núñez. *Naufragios.* Madrid: Alianza, 1998.

Cabrillana, Nicolás, ed. *Documentos notariales referentes a los moriscos 1569–71.* Granada: Universidad de Granada, 1978.

Cachey, Theodore. "Tasso's *Navigazione del Mondo Nuovo* and the Origins of the Columbus Encomium." *Italica* 69.3 (1992): 326–43.

Camamis, George. *Estudios sobre el cautiverio en el Siglo de Oro.* Madrid: Gredos, 1977.

Caro Baroja, Julio. *Los moriscos del reino de Granada.* Madrid: Istmo, 1976.

Carrasco-Urgoiti, María Soledad. *The Moorish Novel: "El Abencerraje" and Pérez de Hita.* Boston: Twayne, 1976.

Cervantes, Miguel de. *El ingenioso hidalgo Don Quijote de la Mancha,* 2 vols. Ed. Martín de Riquer. Buenos Aires: Ed. Kapelusz, 1973.

El trato de Argel. Teatro completo. Ed. Florencio Sevilla Arroyo and Antonio Rey Hazas. Barcelona: Planeta, 1987.

Los baños de Argel. Teatro completo. Ed. Florencio Sevilla Arroyo and Antonio Rey Hazas. Barcelona: Planeta, 1987.

Los trabajos de Persiles y Sigismunda. Ed. Juan Bautista Avalle-Arce. Madrid: Castalia, 1969.

The Trials of Persiles and Sigismunda, A Northern Story, Trans. Celia Richmond

Weller and Clark A. Colahan. Berkeley: University of California Press, 1989.

Chejne, Anwar G. *Islam and the West: The Moriscos.* Albany: State University of New York Press, 1983.

Chew, Samuel. *The Crescent and the Rose: Islam and England during the Renaissance.* New York: Oxford University Press, 1937.

Cheyfitz, Eric. *The Poetics of Imperialism: Translation and Colonization from* The Tempest *to* Tarzan. New York: Oxford University Press, 1991.

Clendinnen, Inga. "Landscape and World View: The Survival of Yucatec Maya Culture under Spanish Rule." *Comparative Studies in Society and History* 22 (1980): 374–93.

Clissold, Stephen. *Conquistador: The Life of Don Pedro Sarmiento de Gamboa.* London: Derek Verschoyle, 1954.

Concha, Jaime. "El otro nuevo mundo." *Homenaje a Ercilla.* Concepción, Chile: Universidad de Concepción, 1969. 31–82.

Córdoba, Pedro. "Las leyendas en la historiografía áurea." *Criticón* 30 (1985): 235–53.

Covarrubias, Sebastián de. *Tesoro de la lengua castellana o española* (1611). Ed. Martín de Riquer. Barcelona: Alta Fulla, 1998.

Cummins, John. *Francis Drake: The Lives of a Hero.* London: Weidenfeld and Nicolson, 1995.

Daborne, Robert. *A Christian Turn'd Turk.* London: William Barrenger, 1612.

D'Amico, Jack. *The Moor in English Renaissance Drama.* Tampa: University of South Florida Press, 1991.

Dee, John. *General and Rare Memorials Pertaining to the Perfect Art of Navigation. John Dee: Essential Readings.* Ed. Gerald Suster. London: Crucible, 1986.

Dekker, Thomas. *If This Be Not a Good Play, the Devil Is in It* (1612). *The Dramatic Works of Thomas Dekker*, III. Ed. Fredson Bowers. Cambridge, England: Cambridge University Press, 1958, 4 vols.

Durling, Robert. *The Figure of the Poet in the Renaissance Epic.* Cambridge, Mass.: Harvard University Press, 1965.

Earle, Peter. *Corsairs of Malta and Barbary.* London: Sidgwick and Jackson, 1970.

Elliott, J. H. *Imperial Spain 1469–1716.* London: Penguin, 1990.

Entreambasaguas, Joaquín. *Estudios sobre Lope de Vega.* Madrid: Gráficas Sol, 1946.

Epalza, Míkel. *Los moriscos antes y después de la expulsión.* Madrid: Mapfre, 1992.

Ercilla, Alonso de. *La Araucana.* Ed. Isaías Lerner. Madrid: Cátedra, 1993.

Evans, J. Martin. *Milton's Imperial Epic: Paradise Lost and the Discourse of Colonialism.* Ithaca: Cornell University Press, 1996.

Ferguson, Margaret. *Trials of Desire: Renaissance Defenses of Poetry.* New Haven: Yale University Press, 1983.

Flecniakoska, Jean-Louis. "Lope de Vega Propagandiste Nationaliste: *La Dragontea.*" *Hommage des Hispanistes Français à Noel Salomon.* Barcelona: LAIA, 1979. 321–33.

Forcione, Alban. *Cervantes, Aristotle and the "Persiles."* Princeton, N.J.: Princeton University Press, 1970.

Foucault, Michel. "On the Genealogy of Ethics: An Overview of Work in Progress." *Michel Foucault: Beyond Structuralism and Hermeneutics*, second edition. Ed. Hubert L. Dreyfus and Paul Rabinow. Chicago: University of Chicago Press, 1983.

Friedman, Ellen G. *Spanish Captives in North Africa in the Early Modern Age.* Madison, Wis.: University of Wisconsin Press, 1983.

Fuchs, Barbara. "Conquering Islands: Contextualizing *The Tempest,*" *Shakespeare Quarterly* 48.1 (Spring 1997): 45–62.

Fuller, Mary C. *Voyages in Print: English Travel to America, 1576–1624.* Cambridge, England: Cambridge University Press, 1995.

García, Ismael. "*La Dragontea*: Justificación y visicitudes." *Lope de Vega y los orígenes del teatro español, Actas del I Congreso Internacional sobre Lope de Vega.* Ed. Manuel Criado de Val. Madrid: EDI-6, 1981. 591–603.

García Arenal, Mercedes. "Moriscos e indios: Para un estudio comparado de métodos de conquista y evangelización." *Chronica Nova* 20 (1992): 153–75.

Garcilaso de la Vega, El Inca. *Comentarios reales de los Incas.* Ed. Aurelio Miró Quesada. Sucre, Venezuela: Biblioteca Ayacucho, n.d.

———. *Royal Commentaries of the Incas and General History of Peru.* Trans. Harold V. Livermore. Austin: University of Texas Press, 1966.

———. *La Florida del Inca.* Ed. Emma Speratti Piñero. México: Fondo de Cultura Económica, 1956.

———. *Obras completas del Inca Garcilaso de la Vega,* Ed. Carmelo Sáenz de Santa María. Madrid: Atlas, 1960.

Garrad, K. "The Original Memorial of Don Francisco Núñez Muley," *Atlante* 2 (1954): 199–226.

Garrido Aranda, Antonio. *Moriscos e indios: precedentes hispánicos de la evangelización en México.* México: Universidad Nacional Autónoma, 1980.

———. *Organización de la Iglesia en el Reino de Granada y su proyección en Indias.* Seville, Spain: Escuela de Estudios Hispano-Americanos, 1979.

Gerli, E. Michael. *Refiguring Authority: Reading, Writing, and Rewriting in Cervantes.* Lexington, Ky: University Press of Kentucky, 1995.

Giamatti, Bartlett. *The Earthly Paradise and the Renaissance Epic.* Princeton, N.J.: Princeton University Press, 1966.

Gibson, Charles. "Reconquista and Conquista." *Homage to Irving A. Leonard: Essays on Hispanic Art, History and Literature.* Ed. Raquel Chang-Rodríguez and Donald A. Yates. New York: Mensaje, 1977. 19–28.

Gil, Juan. *Mitos y utopías del descubrimiento.* Madrid: Alianza, 1989.

———. "El latín en América: lengua general y lengua de elite." *Primer Simposio de Filología Iberoamericana, Facultad de Filología, Universidad de Sevilla.* Zaragoza: Pórtico, 1990. 97–135.

Girard, René. *"To double business bound": Essays on Literature, Mimesis, and Anthropology.* Baltimore: Johns Hopkins University Press, 1978.

Godoy, Alcántara, José. *Historia crítica de los falsos cronicones.* Madrid: Rivadeneyra, 1868.

Gómara, Francisco López de. *Historia general de las Indias.* 2 vols. Madrid: Espasa Calpe, 1932.

Gonzalbo Aizpuru, Pilar. *Historia de la educación en la época colonial: El mundo indígena.* México: Colegio de México, 1990.

González Echevarría, Roberto. *Myth and Archive: A Theory of Latin American*

Narrative. Cambridge, England: Cambridge University Press, 1990.

Greenblatt, Stephen. "To Fashion a Gentleman: Spenser and the Destruction of the Bower of Bliss." *Renaissance Self-Fashioning.* Chicago: University of Chicago Press, 1980. 157–192.

Marvelous Possessions: The Wonder of the New World. Chicago: University of Chicago Press, 1991.

Greene, Roland. *Unrequited Conquests: Love and Empire in the Colonial Americas.* Chicago: University of Chicago Press, 1999.

Greene, Thomas. *The Descent from Heaven: A Study in Epic Continuity.* New Haven: Yale University Press, 1963.

Guaman Poma de Ayala [Waman Puma], Felipe. *El primer nueva corónica y buen gobierno.* Eds. Rolena Adorno and John V. Murra. Quechua trans. and textual analysis Jorge L. Urioste. México: Siglo Veintiuno, 1980.

Hadfield, Andrew. *Edmund Spenser's Irish Experience: Wilde Fruit and Salvage Soyl.* Oxford: Oxford University Press, 1997.

Haedo, Diego de. *Topografía e historia de Argel.* 3 vols. Madrid: Sociedad de Bibliófilos Españoles, 1927.

Hagerty, Miguel, ed. *Los libros plúmbeos del Sacromonte.* Trans. from Arabic, Adán Centurión, Marqués de Estepa. Madrid: Editora Nacional, 1980.

Hakluyt, Richard.*Voyages and Discoveries.* Ed. and introduction Jack Beeching. London: Penguin, 1985.

Hampton, Timothy.*Writing from History: The Rhetoric of Exemplarity in Renaissance Literature.* Ithaca: Cornell University Press, 1991.

Hanke, Lewis. *The Spanish Struggle for Justice in the Conquest of America.* Philadelphia: University of Pennsylvania Press, 1949.

Harvey, L.P. "The Moriscos and *Don Quijote.*" Inaugural Lecture in the Chair of Spanish delivered at King's College, University of London, November 11, 1974.

Hayes, Aden W. "Fitón's Aleph, Ercilla's World." *Revista de estudios hispánicos* 15.3 (October 1981): 349–63.

Hebb, David Delison. *Piracy and the English Government, 1616–1642.* Aldershot, England: Scolar Press, 1994.

Hegyi, Ottmar. *Cervantes and the Turks.* Newark, Del.: Juan de la Cuesta, 1992.

Helgerson, Richard. *Forms of Nationhood: The Elizabethan Writing of England.* Chicago: University of Chicago Press, 1992.

Heredia Herrera, Antonia M. "La carta como tipo diplomático indiano." *Anuario de estudios americanos* 34 (1977): 65–95.

Heywood, Thomas. *The Fair Maid of the West.* Ed. Robert K. Turner. Lincoln, Nebr.: University of Nebraska Press, 1967.

and Rowley, William. *Fortune by Land and Sea.* Ed. Herman Doh. New York: Garland, 1980.

Howard, Jean. "An English Lass Amid the Moors: Gender, Race, Sexuality, and National Identity." *Women, "Race," and Writing in the Early Modern Period.* Ed. Margo Hendricks and Patricia Parker. London: Routledge, 1994. 101–17.

Hulme, Peter. *Colonial Encounters: Europe and the Native Caribbean, 1492–1797.* London: Routledge, 1986.

Hume, Ivor Noël. *The Virginia Adventure.* New York: Knopf, 1994.

James VI. *The Poems of James VI of Scotland*, 2 vols. Ed. James Craigie. Edinburgh, n.p., 1955.

Jameson, A. K. "Lope de Vega's *La Dragontea*: Historical and Literary Sources." *Hispanic Review* 6 (1938): 104–19.

Janik, Dieter. "Ercilla, lector de Lucano." *Homenaje a Ercilla*. Concepción, Chile: University of Concepción Press, 1969. 83–109.

Javitch, Daniel. "Cantus Interruptus in the *Orlando Furioso*." *MLN* 95 (1980): 66–80.

Jones, Emrys. " 'Othello,' 'Lepanto' and the Cyprus Wars." *Shakespeare Survey* 21 (1968): 47–52.

Kagan, Richard L. "Clio and the Crown: Writing History in Habsburg Spain." *Spain, Europe and the Atlantic World: Essays in Honour of John H. Elliott*. Ed. Richard L. Kagan and Geoffrey Parker. Cambridge, England: Cambridge University Press, 1995. 73–99.

Lucrecia's Dreams: Politics and Prophecy in Sixteenth-Century Spain. Berkeley: University of California Press, 1990.

Kendrick, T.D. *St. James in Spain*. London: Methuen, 1960.

Knolles, Richard. *The Generalle Historie of the Turkes*, second edition. London: Adam Islip, 1610.

Lagos, Ramona. "El incumplimiento de la programación épica en *La Araucana*." *Cuadernos Americanos* 40 (Sept.–Oct. 1981): 157–91.

Larkin, J. F. and Hughes, P. L., eds. *Stuart Royal Proclamations*. Oxford: Oxford University Press, 1973.

Las Casas, Bartolomé de. *Obras escogidas de Fray Bartolomé de Las Casas*, V. Ed. Juan Pérez de Tudela Bueso. Madrid: Atlas, 1958.

Lea, Henry Charles. *The Moriscos of Spain: Their Conversion and Expulsion* (1908). New York: Greenwood Press, 1968.

Leonard, Irving. *Books of the Brave*, second edition. Berkeley: University of California Press, 1992.

Lerner, Isaías. "América y la poesía épica áurea: La versión de Ercilla." *Edad de Oro* X (1991): 125–40.

Lewis, Bernard. *Islam and the West*. New York: Oxford University Press, 1993.

Lezra, Jacques. *Unspeakable Subjects: The Genealogy of the Event in Early Modern Europe*. Stanford: Stanford University Press, 1997.

Lloyd, Christopher. *English Corsairs on the Barbary Coast*. London: Collins, 1981.

Lockhart, James. "Encomienda and Hacienda: The Evolution of the Great Estate in the Spanish Indies." *Hispanic American Historical Review* 49 (August 1969): 411–29.

Lope de Vega, Félix. *La Dragontea*. 2 vols. Burgos: Museo Naval, 1935.

López-Baralt, Luce. *Islam in Spanish Literature, from the Middle Ages to the Present*. Trans. Andrew Hurley. New York: Brill, 1992.

López Baralt, Mercedes. *Guaman Poma, autor y artista*. Lima: Fondo Editorial de la Pontificia Universidad Católica del Perú, 1993.

Lucan, *Civil War*. Trans. P. F.Widdows. Bloomington: Indiana University Press, 1988.

Luna, Miguel de. *La verdadera historia del Rey Don Rodrigo*. Zaragoza, n.p., 1602.

MacCormack, Sabine. "The Fall of the Incas: A Historiographical Dilemma."

History of European Ideas 6.4 (1985): 421–45.

Mármol Carvajal, Luis del. *Historia del rebelión y castigo do los Moriscos del reyno de Granada.* Málaga: Juan René, 1600.

Márquez Villanueva, Francisco. *Personajes y temas del Quijote.* Madrid: Taurus, 1975.

"La voluntad de leyenda de Miguel de Luna." *Nueva revista de filología hispánica* 30.2 (1981): 359–97.

"El problema historiográfico de los moriscos." *Bull. Hisp.* 86 (1984): 61–135.

Mas, Albert. *Les Turcs dans la littérature espagnole du siècle d'or,* 2 vols. Paris: Centre des Recherches Hispaniques, 1967.

Massinger, Philip. *The Renegado. The Plays and Poems of Philip Massinger,* II. Ed. Philip Edwards and Colin Gibson. Oxford: Oxford University Press, 1976.

Matar, Nabil. *Islam in Britain, 1558–1685.* Cambridge, England: Cambridge University Press, 1998.

Turks, Moors, and Englishmen in the Age of Discovery. New York: Columbia University Press, 1999.

Mejías-López, William. "El Fitón de Alonso de Ercilla: ¿Shamán araucano?" *Atenea* 462 (1990): 97–117.

Menéndez Pelayo, Marcelino. *Orígenes de la novela.* Madrid: Bailly-Baillère, 1925.

Menocal, María Rosa. *Shards of Love: Exile and the Origins of the Lyric.* Durham: Duke University Press, 1993.

Mignolo, Walter. "Teorías renancentistas de la escritura y la colonización de las lenguas nativas." *Primer Simposio de Filología Iberoamericana, Facultad de Filología, Universidad de Sevilla.* Zaragoza: Pórtico, 1990. 171–99.

The Darker Side of the Renaissance: Literacy, Territoriality, and Colonization. Ann Arbor: University of Michigan Press, 1995.

Miró Quesada, Aurelio. *El Inca Garcilaso y otros estudios garcilasistas.* Madrid: Ediciones Cultura Hispánica, 1971.

Monroe, James. *Islam and the Arabs in Spanish Scholarship.* Leiden, The Netherlands: Brill, 1970.

Montrose, Louis A. "The Elizabethan Subject and the Spenserian Text." *Literary Theory/Renaissance Texts.* Ed. Patricia Parker and David Quint. Baltimore: Johns Hopkins University Press, 1985.

Moreno Báez, Enrique. "El manierismo de Pérez de Hita." *Homenaje a Emilio Alarcos,* II. Valladolid: Universidad, 1965–67. 353–67.

Murrin, Michael. *History and Warfare in Renaissance Epic.* Chicago: University of Chicago Press, 1994.

O'Hara, James J. *Death and the Optimistic Prophecy in Virgil's Aeneid.* Princeton, N.J.: Princeton University Press, 1990.

Osorio Romero, Ignacio. *La enseñanza del latín a los indios.* México: Universidad Nacional Autónoma de México, 1990.

Pagden, Anthony. *The Fall of Natural Man: The American Indian and the Origins of Comparative Ethnology.* Cambridge, England: Cambridge University Press, 1986.

Spanish Imperialism and the Political Imagination. New Haven: Yale University Press, 1990.

Lords of All the World: Ideologies of Empire in Spain, Britain and France c. 1500–c.1800. New Haven: Yale University Press, 1995.

Parker, Patricia. *Inescapable Romance.* Princeton, N.J.: Princeton University Press, 1979.

Pazzis Pi Corrales, Magdalena. *Felipe II y la lucha por el dominio del mar.* Madrid: San Martín, 1989.

Pérez de Hita, Ginés. *Guerras civiles de Granada,* 2 vols. Ed. Paula Blanchard-Demouge. Madrid: Bailly-Baillière, 1913.

Pérotin-Dumon, Anne. "The Pirate and the Emperor: Power and the Law on the Seas, 1450–1850." *The Political Economy of Merchant Empires.* Ed. James D. Tracy. Cambridge, England: Cambridge University Press, 1991.

Pierson, Peter. *Commander of the Armada: The Seventh Duke of Medina Sidonia.* New Haven: Yale University Press, 1989.

Pinard de la Boullaye, R. P. "Le mouvement historique en ethnologie." *Semaine Internationale d'Ethnologie Religieuse* 1925: 33–46.

Porras Barrenechea, Raúl. *El cronista indio Felipe Huaman Poma de Ayala.* Lima: Lumen, 1948.

Potter, Lois. "Pirates and 'Turning Turk' in Renaissance Drama." *Travel and Drama in Shakespeare's Time.* Ed. Jean-Pierre Maquerlot and Michèle Willems. Cambridge, England: Cambridge University Press, 1996. 124–40.

Pratt, Mary L. "Arts of the Contact Zone." *Profession* 1991: 33–40.

Quint, David. "Astolfo's Voyage to the Moon." *Yale Italian Studies,* o.s. 1 (1977): 398–408.

Origins and Originality in Renaissance Literature. New Haven: Yale University Press, 1983.

Epic and Empire: Politics and Generic Form from Virgil to Milton. Princeton, N.J.: Princeton University Press, 1993.

"Narrative Interlace and Narrative Genres in *Don Quijote* and the *Orlando Furioso.*" *Modern Language Quarterly* 58.3 (September 1997): 241–68.

Rabb, Theodore K. *Enterprise and Empire.* Cambridge, Mass.: Harvard University Press, 1967.

Ricard, Robert. "Contribution à l'étude des fêtes de "Moros y Cristianos" au Mexique." *Journal de la Société des Americanistes* 26 (1932): 51–84.

Roach, Joseph. *Cities of the Dead: Circum-Atlantic Performance.* New York: Columbia University Press, 1996.

Rodríguez Prampolini, Ida. *Amadises de América: La hazaña de Indias como empresa caballeresca,* second edition. Caracas: Centro de Estudios Latinoamericanos Rómulo Gallegos, 1977.

Root, Deborah. "Speaking Christian: Orthodoxy and Difference in Sixteenth-Century Spain." *Representations* 23 (Summer 1988): 118–34.

Rhu, Lawrence. *The Genesis of Tasso's Narrative Theory: English Translations of the Early Poetics and a Comparative Study of Their Significance.* Detroit: Wayne State University Press, 1993.

Saiz Sidoncha, Carlos. *Historia de la piratería en América española,* 3 vols. Madrid: Ed. San Martín, 1985.

Sánchez Alonso, B. *Historia de la historiografía española.* Madrid: Consejo Superior de Investigaciones Científicas, 1944.

Senior, C. M. *A Nation of Pirates.* New York: Crane, Russak, and Co., 1976.

Seno, Ariella dal. "L'umanesimo etnografico e l'*Araucana* di Alonso de Ercilla."
   Tre studi sulla cultura spagnola. Milan: Varese, 1967.
Shakespeare, William. *The Tempest*. Ed. Stephen Orgel. Oxford: Oxford University Press, 1987.
Sieber, Diane E. "The Frontier Ballad and Spanish Golden Age Historiography."
   Hispanic Review 65.3 (Summer 1997): 291–306.
Smith, John. *Generall Historie of Virginia, New-England and the Summer Iles*. 2
   vols. London, n.p. 1629.
   A Select Edition of his Writings. Ed. Karen Ordahl Kupperman. Chapel Hill:
   University of North Carolina Press, 1988.
Smith, Paul Julian. "'The Captive's Tale': Race, Text, Gender." *Quixotic Desire:
   Psychoanalytic Perspectives on Cervantes*. Ed. Ruth Anthony El Saffar and
   Diana de Armas Wilson. Ithaca: Cornell University Press, 1993.
Spitzer, Leo. "Linguistic Perspectivism in *Don Quijote*." *Linguistics and Literary
   History: Essays in Stylistics*. New York: Russell and Russell, 1972.
Stern, Steve J. *Peru's Indian People and the Challenge of Spanish Conquest*.
   Madison, Wis.: University of Wisconsin Press, 1982.
Tanner, Marie. *The Last Descendant of Aeneas: The Hapsburgs and the Mythic
   Image of the Emperor*. New Haven: Yale University Press, 1993.
Tasso, Torquato. *Gerusalemme liberata*. Ed. Lanfranco Caretti. Milano: Mondadori, 1979.
   Jerusalem Delivered. Trans. and ed. Ralph Nash. Detroit: Wayne State University Press, 1987.
   Gerusalemme conquistata. Ed. Luigi Bonfigli. Bari: G. Laterza, 1934.
   Scritti sull'arte poetica. Ed. Ettore Mazzali. Torino: Giulio Einaudi, 1977.
   Discourses of the Heroic Poem. Trans. Mariella Cavalchini and Irene Samuel.
   London: Oxford University Press, 1973.
Tate, Robert B. "Mythology in Spanish Historiography of the Middle Ages and
   the Renaissance." *Hispanic Review* 22 (Jan. 1954): 1–18.
Taussig, Michael. *Mimesis and Alterity: A Particular History of the Senses*. London: Routledge, 1993.
Thompson, I.A.A. "Castile, Spain and the Monarchy." *Spain, Europe and the
   Atlantic World: Essays in Honour of John H. Elliott*. Ed. Richard L. Kagan
   and Geoffrey Parker. Cambridge, England: Cambridge University Press,
   1995. 125–59.
Torre Revello, José. *El libro, la imprenta y el periodismo en América durante la
   dominación española*. Buenos Aires: Publicaciones del Instituto de Investigaciones Históricas, 1940.
Tylus, Jane. "Reasoning Away Colonialism: Tasso and the Production of the
   Gerusalemme liberata." *South Central Review* 10.2 (1993): 100–14.
Varner, John Grier. *El Inca: The Life and Times of Garcilaso de la Vega*. Austin:
   University of Texas Press, 1968.
Weckmann, Luis. *La herencia medieval de México*. México: Colegio de México, 1984.
Weinberg, Bernard. *A History of Literary Criticism in the Italian Renaissance*, 2
   vols. Chicago: University of Chicago Press, 1961.
White, Hayden. *Tropics of Discourse: Essays in Cultural Criticism*. Baltimore:

Johns Hopkins University Press, 1978.

Williams, Diane S. "Beyond the Limits of Genre: The Rhetoric of History in the Guerras Civiles de Granada." Diss., Princeton University, 1993.

Wilson, Richard. "Voyage to Tunis: New History and the Old World of *The Tempest*." ELH 64 (1997): 333–57.

Wright, Irene A., ed. and trans. *Spanish Documents concerning English Voyages to the Caribbean 1527–1568*. London: Hakluyt Society, 1928.

Documents concerning English Voyages to the Spanish Main 1569–1580. London: Hakluyt Society, 1932.

Further English Voyages to Spanish America 1583–94. London: Hakluyt Society, 1951.

Zamora, Margarita. *Language, Authority and Indigenous History in the* Comentarios reales de los Incas. Cambridge, England: Cambridge University Press, 1988.

Zatti, Sergio. *L'uniforme cristiano e il multiforme pagano: Saggio sulla* Gerusalemme liberata. Milano: Il Saggiatore, 1983.

L'ombra del Tasso: Epica e romanzo nel Cinquecento. Milano: Mondadori, 1996.

Index

Adorno, Rolena, 85, 89, 94, 96
Aguirre, Lope de, 67
Algiers, 57, 123, 139, 145, 154–62
Almagro, Diego de, 66, 68, 80
Alpujarras, rebellion of the, *see* Moriscos
  see also Pérez de Hita, Ginés, *Guerras
  civiles de Granada*
Althusser, Louis, 65
Amazons, 19
Anne, Queen of England, 1, 2
Annius of Viterbo, 100
Ariosto, Ludovico
  Orlando Furioso, 16–19, 24–27, 33, 38,
  41–42, 143, 148
Aristotle
  Poetics, 24, 83
Armada, Spanish, 139, 141, 148, 152
Atahualpa, 83, 84
Audiencia, 101
Auerbach, Erich
  Mimesis, 5
Austria, Don Juan de, 50, 53, 55

Barbary States, 2, 11, 14, 57, 96, 103,
  122–24, 132, 134, 137, 139, 140, 145,
  152–63; *see also* corsairs
Bhabha, Homi, 6
Bible, 8, 15–16, 18, 20–21, 28, 83, 108,
  143–47, 150–51
Black Legend, 14, 139
"blood purity"
  and conversion to Christianity, 99, 112,
  162
  and difference, 69, 93–94, 112, 162
  and mixed blood, 87, 92–94, 99, 112
  and the New World, 10, 86, 92, 99
  and nobility, 10, 87, 94
  racial distinctions by, 10, 69, 93, 94, 99,
  112, 158, 162
Braudel, Fernand, 122

Cádiz, 120, 130

Camões, Luis Vaz de
  Os Lusiadas, 143
Canary Islands, 29, 141
  see also Fortunate Islands
captivity, 11, 57–58, 81, 121, 140, 145,
  152–63
Castillo, Alonso del, 113–14, 117
Catholicism, 11, 23, 25, 49
  and Counter-Reformation, 21, 24
  in the New World, 13–23, 65, 66, 75, 90,
  91
  religious orders, 20–23, 108, 109, 134,
  137
  and Spanish national identity, 103–16,
  122, 131, 137, 150–51, 160–64
censorship
  in the New World, 8, 13–16, 19, 24, 108
  and Protestantism, 23
Centurión, Adán, Marquess of Estepa, 116
  see also Sacromonte
Cervantes Saavedra, Miguel de, 11, 12, 16,
  134, 154–63, 165
  Los baños de Argel, 154, 156–58
  Don Quijote, 16, 19, 59, 158
  "The Captive's Tale", 57, 158–61
  Los trabajos de Persiles y Sigismunda,
  161–62
  El trato de Argel, 154–57, 162–63
Charles V, King of Spain and Holy
  Roman Emperor, 7, 36–37, 68, 87, 96
Chile, 9, 37–38, 43–45, 49, 62, 69
Columbus, Christopher, 28–29, 147
Conquista, 1, 7–9, 14, 18–20, 23, 34, 36–37,
  44, 46, 139–47
  history and criticism of, 64–70, 72, 74–80,
  83, 85, 89–93, 96
  and Reconquista, 7, 8, 19, 74, 78, 108,
  140–41, 145–46
conversion, 11, 19, 49, 56, 99, 124–26, 134,
  140, 145, 150, 153
  in Cervantes Saavedra, Miguel de,
  154–61

Cambridge Studies in Renaissance Literature and Culture

General Editor
STEPHEN ORGEL
Jackson Eli Reynolds Professor of Humanities, Stanford University

1. Douglas Bruster, *Drama and the market in the age of Shakespeare*

2. Virginia Cox, *The Renaissance dialogue: literary dialogue in its social and political contexts, Castiglione to Galileo*

3. Richard Rambuss, *Spenser's secret career*

4. John Gillies, *Shakespeare and the geography of difference*

5. Laura Levine, *Men in women's clothing: anti-theatricality and effeminization, 1579–1642*

6. Linda Gregerson, *The reformation of the subject: Spenser, Milton, and the English Protestant epic*

7. Mary C. Fuller, *Voyages in print: English travel to America, 1576–1624*

8. Margreta de Grazia, Maureen Quilligan, and Peter Stallybrass (eds.), *Subject and object in Renaissance culture*

9. T. G. Bishop, *Shakespeare and the theatre of wonder*

10. Mark Breitenberg, *Anxious masculinity in early modern England*

11. Frank Whigham, *Seizure of the will in early modern English drama*

12. Kevin Pask, *The emergence of the English author: scripting the life of the poet in early modern England*

13. Claire McEachern, *The poetics of English nationhood, 1590–1612*

14. Jeffrey Masten, *Textual intercourse: collaboration, authorship, and sexualities in Renaissance drama*

15. Timothy J. Reiss, *Knowledge, discovery and imagination in early modern Europe: the rise of aesthetic rationalism*

16. Elizabeth Fowler and Roland Greene (eds.), *The project of prose in early modern Europe and the New World*

17. Alexandra Halasz, *The marketplace of print: pamphlets and the public sphere in early modern England*

18. Seth Lerer, *Courtly letters in the age of Henry VIII: literary culture and the arts of deceit*

19. M. Lindsay Kaplan, *The culture of slander in early modern England*

20. Howard Marchitello, *Narrative and meaning in early modern England: Browne's skull and other histories*

Lightning Source UK Ltd.
Milton Keynes UK
UKOW03f1849200814

237273UK00001B/63/A